Praise for *Screen Time*

"[Lisa Guernsey's] approach is a gift to parents because she encourages them to decide what the best media choices are for their particular child."
—*Television Quarterly*

"A science journalist and mother of two, Guernsey manages to extricate straightforward information and guidelines from the morass of research, articles and debates on screen media and child brain development. Easily digestible chapters are smartly structured around 12 pervasive concerns of interviewees from all walks of life."
—*Publishers Weekly*

"Guernsey's exploration of the world of electronic media and its positive and negative impact on young children is one we will all benefit from."
—Robert Kesten, Executive Director,
Center for SCREEN-TIME Awareness

"Written with passion and precision, humor and humility. . . . A calming and reassuring new resource for parents."
—Claire Green,
President, Parents' Choice Foundation

"This journey into the best research on the impact of media on young children will serve as an essential guide to all those who care about kids."
—Ellen Galinsky,
President, Families and Work Institute

Screen Time

Screen Time

How Electronic Media — From Baby Videos to Educational Software — Affects Your Young Child

LISA GUERNSEY

BASIC BOOKS

A Member of the Perseus Books Group
New York

Books published by Basic Books are available at special discounts for bulk
purchases in the United States by corporations, institutions, and
other organizations. For more information, please contact the
Special Markets Department at the Perseus Books Group,
2300 Chestnut St., Suite 200, Philadelphia, PA 19103.

Previously published as *Into the Minds of Babes:
How Screen Time Affects Children from Birth to Age Five*

Designed by Trish Wilkinson
Set in Adobe Caslon

The Library of Congress has catalogued the hardcover as follows:
Guernsey, Lisa.
    Into the minds of babes : how screen time affects children from birth to
age five / Lisa Guernsey.
        p.   cm.
    Includes bibliographical references and index.
    ISBN-13: 978-0-465-02798-9 (hardcover : alk. paper)
    ISBN-10: 0-465-02798-9 (hardcover : alk. paper) 1. Television and children.
2. Child development. 3. Video recordings for children. 4. Educational
television programs. 5. Educational videos. I. Title.
HQ784.T4G83 2007
302.23083—dc22   2007021043

ISBN: 978-0-465-02980-8 (paperback)
ISBN: 978-0-465-03134-4 (e-book)

10 9 8 7 6 5 4 3 2 1

To Janelle and Gillian

Contents

Foreword to the Paperback Edition   *xi*

Preface, or the Three Cs: Content, Context and Your Child   *xv*

1   **What Exactly Is This Video Doing to My Baby's Brain?**   1

    • *ADHD and autism—should I be worried?*

    • *Why do pediatricians say no screen time before age 2?*

    NOTES, 25

2   **Is TV Turning My Tot Into a Zombie?**   27

    • *Why does it look like my child is tuning out?*

    • *At what age do children become mentally engaged?*

    NOTES, 42

3   **Could My Child Learn from Baby Videos?**   45

    • *How and when do toddlers learn from audiovisual media?*

    • *What is the "video deficit?"*

    NOTES, 65

4   **My Toddler Doesn't Seem to Notice When the
    TV Is On—or Does He?**   67

    • *What is the impact of background television?*

    • *How does noise affect language development?*

    NOTES, 84

5   Which Videos Are Too Scary for My Child?   87

   • *What content is most upsetting to young children?*
   • *What should I do when they get frightened by what they see?*
   NOTES, 111

6   What Is Educational About "Educational" TV?   113

   • *What are the features of a well-designed preschool show?*
   • *Have children really been shown to benefit from
     educational shows?*
   NOTES, 132

7   Could the Right DVD Teach My Child to Speak, or
     Better Yet, Become Bilingual?   135

   • *What exactly leads to language development?*
   • *Will foreign-language videos give my children an edge?*
   NOTES, 149

8   Can Electronic Media Enrich My Child's Vocabulary?   151

   • *At what age can a video make the most difference?*
   • *Under what conditions do children learn words from TV?*
   NOTES, 170

9   Could This Program Teach My Child to
     Be a Good Person?   173

   • *Is there any evidence that videos can inspire good character?*
   • *How are TV, pretend play and good behavior connected?*
   NOTES, 191

10 Is Interactive Media Worthwhile—or at Least
     Better Than TV?   193

   • *Are screen-based toys of any use to babies?*
   • *Is educational software a good idea for preschoolers?*
   NOTES, 213

11   Will Screen Time Make My Children Fat?   215

    • *Are there real connections between TV and obesity?*
    • *Does the location of the TV matter?*

    NOTES, 231

12   How Do Real Families Make Smart Media Choices?   233

    • *How do they cope with siblings? sickness? single parenthood?*
    • *What are some examples of limits that stick?*

    NOTES, 252

Epilogue   *253*
Appendix I: Movie Review Web Sites   *277*
Appendix II: Web Site Reviews of Interactive Media   *279*
*Appendix III: Resources on the Use of Electronic
    Media with Children Who Have Special Needs*   *281*
Acknowledgments   *283*
Bibliography   *285*
Index   *299*

Foreword to the Paperback Edition

During the past fifteen years, baby media have exploded. Since the introduction of the *Baby Einstein* video in 1997, we've seen a variety of screen media directed to infants and toddlers, including a variety of television shows (*Teletubbies* and *Classical Baby*), entire cable channels such as *Baby First TV*, and computer software and applications for iPads and cell phones (such as *Elmo's Monster Maker* App). From their introduction, such baby media made explicit claims about wanting to provide children with educational or informational programming in an entertaining presentational style that elicits the children's attention and demonstrates to the parents that children are engaged and learning something, whether with colors, numbers, letters, or words. Also from their introduction, baby media have been controversial. In 1999 the American Academy of Pediatrics recommended *no* screen time for babies two and younger and a limit of two hours of screen time for older children, sending American parents into a quandary about the appropriateness of baby media. Much of this activity occurred without explicit research on whether babies are learning from such baby media and whether such media have either short-or long-term influences on children's development.

Any examination of the research literature on children's use of television in its early days (such as the 1950s studies reported in *Television in the Lives of Children* by Wilbur Schramm, Jack Lyle, and Edwin Parker) demonstrates that people were recognizing babies and toddlers as viewers of television from the moment TV sets were introduced into American homes (but without any hand-wringing over the fact). Furthermore, young children of the 1950s were asking for their favorite programs by the time they started talking around 2 years of age and were regular viewers of television by 2.8 years. But the number of programs expressly intended for very young children was relatively few: not until the 1960s and the arrival on national TV of both *Fred Rogers Neighborhood* and *Sesame Street* were programs being developed to educate the very youngest in the audience.

What did accelerate in the past fifteen years is both the number of baby media outlets and the amount of time children under six are spending with media. According to the 2011 Common Sense Media study of media use by children from birth to age eight, children under two years old spend on average nearly an hour a day (fifty-three minutes) with screen media (including TV, DVDs, computers or videogames) and nearly four out of ten babies under age two watched some screen media every day. And yet, until the past half dozen or so years, there was little research documenting the influence of screen media on these very young child viewers.

Indeed, the media market coupled with parental concerns about what is appropriate for young children and the admonitions of the 1999 AAP report led to studies of young children's learning from baby videos as well as television shows babies watch. Can babies learn novel words from baby videos? At what age do very young children demonstrate attention to the formal production characteristics of videos such as camera movement? Can babies imitate behaviors they see on-screen?

It was into this mix of increasing baby media outlets and little research (but lots of opinion) that Lisa Guernsey—both a mother of young children and a journalist—set out to make sense of what we do and don't know about media use by very young children.

With this volume she fairly summarizes the growing body of re-search, which suggests that children's learning from the baby videos currently in the marketplace has some limitations and de-pends on the viewing context and presence of adult guides, age ap-propriateness of the content, and the particular cognitive and social emotional development of the child. Lisa also explores and deci-phers the research on educational media for preschoolers. Both ac-ademics and parents can find the literature reviewed here accessible and understandable. Indeed, Guernsey's book was the first and best compilation of what academics know about babies' and very young children's use of and learning from screen media as well as a report on the various parental practices when parents do let their very young children watch screen media.

This book is noteworthy in that its first edition made public how much research has been done but also how much more we need to understand about both the short-term and long-term influences of screen media on children's development. It helped spark the growth of this research literature, as is evident in this edition. And like the first edition, this edition provides parents with scientific evidence for their questions about the effects of baby media prod-ucts.

Attitudes about screen media for young children are changing. Screen media are very much a part of American children's lives, and parenting in this age of media technology requires an under-standing of the influence of such media on our children. This book helps advance that understanding for all parents and concerned adults.

ELLEN WARTELLA
Northwestern University
December 2011

Preface, or the Three Cs:
Content, Context and Your Child

My introduction to Baby Einstein came in a moment of panic. I was a new mother with a colicky 5-week-old baby, desperate for anything that might calm her. "Try *Baby Mozart*," advised one of my closest friends, who had just emerged—alive—from six months of colic with her daughter. "We call it baby crack."

On went the video, opening a window onto a terrain that I never knew existed before: the world of electronic media for the very young. Since then, as my daughter has grown and her younger sister arrived, companies have produced more and more multimedia programs for the stroller set. Videos promoting cognitive growth have been designed for babies as young as 2 months old. Television shows like *Teletubbies, Boohbah* and *Oobi* target toddlers. Videos for iPods, computer software, and games for portable devices, with screens no bigger than a box of raisins, are being made for 2- and 3-year-old kids.

In 1999, at the first rumble of this media avalanche, the American Academy of Pediatrics came out with some professional advice for parents. It recommended no screen time—including TV, video or computer time—for children under the age of 2. Five years later, a report in the journal *Pediatrics* linked children's attention problems to how much TV they watched when they were very young. Meanwhile, child-advocacy groups have continued to turn up the sirens, issuing warnings about the academic and health problems children will soon face if they are settled down in front of TV and computer screens at such an early age.

I felt caught in the middle. On one side, I was getting hit by the heavy marketing of video companies. I recognized that they were simply trying to make a buck in the baby market, but that didn't mean that I was immune to the lure of products labeled "educational." On the other side, I was inclined to trust and practice the advice of pediatricians. But raising children is not always a walk in the park, and I was becoming acutely aware of how much time and energy it takes to care for babies and toddlers. When an afternoon goes haywire, you can't exactly tell an 18-month-old to go read a book. Three-year-olds who have given up naptime demand far more attention than a weary body can give. Video programs, however, have an uncanny way of turning chaos into tranquility. And so screen time became part of the routine at our house beneath a barrage of health warnings, marketing promotions and mixed feelings. With the insertion of every DVD, I felt guilty. With every statement about the videos stimulating my children's brains, I felt I was being taken for a ride. And yet with every minute of quiet, I couldn't help but breathe a sigh of relief.

My first daughter, Janelle, was born in April 2002. My second, Gillian, arrived almost two years later in March 2004. It was on a spring morning a few months after Gillian's birth, while trying to steal a couple of minutes with the newspaper, that I came across the *Pediatrics* study linking children's attention problems to early-age TV viewing. Gillian was strapped into a bouncy chair at the time, facing the TV, while her 25-month-old sister watched Playhouse Disney. I was both worried and fascinated. I wanted details.

I had spent ten years reporting on how the Internet and computer technology had changed the lives of school-aged children, college students and adults. Now, as I experienced parenthood, questions about technology's impact seemed more real and more complicated, especially regarding the very young. Babies communicate through little more than smiles and cries. How could anyone know what was going on in their heads as they watched and listened to these videos? What were they absorbing? Was it making any sense in the least? Was it doing harm?

I did some interviews, read some journal articles, and wrote a story about toddlers and television for the *Washington Post* in November of 2004. I thought that was the end of it. But it was only the beginning. Parents emailed me in droves, pressing the point about how difficult it was to avoid TV and still balance the realities of daily life with young children, especially when parents used television to stay in touch with the world and enjoyed watching programs with their kids. There was much more to say and, as I soon learned, much more research to discover.

What started as a couple of additional interviews became a two-year obsession. I found myself on a quest to learn everything I could about screen media and children under the age of 5. I talked with language-acquisition experts and developmental psychologists, visiting their laboratories and hounding them with email questions. I interviewed cognitive scientists, educational psychologists, communication scholars and social workers. I met with the producers of children's videos and designers of computer software for kids. I took notes on how my own kids responded to what they saw on screen. I watched more children's TV than my children did. I knew I had lost all semblance of normalcy when I sent my daughters and our babysitter out to the playground so that I could watch a couple hours of Nick Jr. Instead of setting up play dates, I was scheduling viewings of BabyFirstTV on my friend's satellite network when my children were in preschool.

I also talked to as many parents as I could, in their homes, on the phone and via email. Their questions were what kept me going. Many of them knew about the *Pediatrics* study and the AAP recommendation. "We all know that the AAP says it is bad," said the father of a 9-month-old girl in Washington DC. "But help us understand why. And how certain is the research on that question? What effect does screen time really have on the brain?"

Children under age 4 are spending an average of 1 hour and 25 minutes in front of a screen each day, according to a survey conducted in 2005 by the Henry J. Kaiser Family Foundation.[1] Should we be alarmed or encouraged by that number? It is hard to know, since it is not even clear whether this is a dramatic increase over times past. Historical comparisons are nearly impossible to make, given that very few surveys from previous decades contained questions about television use around infants and toddlers, and most of those that did never asked parents to differentiate between actually putting a child in front of the TV to watch a program or having the child simply present in a room where a television set was on. A set of national data from the 1990s, for example, showed that children aged 1½ watched more than two hours of TV a day—a higher amount of screen time than what parents report today.[2]

The more I learned, the less use I found for focusing so intently on the quantity of screen time. Instead, I started to see three channels of inquiry that shed light on what screen time really means to a child's development. I call them the three Cs: "content," "context" and "your child." The studies on how children respond to content led me to ask: What exactly are our daughters watching? Can they make sense of it? Will they try to imitate what happens on screen? Could they learn from it? Are they learning what we think they are learning?

The studies that delved into context made me wonder: What would our children be doing if they weren't watching a video? Where are they watching? Is an adult helping them figure out what they see? Are they really watching, or is the TV background noise? How does the time our child spends with media compare to the time she spends on other activities? Is she getting enough quiet time for pretend play?

And then there was the recognition that every child is different, leading me to ask: Is this appropriate for this particular daughter's age, her stage of development, or her temperament? How much stimulation can she take? What scares her? What types of media experiences trigger the most curious questions, the most playful reenactments, the most engagement, the most joy?

With the three Cs in mind, I organized this book around twelve of the most frequently asked questions that I either heard from parents or grappled with myself over the past two years. My aim was to keep answers rooted in research. At the outset, some people warned me that I would have little to go on, since media research on very young children is hard to come by. The research on infants is, indeed, in its infancy. But there are many fascinating studies that have started the research ball rolling, along with a flurry of new science on cognitive development, including how children see, hear, learn language and play. These studies gave me a framework for thinking about how children respond to media, not to mention new lenses of understanding through which I could see how to help my own kids.

I can't promise that parents will find answers to all of their media questions in this book. Cognitive scientists and developmental psychologists are only starting to uncover the holes in their understanding of how very young children are affected by media. Debates are already raging on how to interpret what we know so far. New experiments are underway this year, and scientists are seeking the funding to embark on national, large-scale studies. In short, easy answers are hard to come by. But what I hope this book can offer are some shafts of light, some helpful glimpses into the research on media and the minds of babes.

Today, as I read over the *Washington Post* story I wrote more than two years ago, I feel like a different person. While writing that story, with just a few months of research behind me, my focus was on the hype about harm, and my guilt was palpable. Today, after getting a much fuller picture of when and how children can learn from video, I can make better choices. Understanding the major caveats that come with reports on the risks of TV, I can relax. I feel a greater sense of confidence and control about how to use and enjoy screen media around my kids. I hope that, armed with a greater awareness of how children respond to and are affected by what they watch, you will, too.

NOTES

1. These numbers are from a phone interview with Victoria Rideout of the Kaiser Family Foundation. The numbers published on page 9 of the 2006 report, "The Media Family," break out the statistics in smaller age groups: the average amount of screen time per day used by children 0 to 1 year old is 49 minutes, and the average for children 2 to 3 years old is 1 hour, 51 minutes. When you subtract the survey participants who said that their children had no screen time at all, the numbers rise to 1 hour and 20 minutes for children age 0 to 1, 2 hours and 7 minutes for children age 2 to 3, and 1 hour and 51 minutes for the combination of those two groups (children age 0 to 3).

2. Anderson and Pempek, 2005, pp. 506–508.

Chapter One

What Exactly Is
This Video Doing to
My Baby's Brain?

In 1999, the American Academy of Pediatrics (AAP) decided to take a stand on how much time children should spend in front of TVs, computers and videogames. The academy's public education committee released a report with many conclusions, but the one many newspapers reported as a front-page story was the suggestion that children younger than 2 years of age should not have any screen time at all. None. Nada. Zilch.

"Pediatricians should urge parents to avoid television viewing for children under the age of 2 years," the recommendation said. "Although certain television programs may be promoted to this age group, research on early brain development shows that babies and toddlers have a critical need for direct interactions with parents and other significant caregivers (e.g., child care providers) for healthy brain growth and the development of appropriate social, emotional and cognitive skills. Therefore exposing such young children to television programs should be discouraged."[1]

You might think that statement would close the book on the issue. After all, when doctors tell us that our kids should take antibiotics, get vaccinated or see a specialist, the overwhelming majority of us comply. But in this case, parents seemed to wave away the recommendation, or not even know about it. In 2004, when I first became aware of the AAP's edict, conversations with parents on the playground and in playgroups led me to believe that it was having little effect. Even my children's pediatricians seemed less than inclined to push the recommendation—the waiting room featured a television set that was usually showing a Disney movie. Later data showed that my peer group was not the only one ignoring the advice; a survey conducted nationwide in 2005 by the Henry J. Kaiser Family Foundation indicated that more than 60 percent of parents allow their children, ages 6 to 23 months, to be exposed to some TV or video media each day.[2]

I was one of them. My first daughter, Janelle, was born in April 2002, and a month later I was positioning her in front of the TV screen. She was a colicky baby. If she wasn't sleeping, she was usually fussing or crying. My husband and I tried everything—car trips, stroller rides, swaddling, massages, white noise, lullabies, pacifiers. I held her and rocked her for hours upon hours. Worried that there was something in my breast milk, I changed my diet. Our pediatrician wondered if she was suffering from acid reflux and prescribed Zantac. Little worked, and I was distraught. For a few months there were only two things that were guaranteed to provide fifteen minutes of calm. One was techno music by the pop singer Moby, cranked up to full volume on the stereo. The other was the Baby Einstein video called *Baby Mozart*. The video delivered an on-screen montage of toys and mobiles set against a white or black background. Janelle would stop fussing and turn her head to the screen. It was as if a switch had been turned off, halting the crying. A friend called the video "baby crack," and now I knew why.

This was before I learned about the AAP's no-TV recommendation, but even if I had known about it back then, I'm not sure it would have made a difference. All I cared about was that my baby seemed less unhappy. I wasn't going to question it. By the time Janelle was 6 months old, she had shaken the colic, and we were finally experiencing the joys of a happy child. With the benefit of hindsight and experience, I now think Janelle was experiencing acid reflux and digestion problems while also picking up on my own anxiety. But during those difficult six months, I was frankly too exhausted to understand that, let alone wonder what the TV might be doing to her.

Three years later, in April 2005, I attended the biennial meeting of the Society for Research in Child Development in Atlanta. The meeting draws child-development specialists from around the world, taking over two hotels for four days. It was there that I discovered just how much debate surrounds the AAP's advice against screen time. Whenever it was mentioned, some attendees would nod in agreement, while others would shake their heads. During one session, within a few minutes of a presenter concluding that the rule was "well taken," another stood up to declare that she disagreed with it.[3] On both sides, panelists admitted that there was very little evidence of harm or benefit to screen time.

Scientists at other times and places have also questioned whether the AAP's recommendation was a smart move. Why draw such a hard line, they ask? Why put parents in a bind of guilt when so little is known? One evening after participating in a journalism conference about child development, I cornered Jack Shonkoff, the chair of a committee at the National Academies of Science that was charged with examining research on early child development. I asked him what he thought of the rule. "Shame on them," he said, shaking his head. To jump the gun by telling parents not to expose their babies to TV of any kind, he suggested, seemed to scare parents more than help them.

The AAP has been stunned by the criticism. "They've come back at us tooth and nail," said Donald Shifrin, one of the physicians who served on the AAP's media committee. "We thought it was a fairly benign thing to suggest." The recommendation, he explained, was designed with the interests of children in mind, children so young they can't speak for themselves. Decades of research had shown that what babies need most is attentive, loving care from their parents, and no research had ever pointed to any advantage in exposing children under age 2 to a television set. With little else to go on, the AAP decided to take a "caveat emptor" position, sounding a warning about electronic media that it hoped would cause parents to think harder about what, when and why they were watching with their young kids.

"We thought it was fairly safe," Shifrin continued. "We thought that was the end of the story. We figured, we don't have any research to show this, but who is going to argue with this recommendation? Well, it hit the front page of the *New York Times* and it was an unbelievable lightning rod. And we were like, are we missing something here? Explain this to me: You actually want youngsters in front of the television?"

~⁓

Once my children were old enough to start crawling and toddling around the house, I couldn't help but be amazed at the way they were effortlessly absorbing a huge amount of information in what felt like the blink of an eye. Their ability to understand words spoken to and around them made me wonder about the impact of the flash of pictures and sounds from a video screen. What kind of wiring and rewiring was happening inside their little heads?

Scientists admit that they are in the dark about much regarding brain development. The media's impact on the developing brain is not easy to measure—partly because much of the science on the brain is still so new. Consider this apology in *From Neurons to Neighborhoods*, a landmark book from 2000 about the science of early childhood development: "There is one very important context for early development that is not addressed in this report, namely the media. . . . We are only beginning to understand the repercus-

sions of these trends for family life and child well-being. Our neglect of this topic is not a signal of any lack of concern; this is clearly
an issue that warrants substantial attention."[4] Not only is the science itself in its infancy, but media that is designed for babies has
only truly arrived in the past decade. Scientists say they have not
had enough time to see the long-term effects of these new products.
The first Baby Einstein video came out in 1997, so most of the babies exposed to the DVDs have not even graduated from elementary school. And while the evening news, soap operas and sitcoms
have been part of family routines for decades, increases in the
amount and variety of media available to households have led child-
development experts to raise alarms. Only in the last few years have
scientists started to lobby aggressively for the funding to do large
scientific studies of the media's effect on very young children.

But a good deal has come to light recently about brain development in young children generally. In the past decade, new research
has persuaded parents, educators and politicians that the preschool
years are very important for healthy brain development. An oft-
quoted statistic is that 90 percent of a child's brain is formed before
age 5.[5] Cities and states across the country are calling for better
post-natal care and more access to preschools so that children of all
walks of life can reap the benefits of healthy brain growth—and
the social, emotional and language development that goes with it.

William T. Greenough, a professor of neurobiology at the University of Illinois at Urbana-Champaign, is one of the scientists
responsible for this explosion of interest in the brain. Starting in the
1970s, he conducted several studies that compared the brains of rats
that were raised in "impoverished" versus "enriched" environments.
The impoverished rats, once they could be weaned from their mothers, were reared in small empty cages with no other rats for one or
two months. The enriched rats spent the same amount of time in
larger cages with other rats, surrounded by toys that encouraged exploration and play. After the rats died, scientists looked at their

brains and found that there was an unmistakable difference between them. The impoverished brains—particularly in a region called the cerebral cortex—were notably smaller than the enriched ones.

Picture the brain, whether rat or human, as a tangle of tiny rope fragments that are frayed at each end. Each piece of rope is a nerve cell, or neuron. The frayed ends are the axons and dendrites, branching out to meet—but not quite touch—the axons and dendrites of other neurons. The junctions between their tips are called synapses—channels through which bits of information are passed from one neuron to another.

Without those connections, information can't pass from one nerve cell to another. Learning can't happen. When a baby is born, its brain has a lot of developing still to do—and a lot of synapses to create. During a baby's first few years of life, they are being formed at a furious rate. One estimate is that 1.8 million synapses are produced per second from two months after conception until the baby is 2 years old.[6] After those first few years, the number starts to drop as unused connections atrophy. The brain is, essentially, deciding which junctions offer the most useful paths to understanding the world. The others—think of them as the dead-ends, the distracters—are pruned away. By adulthood, only half of the synapses are left.

The enriched rats in Greenough's experiments, it turns out, had bigger brains because they had bigger neurons, with more dendrites and more synapses.[7] Input from the rats' environment helped sprout and strengthen those connections. For the impoverished rats, on the other hand, it appeared that the brain suffered from lack of stimulation. Nothing prompted the growth of the neurons, so they just sat there, lacking miserably in the synapse department.

In the debate over nature versus nurture, the majority of scientists now believe that, while our genes play a large role in how we turn out, experience matters quite a bit, too. When you extrapolate from the results of studies like Greenough's—when you leap from caged rats to human beings—it becomes clear why people believe that children's earliest experiences can, literally, shape their brains. So it is easy to understand the anxiety surrounding the growing use of video and computer media around babies and toddlers. What happens if screen time is a significant portion of a child's early environment? What connections are being reinforced by TV shows, DVDs and videogames? And are they replacing "better" connections that come from real-world interactions? When the TV is on, are any synapses being pruned away? Could those being discarded be the very ones that might help a child become a sensitive, thinking person in the real world?

When I first read about synapse-pruning, I was awash in waves of guilt. I could no longer escape the idea that every interaction was shaping my baby's brain. I sank into my chair. I tried to block out those bad parenting moments, those days of sleep deprivation and short tempers and no patience, those hours when I was desperate to stick my baby in a bouncy chair, ignore her and lose myself in a cup of coffee for half an hour.

But when I talked with Greenough about his research, the guilt started to subside, at least a little. Extrapolating from rat research to the art and science of child rearing is a tall order. "These conditions were extreme," Greenough reminded me. Indeed, the small-brained rats' environment was quite impoverished. These poor animals had nothing to do and no other furry rodents to interact with for the vast majority of their days. This case wasn't one of not having the newest toys or not getting enough attention once in a while; this was real neglect.

It is a stretch to equate watching television with such dismal conditions, unless, of course, a baby is watching alone in an empty room for months at a time with no social interaction of any kind. But, still, I wondered about the effects of something less extreme, like a daily dose of *Barney*. Was there some smaller, difficult-to-detect harm that might come of screen time? After all, I thought, if pediatricians are telling parents to avoid even turning on the tube around children under age 2, they must have seen some signs of real harm. But in interview after interview, I heard the same refrain: There is little, if any, evidence of direct harm from a video screen. There is no science yet to show that the neural connections being made when young children view video images are mechanically different from those made when they watch flames flicker in the fireplace or ceiling fans spin on the ceiling. There are no credible studies showing a brain being wired "wrong" by watching television. Dig behind the scary headlines about TV causing attention deficit disorders or autism, and the depth of the fear seems out of proportion to the actual findings.

What I did learn, however, is how much parents need to be aware of screen time's indirect impact—the way it shapes their interactions with their children, which then shape their children's brains. This isn't about shielding a child's eyes from a TV screen for fear of toxic exposure. This is about giving children as many opportunities as possible to explore, play and interact with others. Looking at the science checked my guilt. But it also opened my eyes to a fuller awareness of what my daughters might be doing instead of spending time in front of the screen.

⁓

Ask today's parents what worries them most about screen time for their babies or toddlers and the answer is often ADHD—attention deficit/hyperactivity disorder. In the spring of 2004, an article from the journal *Pediatrics* reported that children who had watched a lot of television as toddlers were having attention problems at age 7. The study seemed to provide the first evidence that something about the images and sounds on television could, in fact, rewire a child's brain. On CNN, Anderson Cooper interviewed Sanjay Gupta, CNN's medical advisor, about the report, and both men warned parents not to expose their children to too much TV.[8]

The study was led by Dimitri A. Christakis, a physician who was then a researcher at the University of Washington's Child Health Institute. He and his co-authors analyzed data about more than 1,000 children from a national survey that spanned many years. The study did not provide any evidence that television caused the attention disorders, but it did show a link between the two. For each hour of television that toddlers watched daily, their risk of having attention problems was increased by almost 10 percent. Put another way, a child who watched two hours of TV per day before age 3 would be 20 percent more likely to have attention problems at age 7 than a child who watched no TV.

It was enough to make many families with toddlers incredibly nervous. But it was even more unsettling to many parents of older children who had been diagnosed with ADHD. These families were already coping with negative perceptions, since some people typically discount any medical basis for the disorder, assuming instead that ADHD children are simply out of control as the result of poor upbringings. Now parents had to contend with assumptions about their inability to turn off the tube. Some started harboring new guilt, mentally calculating hours of TV use when their children were very young. Others simply felt angry. "Stupid" was the way the study was described by one social worker who counsels parents and teachers about how to work with ADHD children (and who has a husband and two children with the disorder). "It's not even worth talking about," she told me. "It's so simplistic." To her, the article and the media frenzy surrounding it were simply another case of ignorant people believing that ADHD simply comes down to poor parenting.

A few months after the *Pediatrics* study appeared, Russell A. Barkley, a clinical scientist and authority on ADHD, wrote a critique of the paper that singled out several problems with it. He pointed out, for example, that the study had nothing to do with the clinical diagnosis of ADHD because it relied on parents' reports of the way their kids behaved. He called the study "a classic example of how investigator bias, a media propensity for sound bites and glibness, both coupled with a deeply held societal desire to blame parents for the problems of their children can all lead to the public being fed an exceptionally mistaken impression—that TV causes ADHD."[9]

The study started getting bad reviews from other places, too. Several developmental psychologists criticized the way the study's authors crunched their numbers. Specialists in the field of media and communications dismissed the study because it did not differentiate between good and bad television content, between background and foreground television, and between what was shown on television in the 1990s—when the data were collected—and what families watch today.

Critics also hinted at another limitation: the study was led by a pediatrician, someone whose badge says MD, not PhD. Tensions have always existed between medical practitioners, who have been known to roll their eyes at "navel gazing" scholars, and academic psychologists, who shake their heads at what they see as doctors' myopic focus on physical health. The relationship between pediatricians and child-development specialists is no different. So when Christakis's study hit the newspapers that spring, psychologists and child-development specialists were inclined to be suspicious. For years, academics had published studies about media and children that got no attention. Now, out of the blue, a pediatrician appears with a questionable study, and suddenly everyone takes notice. In private circles, developmental psychologists were asking themselves, Just who is this Christakis guy, anyway?

Dimitri Christakis is a pediatrician with a master's degree in public health who now serves as the director of the Child Health Institute. He and the co-director at the center, Frederick J. Zimmerman, have published several studies about television over the last several years. Although many of their studies highlight negative aspects of large quantities of screen time, in 2006 they wrote a book,

The Elephant in the Living Room, that highlights both the positive and negative impacts of television on children. When I read it, I came away with the feeling that they have more nuanced views on TV than the headlines about their studies might lead one to believe.

In my work for this book, I talked to Christakis several times about his approach to research. He started his career as an epidemiologist, someone who systematically studies the causes of diseases and how to control them. I realized that, when he started looking at the interplay of television and children's health, he couldn't help but think of television as something that caused problems—a toxin. In one of our first interviews, for example, he likened studies about the effect of television to studies on the effects of smoking: "When the first studies came out linking smoking to lung cancer," Christakis said, "people were making the same criticisms that have been made here." In those days, more than fifty years ago, people dismissed reports about the effects of smoking by pointing out that the data could only show a link between the two; there was no experimental research proving that smoking actually caused cancer. In regard to television and children's outcomes, "I think that's where we are right now," Christakis said.

The lung cancer comment alarmed me, but reading through Christakis's study linking television to attention problems calmed me back down. Why? First, consider the data used by Christakis and his colleagues. The study looked at responses from a random sample of parents around the country in the 1980s who had answered questions annually about their children's temperaments, behavior problems, math and reading skills, even whether their kids made their bed in the morning. The question about television use was framed as: How much time would you say your child spends watching TV on both a typical weekday and weekend day?

The questions about behavior problems were not related to ADHD—in fact, ADHD wasn't even mentioned. Five of the questions came from a well-regarded scale of behavioral problems relied upon by clinicians. Did the children have difficulty concentrating? Were they easily confused? Were they impulsive? Did they have trouble with obsessions? Were they restless? The mothers with answers that deviated dramatically from the mean—who, to put it simply, described the most extreme situations—were deemed to have children with attentional problems. These questions about hyperactivity, Christakis and Zimmerman wrote, are "similar to symptoms that are consistent with a diagnosis of ADHD."[10]

But Russell Barkley and other ADHD experts say that that conclusion is not valid. Yes, the disorder may be characterized by impulsivity, restlessness and an inability to concentrate, but it has little to do with being easily confused or obsessive. "I worry that we're connecting this global, inaccurate measure of viewing with a scale of attention problems that includes items that have nothing to do with attention problems," said Elizabeth Lorch, a psychologist at the University of Kentucky who studies ADHD children and television.

Still, behavioral problems—no matter what they are called—are worth worrying about. So, let's consider how the researchers came to their conclusions. First, they pinpointed a group of mothers with 7-year-old children who may not have had ADHD but who at least fell on the very high end of a scale of behavior problems. Then the researchers looked into the past history of each child. They didn't just consider the number of hours of television watched at ages 1 and 3; they also explored whether the hyperactivity might be explained by, say, the fact that the mother had been using illegal drugs when pregnant, that she was depressed, or that the child was growing up in a household with low socioeconomic status.

After all such factors were taken into account and the researchers had run the statistics through a set of mathematical formulas vetted by the university's review board, Christakis and his team still found a relationship between television viewing and what they called attentional problems. The two variables were correlated. When one went up, the other went up. The more television a child watched as a toddler, the more likely the child would be described as having problems at age 7.

Reported that way, the results sound pretty bad. But try turning it around: the more attention problems a child had, the higher probability that the mother resorted to turning on the television. In other words, couldn't the attention problems have led to the television use instead of the other way around?

This is what researchers mean when they say there is no proof of cause and effect. Christakis and his team did issue this warning within their paper. But they still concluded with this advice: "Limiting your children's exposure to television as a medium during formative years of brain growth . . . may reduce children's subsequent risk of developing ADHD."

Barkley, the ADHD expert, gets angry whenever he reads that last line. "Christakis really should have at least gotten some advice about known causes of ADHD," he said. Christakis, he continued, published results that show no cause and effect regarding a disorder that is not even in his specialty, and then he went so far as to offer advice on preventing the disorder. "That," Barkley said, "is the height of chutzpah."

What are the known causes of ADHD? Genes are the main culprit, according to the latest scientific studies. People with attention deficit disorder are simply born with it, even though the disorder may not be diagnosed until they hit elementary school. Some evidence is emerging that toddlers and even infants may show some of the traits that accompany attention problems, but specialists usually refrain from making a diagnosis until children are old enough to be expected to start organizing their lives and regulating their behavior. Anyone who has a toddler can tell you that they are, by definition, impulsive.

ADHD is "the most genetically influenced trait discovered to date in psychology," said Barkley. He mentioned that, if you average all the studies that test whether ADHD is heritable—which includes more than thirty studies around the world—you can attribute genetics to 80 percent of the variation between people with the disorder and those without. The most recent studies, he added, show that the number may be as high as 90 or 95 percent. Other researchers, using more conservative estimates with formulas to correct for various biases, show the heritability to be around 60 or 70 percent.[11]

Those results, though, beg the question: What about the other 5 to 40 percent? Couldn't a person's home environment contribute to part of that chunk? Could it be that a child with "ADHD genes," so to speak, is more susceptible to a negative influence in the environment?

That argument is exactly what Christakis professes, in fact. He wonders if television viewing might play a role in worsening attention problems among children already genetically predisposed to having them. "The issue shouldn't be, 'Was this study about ADHD or not?'" he told me. Instead, it should be about parents creating the best environments for their children given their individual needs. Parents, he said, should be asking themselves, "Am I doing everything I can to maximize their genetic predisposition to focus on something and pay attention? Because that is a good thing for life."

The nongenetic causes of ADHD are a subject of intense study among scientists. Joel T. Nigg, a neuro-psychologist at Michigan State University, is one such researcher. He has dedicated much of his career to exploring how environmental and genetic factors come together to cause ADHD. In his 2006 book, *What Causes ADHD: What Goes Wrong and Why?* he sifts through a wealth of studies that might offer some hints—including the scanty information available on electronic media. It is possible, he volunteered, that high amounts of screen time can affect children more "vulnerable" to ADHD, though he added that there is very little evidence of that being the case. He points out, for example, that the science is conclusive about the negative impacts of violent television on children's behavior, but no direct evidential line connects children who act out because they watch violent television and children who end up with diagnoses of ADHD.[12]

When I pressed him on whether I should be worried, whether those half-hours that I exposed my daughter to *Baby Mozart* were a big mistake, he said, "There is very little to go on. You've got a lot of speculation and a couple of intriguing and very flawed studies." He mentioned that he has found far more evidence that, in addition to genetics, ADHD is caused by other environmental factors like alcohol use during pregnancy, chemical pollution and, especially, the presence of lead paint in the home. Scientists have also found connections between ADHD and premature birth, but again those studies simply suggest a link between the two factors and give no real hints of what drives the onset of ADHD.[13]

ADHD experts are much more convinced that attention disorders might cause television use, instead of the other way around. Even at the tender ages of 1 and 3—the age of the children in Christakis's study—these kids may have been tough for their parents to manage. Perhaps naptimes were a struggle. Maybe these children were not content with a pile of toys and would instead start climbing the stairs, the furniture and the baby gates—behavior parents considered more dangerous than watching TV. Research on older children with attention problems has shown that parents use TV to give themselves a break, so it's not inconceivable that the same happens with parents of younger children.[14] "The relationship between early television viewing and later attention problems may be linked to child temperament as much or more than television causing children to be inattentive," wrote Tara Stevens and Miriam Mulsow, two ADHD researchers at Texas Tech University in a 2006 analysis of the viewing habits of kindergartners.[15]

Given the genetic basis of ADHD, it's also highly plausible that at least one of the parents had attention problems, too. Between 20 and 35 percent of parents with affected children have ADHD, Barkley said. People who study the disorder say that, compared to normal adults, a person with an attention disorder is more likely to—you guessed it—watch TV.[16] Why? It's been postulated that television becomes a comfort to people with attention disorders because they typically read less (since they are always getting distracted) and have a hard time making friends (due to their impulsivity).[17] And if the parent of a 1-year-old is watching television, it's a pretty good bet that his or her baby is being exposed to it as well.

Just as I had become persuaded that discrete amounts of nonviolent screen time are highly unlikely to do real harm, another alarming study appeared about young children and television. This one looked at autism. Conducted in 2006 by economists at Cornell University, the study crunched a series of statistics that came up with associations between autism, precipitation rates, and cable television subscriptions. Using 2003 data from California, Oregon and Washington, the study showed that in counties with relatively higher amounts of rain or snowfall—where children were presumably spending more time inside watching TV—there were higher rates of autism. The economists then compared cable subscription data from the 1970s and 1980s for counties in California and Pennsylvania (no word on why those states were chosen) and found that children in the counties with more cable subscriptions were also more likely to have autism.[18]

A flood of caveats accompanied this study—so many that the major media outlets did not even report on it. I read about it in the online magazine *Slate*. The study had not been published by an academic journal, merely posted on a Cornell Web site. It had not been subjected to peer review by other scholars, and it was done by economists, not child-health experts. It was not based on any data about whether the children actually watched television—let alone how much and what kind. Some experts suspected that the connection was spurious. They argued that the rise in autism rates could be due to doctors' newfound awareness of the disorder by the 1980s. Even if, as the study's authors contended, the analysis had taken that point into account, critics argued that other possible culprits weren't considered—like the mother's or father's age when the children were born, the rate of vaccinations, the rate of premature births, or environmental toxins. Whenever I asked experts in child development what they thought of the study's conclusions, many simply shook their heads, incredulous that it would be taken seriously.

In my mind, the biggest reason to take the autism-TV study with a huge grain of salt is the same one for being skeptical of headlines about attention deficit problems: the data may show an association between autism and television, but that does not mean that TV causes autism.[19] From what I have heard from parents with autistic children, it sounds quite possible that the disorder is leading to television use at young ages instead of the other way around. The behavioral problems often associated with autism are enough to break your heart, as was driven home to me by an email I received from a mother in Maryland whose 3-year-old son is autistic: "Out of complete desperation we began turning on the TV because it was the ONLY thing that would decrease his screaming and out of control behavior," she wrote. "We mostly put on *Baby Mozart*–style tapes, but he would watch things like *Teletubbies* and *Elmo* and *Wiggles*. To be honest he would watch 2–4 (OK sometimes more I admit it!) hours of TV a day (and night, like MIDDLE of the night . . . it was a rough two plus yrs)."

In fact, not only are many autistic children calmed by videos, but evidence suggests that they may be able to benefit from some of them. Take the popular video series *Thomas & Friends*. Thomas is a train engine with a face. With wide eyes, arched triangle brows and doughy cheeks, Thomas has become the celebrity du jour for 2- and 3-year-old boys. Surely some girls are enamored of Thomas, too, though I have to admit that my daughters haven't had anything close to the same infatuation as many of their male peers, who are obsessed with their Thomas model trains and have watched the show so often that they can recount every engine type and rail line with authoritative precision. Dare I mistake Percy (the happy green saddle-tank engine) for James (the arrogant scarlet one that can pull freight cars), and my friend's son will immediately correct me, his eyes filled with disdain for my ignorance.

Parents of nonautistic Thomas-loving boys may think that their children's behavior represents the height of obsession, but parents with autistic children who love Thomas can do them one better. A mother in New York City with an autistic 3-year-old told me that he is incessantly "scripting" Thomas, meaning that he repeats the dialogue from the show over and over again, throughout the day, no matter where they are. At one point, she said, her family got so exhausted by the Thomas talk that she instituted a "Thomas moratorium," holding off on the videos for several days. Eventually, she said, she relented. That was when she discovered that watching the train engines was having a positive effect. It was helping her son learn how to recognize facial expressions.

One of the primary characteristics of children who have autism spectrum disorder is their struggle to read other people's emotions and imagine what they are thinking. "The difference between a happy face and a sad face is very clear on Thomas, and they need that clarity," this mother told me. When watching the video, she said, her son will now spontaneously point to a frowning face and say, "He's sad." "And that's terrific," she continued, "because that's something that spectrum kids have a hard time with."

In 2002, a study by the National Autistic Society in the United Kingdom examined how children with autistic spectrum disorder relate to Thomas. The report concluded that Thomas often serves as a "gateway to learning" for children with autism spectrum disorder. Because children with the disorder are often attracted to objects arranged in straight lines and characters with exaggerated expressions—not to mention the predictable routines and roles played by the trains—the video series seems to hold just the right combination of elements for autistic kids.[20] Simon Baron-Cohen, director of the Autism Research Centre at Cambridge University, has taken a keen interest in the connection between shows like *Thomas* and autism. Recently, he launched a new line of DVDs specifically designed for autistic children called *The Transporters*. The videos feature animated buses, trams, boats and planes with faces. Episodes are just five minutes long, similar to those in the Thomas series, and each transporter emphasizes different human emotions, repeating "I'm sad," or "I'm excited," depending on the narrative. In early clinical trials using the videos for fifteen minutes a day over four weeks, children with high-functioning autism showed big gains in emotional skills. Free copies of the DVDs are now being distributed via the National Autistic Society's Web site to any resident of the United Kingdom.[21]

So, if the fears about ADHD and autism might be overblown, what about concerns that video and TV time are displacing time that a baby should be spending doing something else? In other words, instead of asking, "What is screen time doing to a baby's brain?" maybe we should be asking the opposite question, "What is it not doing?"

If you read the AAP's recommendation closely, this concern is the basis of its "no screen time" advice. Here is also where child-development specialists start to expound on video's potential for harm. Infants need to be given chances to touch, smell, hear, see—sense—the way blocks stack or wheels work or leaves dance in the wind. Toddlers need room and time to explore, to totter up the stairs, to fall on their diaper-padded bottoms and get up again. A child isn't getting much of that, the critics say, if she is strapped into a bouncy chair or stuck in an Ultrasaucer in front of a TV for long periods of time. Think of those brain synapses being picked and pruned. Don't we want to make sure that the brain gets lots of practice making connections that relate to motor skills and spatial relationships?

This all makes sense in theory, but is there any evidence that screen time is, indeed, displacing the time children might spend, say, crawling or toddling around? Do we know if TV time is keeping parents from interacting with their young ones? I observed plenty of babies and toddlers who were quite active in front of a television set, and I was often present when my daughters were watching a video, often even sitting right next to them and talking to them about the images on screen.

Elizabeth A. Vandewater, a researcher from the University of Texas at Austin, said she used to chastise her pediatrician friends for publishing a "no TV" edict without any empirical evidence to back up their recommendation. In 1999, the year of the AAP's recommendation, there was simply no evidence that television was leading parents to spend less time with their babies. So she set out to do the research herself. Her findings, published in *Pediatrics* in February 2006, were based on a national sample of more than 1,700 children from families with a multitude of different socioeconomic backgrounds. The parents had been randomly recruited to fill out twenty-four-hour time diaries of how they spent their days.

Among children under five, she found that there was no relationship between time spent watching television and time spent being read to. Nor did screen time seem to have a dampening effect on a child's time spent in active play. Even in families in which children watched television, they ran around outside and read books as much as families without much TV.

This surprising fact reminded me how easy it can be to assume that experts have it all figured out. More than a generation ago, for example, medical experts sounded warnings about the dangers of children sitting too close to the television set. A *New York Times* story in 1951 carried the headline "TV Called Threat to Child Eyesight" and noted that "long viewing in dark rooms is especially serious for those under 5." Fourteen years later, the *Times* ran another story that debunked that idea by quoting an eye physician, who called it "malarkey."[22] In 2004, the American Academy of Ophthalmology put out a brochure called *Eye Care Facts and Myths*. One myth is about the danger of sitting too close to the TV set. "There is no evidence that this damages their eyes, and the habit usually diminishes as children grow older," the academy says. "Children with nearsightedness sometimes sit close to the television in order to see the images more clearly."[23]

It is worth noting in Vandewater's study, however, that television did appear to be displacing two things. One was the children's time spent with their parents in activities other than television. The other was their time spent in creative play. This included what Vandewater called the "usual childhood creative pastimes," like coloring, playing a musical instrument, playing pretend or dress up, playing with toys, playing board games or making arts and crafts. An hour a day of television viewing among 0- to 2-year-olds was linked to a 9 percent reduction in creative play during the week and an 11 percent reduction on the weekend.[24] Vandewater concluded that the AAP was right to be concerned that screen time would affect babies' time with their parents. She is troubled, too, by the reduction in creative playtime.

Dimitri Christakis, the pediatrician behind the controversial attention disorder study, had also been wondering about how TV affects playtime. One of his hypotheses is that "the television has become the default" mode of entertaining young children. Maybe in poorer families, he said, parents cannot afford blocks and dolls, or don't recognize the value of them. In an unpublished pilot study in 2006, he tested what would happen if low-income mothers were given a set of new blocks—oversized Lego-like blocks called Mega

Bloks—and a handout listing some simple ideas about how to use them with their toddlers. After six months, he compared a group that received blocks to one that did not. The children in the group with the blocks were significantly less likely to have watched television. They also showed gains, compared to the control group, on tests of emergent language skills.[25] Christakis speculated that the gains may have come from the parents talking to their children while playing with them.

I am 100 percent behind any policy or outreach program that enables parents to spend more time playing with their children. But I have to admit that, in our household, the presence of toys was not always a deterrent from turning on the television. There were days when I felt I would have gone nuts without a short break, and the screen delivered. I wondered about parents under much more stress than me. What about families in which the mother is depressed or distracted and unable to interact positively with her children in the first place? When Vandewater announced the results of her survey, she stopped short of lamenting how problems could be solved if there were no TV. "This requires the assumption that turning off the TV would mean more time spent with parents, and requires the assumption that all time spent with parents is 'good time,'" she said. "It's the assumption that if we turn off the TV, all will be fixed."

~⌒

Consider the story of *Sesame Beginnings*, a line of videos for babies developed by the creators of *Sesame Street*. A few years ago, developers at Sesame Workshop found themselves in a bind. The nonprofit organization is known for conducting solid research on how children learn and respond to TV, and *Sesame Street*, which first aired in 1969, has been the subject of multiple peer-reviewed studies showing a positive benefit to its programming among children two years old and up. But by 2000, Sesame Workshop did not have any product on the shelves to compete with the flood of videos aimed at children younger than two. Their worry was that, after a few years, children (and parents) might grow attached to the characters in baby videos from companies like Nickelodeon or Disney, thus choosing preschool programming and products affiliated with those companies rather than *Sesame Street*.

But if Sesame Workshop did create a baby video, would the company honestly be able to say that a baby could benefit from it? Rosemarie Truglio, Sesame Workshop's vice president for research, needed advice. In 2003, she pulled together a roundtable of experts to figure out whether a video could be developed that had a basis in solid research. "They basically sent out a note of caution," Truglio said. "Less is more, and be careful not to over-stimulate infants because they close down and there are not opportunities for learning." Another concern was how to ensure that the videos encouraged, instead of replaced, parent interaction. "We wanted to make sure that if we were going to enter this area, we were going to be different," Truglio said. The question was, different in what way?

The workshop teamed up with Zero to Three, a nonprofit organization that publishes research on the importance of nurturing experiences in children's early years. With Zero to Three's guidance, Sesame Workshop decided that the most appropriate content for children this young would feature peeks into the households of Muppet families playing happily together. One segment, for example, shows a Baby Bird Muppet with a Mommy Bird Muppet. The mother sings, "Who's that baby looking in the mirror?" while Baby Bird squeals and smiles.

The *Sesame Beginnings* videos landed in stores in 2006, and when I saw them for the first time, I couldn't help but think, "Cute!" But my second thought was, wait, these videos are not so much about entertaining babies as about training parents. In scene after scene, the Muppets model what it means to be a good caregiver, with examples of games to play and songs to sing. A few months after the videos arrived in stores, I came across a blog entry from a mother in Kansas who said she sings the "Who's that baby?" song from *Sesame Beginnings* with her 8-month-old "all of the time." I found myself wanting to try out some of the videos' peek-a-boo games with my younger daughter and baby nephew. What's more, the DVD also comes with a Spanish-language track—a development that thrilled several of the social workers I interviewed. They say that videos are more powerful than paper handouts for the families they work with, even when the written advice is in Spanish.

Some child-advocacy groups, however, have labeled these videos as anything but good for families. In April 2006, just after the first videos were released, the controversy swelled, debates raging on television and in newspapers. The AAP complained that parents now had yet another inducement for exposing young children to the screen. A group called The Campaign for Commercial-Free Childhood denounced Sesame Workshop and the organization Zero to Three for trying to build brand preference among babies.

At the height of the *Sesame Beginnings* media storm, I was often asked what I thought about the videos. As shown here, research tells us that what matters is not that the videos exist, but how they might be used—and how often. I'm most mindful of Vandewater's survey data showing that television viewing among children under 2 is linked to a decrease in time spent with parents. That research prompted my mantra for thinking meaningfully about screen time for very young children: content, context, your child. Fruitful discussions about television don't hinge on synapse development, brain growth, or cognitive stimulation. Instead, they come down to those four words and the questions they stir up. Is the content appropriate for your child's age? Is it nonviolent? Is the use of screen time a relatively small part of your child's interaction with you and the real world? Are you considering your child's temperament and sensitivities? Is he overstimulated by what is on the screen? Is television being used as a way to defuse behavioral problems, and if so, is there something underlying those problems that you should see a pediatrician about? Is screen time a default activity that has started to replace the time your child could be playing creatively, or is it a needed substitute for a half-hour of feeling the effects of Mom becoming more and more stressed out?

Perhaps in an ideal world, where mothers and fathers have unlimited time to spend with their perpetually happy infants, it would never cross a parent's mind to use a baby video to catch a break. But in the real world, videos do become babysitters. The answer is moderation. If you are going to pop in a baby video, make sure that your child gets plenty of quality time with you, too.

NOTES

1. Committee on Public Education, 1999, p. 342.

2. Rideout and Hammel, 2006, p. 10.

3. This was an exchange between Tiffany Pempek and Dan Anderson of the University of Massachusetts at Amherst and Deborah Linebarger of the University of Pennsylvania. For more on Anderson and Pempek's work, see chapter 4. More on Linebarger's research is in chapter 8.

4. Shonkoff and Phillips, 2000, p. 221.

5. The 90 percent statistic is often quoted by advocates of more funding for preschool. One recent example: Huber, 2007, http://www.theolympian .com/112/story/61634.html.

6. Eliot, 1999, p. 27.

7. Ibid., p. 32.

8. Barkley, 2004, p.1. The study made headlines in most major newspapers, including the *Washington Post,* the *Chicago Sun Times, USA Today* and the *Wall Street Journal.* Headlines often mentioned "rewiring" of the brain, like this headline on an Associated Press story by Lindsey Tanner that was printed in the *Bergen County Record*: "TV May Rewire the Brains of Very Young Children."

9. Barkley, 2004, p. 10.

10. Christakis et al., 2004, p. 709.

11. Interview with Joel T. Nigg, ADHD expert at Michigan State University, March 13, 2006.

12. Nigg, 2006, pp. 285–286.

13. Bakalar, 2006.

14. Acevedo-Polakovich et al., 2005, p. 20.

15. Stevens and Muslow, 2006, p. 672.

16. This information is from conversations with ADHD experts. I have not found a published study that compares TV use by ADHD adults to TV use by non-ADHD adults. But in a time-diary survey conducted by Elizabeth Lorch of the University of Kentucky, parents of ADHD children were found to watch more television than parents who do not have children with ADHD.

17. Barkley, 2004, p. 9.

18. Waldman, Nicholson, and Adilov, 2006, pp. 1–47.

19. I should note that Waldman et al. argue that their data *can* provide cause-and-effect information. They argue that it is not simply associational data because of the way it is used in their analysis. For example, they write on page 24: "We can be quite certain that autism doesn't cause precipitation." Agreed. But can we be quite certain that autism doesn't cause television viewing? Given what is known about the behavioral patterns of autistic children, their antisocial tendencies and their fixations, it seems at least plausible that television is a coping tool for parents of autistic kids. The association between precipitation and autism is another puzzle; some have argued that environmental toxins associated with rainfall or associated with being indoors may be playing a role.

20. For more information, see the National Autistic Society's 2002 report, "Do Children with Autism Spectrum Disorders Have a Special Relationship with Thomas the Tank Engine, and If So, Why?" Summary can be downloaded from http://www.nas.org.uk.

21. For ordering information, see www.nas.org.uk. Information about Cohen-Baron's DVD series and research is from a news release on the National Autistic Society's Web site, "Animation DVD Helps Children with Autism to Recognize Human Emotions."

22. See "TV Called Threat to Eyesight," *New York Times,* April 6, 1951, and Phyllis Lee Levin, "Preserving Two Good Eyes," *New York Times,* February 28, 1965.

23. *Eye Care Facts and Myths: A Closer Look,* published by the American Academy of Ophthalmology, 2004.

24. Vandewater et al., 2006, p. e186.

25. Dimitri Christakis, Frederick J. Zimmerman, and Michelle Garrison, "Block Play and Language Acquisition, Attention Span and Television Viewing in Toddlers: A Randomized Controlled Trial," unpublished paper, Fall 2006, p. 5.

Chapter Two

Is TV Turning
My Tot Into a Zombie?

W hen babies are born, the philosopher William James once wrote, their world is "one great, blooming, buzzing confusion."[1] He couldn't have been talking about television, since he wrote the words more than a hundred years ago, and his ideas about child development have been debunked and refined as scientists have uncovered more about how much even newborns comprehend. But the idea that young children experience a "buzzing confusion" seems to have transferred to television critics who talk about TV zombies. They say that children become mesmerized by the flashing and buzzing of the screen itself instead of comprehending what is on it.

Jane M. Healy, an educational psychologist, added her voice to this line of thinking in her popular book, *Endangered Minds: Why Children Don't Think and What We Can Do About It*. In a section titled "The 'Zombie' Effect," she wrote that a few studies suggest that television programming may, under certain conditions among certain individuals, "suppress mental activity by putting viewers into a trance." She argued that, when children are faced with content that is difficult or confusing, they may be "physiologically compelled to 'space out.'"[2]

The Plug-In Drug, a best-selling book by journalist Marie Winn, makes a similar argument. Winn writes about what she calls "the television trance," arguing that children are zoned out intellectually when they are sitting in front of a screen. "There is certainly little indication that they are active and alert mentally," she wrote.[3]

These books were written more than a decade ago, but their arguments have shown remarkable staying power. Healy told me that another edition of her book is due out soon, but her argument will be unchanged from its first edition. She has continued to write about the dangers of media, including a commentary on the ill effects of television in the same issue of *Pediatrics* that contained Dimitri Christakis's controversial article linking television with attention problems.[4] Winn came out with a revised edition of her book in 2002, but the "zombie" argument remained intact.

In interviews with parents, I heard echoes of the same concerns. One mother who said she tries to avoid television described her 2-year-old daughter's response to the screen this way: "She gets a glazed look over her eyes and quits blinking. I have to repeat myself a bunch of times to get her attention." This mom is a former social worker with an Ivy League education who stays at home with her children and, from what I've seen in her interactions with them, watches them closely. Surely, I thought, she is sensing something real about the way television is affecting her daughter's ability to pay attention to the world around her. I, too, have witnessed my children so focused on the TV that they hardly notice what is going on in the room. Isn't it reasonable to ask whether something about the screen, with its constant color and movement, is causing them to fixate on it involuntarily?

In November 2006, I attended the annual conference for the National Association for the Education of Young Children. In one session, panelists debated the risk associated with screen time. During the question-and-answer period, an audience member stood up, mentioned Healy's *Endangered Minds* book, and noted how much she had learned from it. Dozens of attendees broke into applause.

But up on the dais, two of the panelists shook their heads. One was Elizabeth Vandewater, director of the Center for Research on Interactive Technology, Television and Children at the University of Texas at Austin. She had recently published a study in *Pediatrics* with data that raised questions about a few commonly held beliefs about screen time, like its supposed risks to reading and physical activity. The other was Deborah Linebarger, a professor from the University of Pennsylvania, who has published in several academic journals and worked with television programs like *Between the Lions* to promote reading among young children. Linebarger grabbed her microphone and argued that media could be a valuable tool. "I disagree with most of what Healy has written," she said. Vandewater followed up with her own criticism of Healy. "None of what she is writing," Vandewater said, "is based on empirical evidence."

The session ended a few moments later with disappointingly little discussion. I decided to get to the bottom of this. I went to the footnotes in the books that had stirred zombie worries but found little actual research to go to. Winn's book cited a 1976 letter to a psychiatry journal and a 1972 *Redbook* magazine article by the noted pediatrician, T. Berry Brazelton. In experiments with newborns exposed to flashing lights, Brazelton had found that babies eventually "shut down" and sleep. He speculated, without offering any further experimental data, that young children may become passive in the face of television, too.

Healy acknowledges in her book that research on the zombie question was "sorely limited."[5] Among the research she does cite is a 1988 report commissioned by the U.S. Department of Education and written by Daniel R. Anderson and Patricia A. Collins. She refers to their report to show that TV has been found to "create passive withdrawal" and attention problems, among other things. But when I read this report, it was clear that such statements occurred there only when flawed research was being rebutted. In a section titled "Attention to Television: A Summary," Anderson and Collins wrote that "the popular accounts of television viewing are wrong. As a rule, children do not just sit and stare at the television vacantly. . . . Children's attention to television generally appears to be a rational rule-guided activity which acts in the service of comprehension and allows engagement in concurrent activities."[6] When I interviewed Healy about the discrepancy between her interpretation and mine, she said that she and Anderson have always disagreed on this point, noting that he performed consulting work for children's television producers. I described the remarks made at the Atlanta meeting in which panelists criticized some of her work, arguing that there was no research behind it. On the zombie effect, she freely admitted to me, "There isn't any, and there wasn't any when I wrote the book. . . . Parents just have to use common sense."

In short, I realized that I would find no solid science behind theories of children mentally spacing out when placed in front of the TV. As I continued to dig for information, what I found instead was just the opposite of what had been proposed in these popular books. It turns out that there is a growing pile of evidence, published in peer-reviewed journals and replicated in multiple studies, that contradicts the zombie theory almost entirely.

～◡

Daniel R. Anderson has, it's true, been paid by television producers for his advice on programming; for example, he was a consultant for Nick Jr. during the creation of *Dora the Explorer*. But his main job is as a developmental psychologist at the University of Massachusetts, where he has spent more than thirty years conducting research funded by agencies like the National Institute of Mental Health and the National Science Foundation on how children respond to television. His research on television began in the spring of 1972, when he was an assistant professor teaching a class on child development. After one of his lectures, in which he talked about how young children in general have trouble sustaining attention, he was approached by an undergraduate with a question. If that is true, the student asked, why is it that my 4-year-old brother can just sit and stare at *Sesame Street*?

"Glibly and with the aplomb of a person who is deeply ignorant," Anderson recalled, "I replied that the child's sustained attention was illusory, the TV was just a distractor that remained in place. A movement or visual change on the TV screen would attract the child's attention, and before she could look away, another movement or change would occur and so she would keep looking."[7]

This was the conventional wisdom at the time, Anderson said. The idea stemmed from three concepts commonly taught in human development and psychology courses: the "novelty preference," "habituation" and the "orienting response." The novelty preference is essentially jargon for the truism that babies love what is new. As the neuroscientist Lise Eliot puts it in her book, *What's Going On in There?* "babies crave novelty. They quickly grow bored with the same old toys or food or four walls, which is one reason that even the fussiest newborn is calmed by a trip outside or in the car."[8] In experiment after experiment, when a baby is offered the choice of something new over something familiar, he will gaze at or grasp for the new one. The only exception to this rule seems to be when the familiar thing happens to be Mom's face or the face of anyone else who evokes feelings of strong emotional attachment.

Habituation is almost the opposite of the novelty preference. Think of it as a fancy word for "been there, done that." When researchers talk about babies habituating to a stimulus, whether it is a toy, a photograph or a spoken word, they are essentially saying that babies have no interest in engaging with it any more. They may turn their gaze and search around for something else to occupy their minds instead. Habituation experiments are common among psychologists who are trying to determine when a baby has learned or processed a piece of information. For example, in testing a baby's color vision, researchers will show a baby a colored card over and over until she seems to habituate and grow bored with it. Then they will pull out another color. If the baby perks up and seems to show interest, that suggests she has recognized that there is a difference between the two colors.[9]

The orienting response is the reaction animals of all kinds exhibit when they are startled or suddenly exposed to a new sight or sound. It's a survival mechanism. Our instinct is to turn our heads and look toward the sound of breaking glass or the sudden flash of light. In infants, this response or reflex is developed by the first three months of age.[10]

Given these well-established concepts, it makes sense that, when a TV is switched on, a baby will almost surely turn to the screen— a classic case of the orienting response. Because what the child sees is probably something new to her, she'll show a novelty preference and keep looking at it. If the image on the screen were to remain perfectly still and the sound unchanging, she might become habituated to it. But video is never still and unchanging. "With television, there is no opportunity for habituation," Anderson told me. "The sound, the picture is never the same."

Sesame Street, for example, is a string of short animated and live-action clips. Colors and movement change on screen with each passing second, letters move and sway, children dance, Muppets appear and disappear. Baby videos are no different. On the *Baby Mozart* video, for example, the screen shows a toy train clicking along a track against a black background. Then there is a cut. The video clip of the train is gone. A puppet is moving on screen instead. Then a toy ferris wheel appears. No more than a minute elapses before the image changes again. For a child who has never seen these objects, or has simply never seen them on screen, there is no chance to get bored.

Still, Anderson started to think more deeply about his student's question. He realized that he didn't actually know for a fact that the visual features on *Sesame Street* were to blame for a child's seeming fixation. He asked a graduate student, Stephen Levin, to review whatever evidence existed on the subject. Levin came back empty handed. There was no research. Anderson was intrigued. He wrote a grant proposal to the National Science Foundation, got the funding, and resolved to study the question himself.

Anderson and Levin recruited seventy-two children, ages 1 to 4 years, to participate in their study. The parents were asked to bring the children to a viewing room in Amherst, Massachusetts (where they lived), to watch a never-before-seen episode of *Sesame Street*. The viewing room held comfortable furniture and toys appropriate for preschool children. A table held juice and crackers for the children and coffee and tea for the adults. Two video cameras recorded the children's movements.

Afterward, the researchers pored over those video recordings. If a child looked at the screen, they marked the time. When the child looked away, they noted that, too. Every onset and offset of looking was recorded. The result was a series of precise notations on exactly how much attention children of varying ages paid to the program. "From 1 to 4 years of age, there was a dramatic increase in attention to the television," Anderson and Levin wrote in a 1976 paper for the highly respected journal *Child Development*.[11] The youngest children were far more interested in the toys, looking at the screen for no more than about a minute at a time, a total of about 10 percent of the time. The older children also played with toys and looked away from the screen at times, but when they did watch, they watched more deliberately. They looked 50 percent of the time,[12] with looks lasting up to seven minutes at a time. It wasn't clear exactly why they turned their attention to the screen. Some visual and auditory features on the screen apparently captured their notice, and some didn't. Anderson needed to learn more.

Over the years, as Anderson has observed children watching television of various kinds under various conditions, he and his colleagues have come up with answers about how and why children become focused on the screen. Yes, the look and sound of the screen does have an effect. Children pay attention to colorful puppets. They like peculiar voices, sound effects, movement, rhyming and repetition. They don't pay attention to long zooms or long periods of inactivity.[13] And contrary to the zombie theory, children do look away from television, as much as 150 times per hour.[14]

More importantly, the researchers found that young children watch television because they are cognitively engaged in it. In one study, for example, they created altered versions of *Sesame Street* that made no sense and showed them to children aged 2, $3^{1}/_{2}$, and 5 years old. Some of the segments were made from chopped up pieces of *Sesame Street* pieced together in random order. Others were segments in which every word was uttered backward. (If someone said the word "fan," for example, it came out as "naf.") Still others were segments in a language the children had never heard before—Greek, in this case. The theory was that, if children paid more attention to the regular programming, it was a near certainty that they were watching because they found some meaning in what they saw.

The result? The children clearly noticed the difference. When the scrambled version was on, they complained that something was wrong with the TV. They looked more frequently and for longer periods of time at the *Sesame Street* program that they could comprehend. Even the 2-year-old children behaved this way. They did not appear to be in the grip of some kind of irrepressible force locking their attention to the screen.[15]

In study after study throughout the last several decades, Anderson and psychologists at other research centers have encountered children who show evidence of being mentally engaged with what they are watching. "They would ask questions, like 'what's going to happen next?' or, 'is that real?'" Anderson told me. "They didn't look like mindless zombies."

David Bickham, a staff scientist at the Center for Media and Child Health in Boston, Massachusetts, credits this work with sharpening the science on how children watch television. It is now widely believed among psychologists and media researchers that, if children don't pay attention, it's typically because they don't understand what they are watching. If they do pay attention, it's because they are able to comprehend at least some of what they see. "Anderson and his colleagues pioneered the theory," wrote Bickham in 2001, "that children's perceptions of the comprehensibility of a message determine their attention to it."[16]

One day, while immersed in these experiments, Anderson noticed something curious about the way these children looked at *Sesame Street*. Anyone familiar with the show knows that it is comprised of multiple segments. At one moment, for example, the program may be broadcasting an animated cartoon about the letter B, then cut to a scene in front of Mr. Hooper's store. You might think that children would be more prone to look away when one of these segments ended and another began. But Anderson noticed that the longer the children had been watching, the more they wanted to keep watching, regardless of the cuts. In controlled experiments, he found that, if children had been watching the screen for about fifteen seconds when those cuts occurred, the children were likely to keep their gaze trained on the television for the second segment. If they had been engaged for less than fifteen seconds, they usually turned away.[17]

Anderson coined a term for this phenomenon: "attentional inertia." When I first heard the term, I couldn't help but think it was bad news. Something about the word "inertia" conjures images of zoned-out human beings too lazy to get off the couch. But Anderson wasn't thinking of it that way. He explained that this behavior is not an unfavorable one at all, but actually a signifier of deepened engagement. In a book about the history of Nickelodeon, Anderson described attentional inertia as "the major mechanism by which a young child will continue to pay attention to the program even when the content is difficult for that child to understand."[18] It can play a role in teaching children new things, he said, but, on the flip side, it can get children to keep watching despite cuts to commercials.

The phenomenon has been observed for activities beyond television as well. Research has shown that it exists when children are playing with toys, and that it occurs in adults, too.[19] We all know how hard it can be to get our spouses to answer a question when they are engrossed in reading a book or responding to email. The mother of the 2-year-old who had trouble getting her daughter to look away from the TV was probably experiencing the same thing. Her child was glued to the screen because she was cognitively engaged in what she saw.

～◯

It seems clear that the zombie theory for children 2 years and older doesn't stand up to scrutiny. But what about babies? Maybe, I thought, automatic mechanisms like the orienting response and the novelty preference are the sole reasons infants and young toddlers pay attention to the screen. Anderson himself readily acknowledges that the research on babies is sparse compared to what is known about preschoolers' ability to be mentally engaged in TV and videos. With babies, he told me, it's "quite possibly a different story."

New research over the past few years is providing some answers. Some of it is happening about 900 miles to the south of Anderson's Amherst lab, at the University of South Carolina. There, a psychologist named John E. Richards has been observing the ages at which babies start to exhibit signs of paying sustained attention to something.

For his tests, Richards asks parents to bring their babies to his laboratory and watch video clips. During each trial, he records exactly how long the babies look at the screen. But he doesn't rely exclusively on these looking times. He measures babies' heart rates, too. He has found that infants' heart rates slow down when they are in a period of sustained attention and engagement. This finding is important because he has also learned that the brains of very young babies—2-month-olds—may not be developed enough to prevent their eyes from fixating on something.[20] Using heart rates as a measure of attention, he said, can thus be more accurate than look lengths in very young children.

In one study, he and his colleague, Erin D. Turner, brought families into their laboratory, hooked up the children to heartbeat monitors, and then asked parents to hold their children on their laps. In front of them were three screens. The center one showed several *Sesame Street* programs. The peripheral screens were intended to be distractions. They showed muted versions of *The Muppet Movie* and a video clip of black-and-white geometric shapes moving on screen.

When the babies' responses were reviewed, several things seemed to be happening in tandem. As soon as the length of a look increased to a point of "attentional inertia," a child would become less distractible and his heart rate would decelerate. As soon as his heart rate started to go back up, the child would be more distractible and less engaged. This was the case across all ages of children, from 2 years old down to 6 months. Even at that young age, they concluded, children show signs of sustained attention to the television.[21]

Anderson and Tiffany Pempek, a doctoral student at Amherst, paired up with Richards's South Carolina lab to answer the next logical questions: Is this sustained attention a sign of mental engagement? Or is it just a baby's version of spacing out? To find out, they decided to do a test very similar to the one they had tried with preschoolers and *Sesame Street*. This time, however, they chose *Teletubbies*.

Teletubbies is a colorful, dreamy, thirty-minute television show that bounced onto the toddler scene in the United Kingdom in 1997. Soon afterward, it was launched on PBS in the United States.

Andrew Davenport and Anne Wood, British writers with decades
of experience in children's programming, designed *Teletubbies* for an
audience of 9-month- to 36-month-old children, making the show
controversial from the start. Its main characters are four pudgy,
huggable creatures with televisions in their tummies who speak in
simple sounds ("eh-oh!") and songs (like "laa-laa-li-laa-laa-li"). According to the creators, "the main concerns [of critics] seemed to
center around these extraordinary creatures—Tinky Winky, Dipsy,
Laa-Laa and Po—being incapable of speaking the Queen's English,
and as a result, future generations' diction would be irreparably
damaged."[22]

I know plenty of parents who cringe at the thought of being
subjected to a half-hour of giggling teletubbies but who grudgingly
acknowledge that their children are enchanted by them. The visual
imagery is almost psychedelic. The singular colors of the characters—red, blue, yellow and neon green—stand out against the golf-
green hills of Teletubby Land. A baby-faced sun smiles down. The
music is lively and repetitive. Midway through the show, the action
temporarily cuts to a live-action video of real children playing or
learning something new, like exploring musical instruments. The
live-action video replays itself after the tubbies gleefully shout,
"Again! Again!" and eventually the viewers are taken back to the
green rolling hills.

When *Teletubbies* hit Australia, a couple of professors of media
and education at Australian universities decided to do a systematic
study on how young children responded to the show. Susan Roberts
of Macquerie University in Sydney and Susan Howard of the University of South Australia recorded twenty toddlers as they watched
an episode in their homes and daycare centers. Reviewing the
recordings later, they took methodical notes on children's attention
levels, verbal or physical responses, and facial expressions. "Some
were rapt and very still, gazing at the screen with a fixed, almost un-
blinking, intensity," Roberts and Howard wrote. "Others could

barely contain themselves with excitement but were nevertheless focused on the screen." Instead of being "mesmerized," they continued, the children's body postures and facial expressions "all indicate engagement with the object of the gaze."[23]

Anderson and Pempek, however, felt that they needed to dig deeper than simply looking at children's responses to the show. They wondered if very young viewers found anything meaningful in what they saw. And, if so, they wanted to know the youngest age at which this comprehension might exist. So they took a ten-minute segment from *Teletubbies*, chopped it into pieces lasting six seconds each, and shuffled them around. This doctored version made no logical sense and followed no narrative line. In the original *Teletubbies* segment, for example, one video shot showed a teletubby throwing a ball, the next shot showed the ball flying through the air, and the next showed the ball bouncing to the ground. But in the incomprehensible version, the sequence went something like this: a shot of a ball flying through the air, a shot of teletubbies standing around, and then a shot of a teletubby contemplating whether to throw a ball.

Babies were exposed to both the mixed-up *Teletubbies* and the original one. The test, like the *Sesame Street* test with preschoolers, was whether the babies would show evidence of discriminating between them. Would there be a difference in the way babies paid attention? Would they look longer, and would their heartbeats decrease while watching the comprehensible show?

The answer, they found, depended on the baby's age. At around 24 months old, babies could clearly see a difference between the two. The original video with its logical, sequential narrative appeared to hold some meaning for them. Babies of 18 months of age could discriminate, too, though on average the differences were not quite as sharp. But with kids 12 months or 6 months of age, there was no sign that they were seeing any difference between a scrambled, incomprehensible sequence of shots and a video that told a simple story.[24] "This suggests that 12-month-olds are not yet perceiving the relationship between shots," Anderson told me. "They are interpreting each snippet of video as one piece. They are living in the present and not constructing any kind of narrative understanding of what they are seeing."

Anderson and Pempek did the same experiment using a *Teletubbies* that featured backward speech, and their findings were confirmed. By 18 months, children had started to notice the difference between the two versions. But at 12 months, there was no evidence that the babies detected any difference. "It appears that they are not very sensitive, linguistically speaking, to the comprehensibility of the language at 12 months," Anderson said.

It is a leap, of course, to say that these results prove that 12-month-olds watching television are simply zombies with no mental engagement. They may be understanding what is happening in the individual six-second shots, or they may at least be recognizing the characters on the screen. In other words, it is unclear how much those snippets of information translate into something that children grasp in any meaningful way. Much more research needs to be done, Anderson commented, before he is willing to make big pronouncements on whether television causes babies to fixate on a screen for no cognitive reason, simply triggering an automatic instinct to watch what is salient and new.

⌐∽

Something was missing from these studies. I was fascinated to hear and read about new studies on babies and their attention to video, but the research didn't get to the depth of questions parents have about their children's responses to video. Nowhere in the dozens of academic papers on young children's attention to television was there any discussion of how different children can be, even within the same age group. I remember how amazed I was as a new mother to compare my friend's 6-month-old boy—who was mellow, relaxed, and often transfixed in quiet contemplation—with my wriggling, wiry, hyper-alert girl of the same age.

In front of videos, babies respond just as differently. I've seen babies who immediately bounce up and down in their "exersaucers" or jumpy swings. I've see babies who get very quiet and focused. Some cry. Some stop crying. Some bang their hands excitedly against their thighs. Some laugh. Some vocalize with ahhs and eehs. Some fall asleep.

After babies are crawling, pulling themselves up, or taking steps, the way they watch differs, too. Many children want to move around. They won't tolerate sitting in front of the screen. Others stop and settle in for a long view. Some point and verbalize. Others don't. Some seem fascinated. Others could not care less. Parents have told me about their toddlers being able to watch a full half-hour show with intense concentration. Other parents have said that their children seem to have no interest in the screen whatsoever.

Rochelle Newman, director of Language Perception and Development Labs at the University of Maryland, recently completed a study of 12-month-olds who were assigned to watch video montages while listening to a fairy tale. She, too, saw a wide span of interest. "There are some infants who don't care at all about TV," she told me, "and some who do." Even the same child, at the same age, can vary from day to day, or hour to hour. Consider this post from the Baby Einstein Web site: "My 20 months old son has adored *Baby Mozart, Baby Bach, Baby Newton,* and *Baby Van Gogh* for 5 months now. He lovingly refers to them as his 'show.' He watches a 'show' anywhere from 5 to 10 times a day. He loves to nap to these 'shows.' Often he will play during his 'show,' but sometimes he plops himself down with his blanket and binky and watches."

None of this would shock child-development specialists except, perhaps, the idea of a 20-month-old watching a show ten times a day. People trained in early childhood education are continually pointing out that children are unique. Each one develops in different ways, with different temperaments and different reactions to different stimuli and environments. It is likely that the way they react to and are affected by media will depend on their individual constitutions.

"Children are not a monolithic group in terms of how they take in and process information," said Claire Lerner, the director of parenting information at Zero to Three, a national organization that focuses on healthy child development. The problem is that research on how children of different temperaments respond to video is essentially nonexistent. So far, researchers are too preoccupied with nailing down some basic knowledge about how and why screen time affects children at different age groups. Questions about differences within those age groups may hang out there for quite some time.

In the meantime, Lerner said, parents should do everything they can to tune into their children, to know them. If you think your child is too focused on the screen, ask yourself if watching is easier for your child than being socially engaged. Or is the content suddenly fascinating to him? Is this a baby who responds well to one type of programming but becomes agitated by another?

After age 2 especially, your child might simply be one who cannot get enough of stories, whether they appear on screen or in books. Just as many children would protest the closing of a book before it is finished, they may want to stay glued to the screen until a show wraps up. In such cases, the scientific evidence is clear: they are not zombies; instead, they're engaged.

NOTES

1. James, 1905, p. 462.
2. Healy, 1990, p. 203.
3. Winn, 2002, p. 17, and accompanying footnote on page 306.
4. Healy, 2004, pp. 917–918.

5. Here is Healy's full quotation from *Endangered Minds* (p. 204): "Taken together, this sorely limited research suggests that children may be physiologically compelled to 'space out' when viewing fatuous, overly difficult or confusing content." Earlier in the chapter, in bullet points on pp. 197–198, she highlights statements from the 1988 report by Anderson and Collins "that didn't make the headlines" but that she sees as evidence of television causing attentional problems.

6. Anderson and Collins, 1988, pp. 11–22.

7. Chapter by Anderson in Hendershot, ed., *Nickelodeon Nation*, 2004, p. 242.

8. Eliot, 1999, p. 340.

9. Ibid., p. 216.

10. Interview with John Richards, cognitive and developmental scientist at the University of South Carolina, March 6, 2006.

11. Anderson and Levin, 1976, p. 810.

12. Chapter by Anderson in Hendershot, *Nickelodeon Nation*, 2004, p. 244.

13. Anderson and Collins, 1988, p. 17.

14. Ibid., p. 32.

15. Chapter by Anderson in Hendershot, *Nickelodeon Nation*, 2004, pp. 247–248.

16. Bickham, Wright, and Huston, 2001, p. 106.

17. Anderson, Choi, and Lorch, 1987, p. 788.

18. Chapter by Anderson in Hendershot, *Nickelodeon Nation*, 2004, pp. 253–254.

19. See Choi and Anderson, 1991; and Anderson and Burns, 1993.

20. This is a behavior called "obligatory looking," which has been shown to occur in the second month of life. Lise Eliot in *What's Going on in There* described it as a baby's gaze "getting stuck," sometimes for thirty minutes or more.

21. Richards and Turner, 2001, pp. 963–972.

22. Web site for Ragdoll Ltd, the company owned by Anne Wood, http://www.ragdoll.co.uk/html/story.html, accessed November 19, 2006.

23. Roberts and Howard, 2005, p. 99.

24. Pempek et al., 2007.

Chapter Three

Could My Child
Learn from Baby Videos?

T he story of Baby Einstein's arrival is legendary. In 1996, a new
mother and former high school teacher named Julie Aigner-
Clark started looking for a video that could expose her baby
daughter to the beauty of art, music and poetry. Finding nothing
on the market that she believed appropriate for a baby, Aigner-
Clark decided to create a video herself. Working in her basement
using borrowed video equipment, computer software and an in-
vestment of a few thousand dollars, she created the first two
videos—*Baby Einstein Language Nursery* and *Baby Mozart*—of
what would become a $25 million company, purchased by Disney
in 2001.[1] By 2006, Baby Einstein products were being distributed
to thirty countries in twenty-five languages, garnering Disney
$250 million in revenue that year.[2] Their success even sparked a
television series for preschoolers called *Little Einsteins*. The Baby
Einstein Company has become an inspiring example for entrepre-
neurial mothers everywhere.

Baby Einstein was born the same year that Don Campbell's
book *The Mozart Effect* was appearing on store shelves. The book
posed the theory that one could become smarter and healthier by
listening to the music of Mozart. It was loosely based on research
from the University of California at Irvine, where scientists had
found that college students performed better on a spatial IQ test

after listening to Mozart for ten minutes. Many respected psychologists have since discredited Campbell's claims, calling them exaggerated, distorted and irresponsible.[3] But they don't seem to be reversing the belief among parents that classical music is good for their babies' brains. Videos and audio CDs for children that feature classical music continue to sell at a brisk pace, and, if searches on Amazon.com are any indication, Mozart has been resurrected as a popular children's entertainer.

Music from Mozart is not the only feature of the *Baby Mozart* video. Aigner-Clark calls her products "video board books," and it's an apt description. Think of those small books with stiff cardboard pages that show simple objects in bright colors: Here's a doggie. Here's a toy train. Here's the color blue. The Einstein videos do the same, with the addition of movement and music.

People buy baby videos for many reasons. They make easy babyshower gifts. They are a surefire way to safely occupy infants while Mom or Dad is in the shower. They placate a fussy baby. And they offer the promise of an "educational" experience. The first line of baby videos, for example, came from a company called Brainy Baby. It started selling videos in 1995, two years before *Baby Mozart*'s debut, and the stated purpose of its products was to cognitively stimulate babies. Here is a description of the company's *Left Brain* video in its 2005 Product Catalog: "Helps develop the left side of the brain by featuring logical images, classical music and gentle voices. Focuses on building such cognitive skills as Logic, Patterns, Letters & Numbers, Sequencing, Analyzing details, and more! 45 minutes. For ages 6 to 36 months."[4]

As a combo deal in 2005, Brainy Baby sold an Infant Learning Pack and Brain Power Pack, with four videos to a box. Other baby videos have made educational claims, too. Baby Einstein says it "creates engaging learning opportunities." Nick Jr.'s *Curious Buddies* video claims it is "specifically designed for babies' social, emotional, cognitive and physical development."[5] A video called *Your*

Baby Can Read, created by an educator named Robert C. Titzer in Louisville, Tennessee, is promoted as a "multi-sensory reading approach [that] may help new synapses form among the visual, auditory, and somatosensory areas of the brain."[6]

It's hard to know how much credence parents put in such promotions. When I resorted to the *Baby Mozart* video for my 5-week-old, I didn't have time to think about what the words on the box meant. But many people believe the products are giving their children a jumpstart on learning. The mother of a 27-month-old told the Baby Einstein Company that her son now "has vocabulary consistent with that of a 3 to 4 year old. . . . He consistently knows 5 colors and 5 shapes. I attribute a lot of this to the material in the program." Her family, she said, had bought every one of the Baby Einstein videos. Another mom wrote about her 20-month-old son: "He is also learning his colors, thanks to *Baby Van Gogh!*"[7]

In 2005, the Henry J. Kaiser Family Foundation decided to look into the claims made by some of these video makers and report on the scientific research behind them. After extensive searches and interviews, the foundation came up with nothing. In a report titled "A Teacher in the Living Room?" it concluded that there was a "paucity of published research documenting the impact of educational media on very young children." Only one company—the nonprofit Sesame Workshop—was apparently doing scientific research on its products that could be made available to the public.[8] And at the time, that research wasn't about babies.

When the foundation released its report in December 2005, it held a forum at its offices in Washington DC on the subject of electronic media and young children. Company representatives were invited to speak. When asked, "Where is the research?" many responded that they chose to rely on testimonials and anecdotes. One of the panelists was Julia Fitzgerald, vice president of marketing for VTech, a technology company that makes electronic gaming systems for young children. "The way we look at research, parents don't really care about data," Fitzgerald said. "They care about one, two or three kids"—their own. She read a quotation from a mother about how her child struggled to learn the ABCs. "With our product," Fitzgerald said, "she had success."

In the minutes after the forum ended, I asked Dennis Fedoruk, the founder of Brainy Baby, what research he did before embarking on production. He handed me a piece of paper listing Web sites and a few trade books about brain growth in children. Over the past decade, scientists have discovered a lot about how babies learn, he told me. The question, he said, was, "How can we make this research beneficial to children in video form?" His answer was to create video montages of animals, shapes and colors. Although his company tested the videos with infants and toddlers to see if they held kids' attention, he acknowledged that no scientific research had been done on what babies were gaining cognitively—let alone whether the right or left sides of their brains were growing as a result.

Representatives for Baby Einstein were conspicuously absent that day, but I remembered the words spoken by the company's general manager, Russell Hampton, in an interview with me a year earlier. The videos were designed to be educational and developmentally appropriate, he had said, but the company did not test whether babies were, in fact, learning anything from them. "We are not a curriculum-based brand," Hampton stated. "We are not a research-based brand."

Six months after the Kaiser forum, an advocacy group called the Campaign for a Commercial-Free Childhood filed a complaint of fraud with the Federal Trade Commission. Three companies were named in the complaint: Disney's Baby Einstein, Brainy Baby and BabyFirst TV, a twenty-four-hour satellite channel. "It is clear as day that these claims are deceptive," said Josh Golin, the campaign's program manager. (The Federal Trade Commission had not made its decision as of this writing.)

Given such a dearth of answers about whether babies learn from these particular videos, I wondered if there wasn't at least some evidence, in some infant lab somewhere, of babies learning from video in general. If so, what did they learn? What type of video "worked?" And at what age did children show signs of remembering, processing and using the information they absorbed?

Over the next several months, I found not just one lab but many that use video with infants and toddlers. Some have conducted studies that speak specifically to the question of whether, or when, babies can learn from video. Their results have opened my eyes. I saw solid evidence that infants and toddlers can imitate something they have seen on TV if the conditions are right. One prerequisite, for example, is repetition—showing the same thing as many as six times in a row. I found a number of studies showing that toddlers can match words to pictures under tightly controlled training conditions— we're talking about slow, unadorned and repetitive auditory information precisely timed to connect with what is shown on screen. But I also found a lot of evidence showing that video exposure is no match for the stimulation children experience in real life. Scientists have so far come up with nothing to suggest that babies are better off watching a baby video than, say, watching Dad fold laundry.

~~~⌒

I started this quest for research with a naïve understanding about how scientists are conducting studies of the developing brain. Given what is now known about how neural synapses are formed and pruned in the earliest years of life, I thought I might find a laboratory wiring up babies to capture data on, say, how many synapses are formed while viewing different types of video. I was mistaken. So far, most brain scanning machines provide scientists with broad, panoramic snapshots of activity in a live human brain. These pictures don't get close to the detail of showing individual neurons. Specialized microscopes have provided a few scientists with week-by-week snapshots of individual neurons in live mouse brains, but holes must be cut in the rodents' skulls to get these pictures, hence little, if any, of this type of research has been done with human beings.[9] Even studies that delve into basic explorations on how children's brains develop are hard to come by, and I came up with none that pose questions about how children process information on video.

But a 2006 study of adult brains could provide a clue. The study used a technique called functional magnetic resonance imaging, or fMRI, which takes pictures of the brain at work. People who undergo fMRI scans are usually told to lie down, face up, on a sliding cot that is inserted into a magnetic tunnel. A viewing screen can be positioned overhead. While they lie still, trying not to flinch, the machine takes pictures of the blood rushing in their head. Because blood contains iron, a magnetic substance, the machine's magnets can trace where the blood is going. The resulting image, lit in multiple colors, shows which areas of the brain are active during that moment.

Daniel R. Anderson and Katherine V. Fite of the University of Massachusetts at Amherst used this brain-imaging machine to figure out what parts of the brain are involved when a person watches a movie. They wanted to know how a viewer makes sense of what he or she sees. Video can be very complex. The screen might depict one person in a particular space, then cut, without warning, to a space that looks entirely different. Consider a scene that shows the outside of a building one second and the inside of it the next. Viewers are required to quickly make sense of the new location and to re-orient themselves in time and space. They may be introduced to new characters or be required to remember ones that haven't been shown on screen for several scenes. They must take in visual cues that change within milliseconds. The whole process is a sort of cognitive gymnastics. Which parts of the brain are working to make sense of it all?

The researchers recruited eight adults for their experiment and had them watch different video clips. One clip was a muted forty-second segment from a Hollywood movie. (The snippets were from *The Package* or *My Girl*, movies no longer in theaters and therefore less likely for viewers to recall.) The segment featured action sequences that didn't require sound or dialogue to be understood, because the researchers wanted to be sure that the brain activity they saw was related to visual comprehension. Another video clip was a forty-second segment of short, scrambled fragments from other movies, some even upside down and/or running backward. Yet another clip was composed of a series of action shots randomly spliced together from still other movies.

While the participants watched, the machine took pictures of their brains. The resulting snapshots from the exposures showed a few red blots scattered at the edges of a gray slice of the brain. To an untrained eye, the images in the three situations don't look all that different, and in each case, of course, the brain was probably working hard to make sense of what was seen. But by using a computer to overlay the images, the scientists could isolate the activity unique to the viewing of the normal forty-second clip. They found seventeen "cortical regions"—parts of the brain—that were activated during the coherent sequences but not during the random shot or scrambled ones. These regions, they concluded, form a cortical network associated with comprehension of the video. Some of these same regions have been linked in other studies to a person's long-term memory of events and ability to evaluate the significance of what is seen.[10] These areas are also, as Anderson writes, "slow to develop through infancy and during the preschool years."

The study raises the question, not of whether young children have the brain power to understand movies, but whether they even have the brain parts to do so. As adults, we may assume that young children are only handicapped by their lack of experience. We figure they just haven't seen as much as we have and therefore don't understand everything. But the reality is that they may not yet have the cognitive equipment to make sense of the experience, whether it is novel or not. Some of Anderson's prior work has shown that, at age 4, children have a basic understanding of film montage, but they have only an elementary understanding at age 3. Making sense of movies involves complex cognitive processes, like those surrounding personal memories, self-reflection and interpretation. "None of this is typically developed in infants," Anderson said.[11]

Anderson cautioned that much is still unknown about exactly what parts of the brain develop in infants and toddlers at what stages. No anatomy textbook shows colorful maps of children's brains with arrows pointing to sections saying, "this area is responsible for X and is developed by age 2," "this area controls Y and is developed by age 3." The science is just too new. And it is rare for young children to be participants in brain imaging research—partly because it's so hard to get them to lie still long enough. The case of the developing brain is still, in many ways, a mystery.

~~~⌒

Let's think for a minute about what it means to learn in the first place. Does it mean to memorize and recall—to see something one day and then recognize it the next? Does it mean to imitate—to watch an action and then replicate it, hours or days later? Does it mean to verbalize—to see an object and label it, pronouncing its name? Does it mean to follow directions? Does it mean to solve a problem? Does it mean to take this information and apply it to the real world?

To do even the simplest of these tasks—like memorize and recall—the brain has to have some basic visual and auditory capabilities. We know, for instance, that even before birth, babies can hear. But do they hear the way we, as adults, hear? Not quite. At 6 months, they are still relatively hard-of-hearing, though their ability to sense quiet sounds gradually improves throughout early childhood.[12] They are also poor at being able to localize sound. Whereas adults can point with relative precision to where a sound is coming from, infants have shown that they cannot separate sounds that originate from spaces less than twenty degrees apart.[13] Their hearing, it is thought, improves to adult levels by age 7.

Just after birth, babies can see, and within a day or two, they can even recognize their mother's face, though, as Lise Eliot of Cornell University put it, "their world probably looks the way it would to you or me if we had to stare out of a frosted window all the time."[14] By 4 months, babies can distinguish colors, and by 6 months, their depth perception and visual acuity is as good as an adult's.[15] But do babies see as we see? Well, it depends on what you mean by "seeing." Many of the objects that people look at are not just things, they are also symbols representing something else. The cover of a book showing a picture of an elephant is not just a piece of cardboard covered in glossy paper with a large patch of gray color in the middle. It is a sign. It tells us that this book is about elephants.

To make sense of media, babies need the ability to make sense of signs. Figuring out how and when babies understand signs has been a life's work for Judy S. DeLoache, a developmental psychologist at the University of Virginia. She wants to know how children develop "pictorial competence," how they learn to read images, how they come to understand symbols. Her work offers intriguing insights on how young children comprehend not only videos but media of all kinds.

Have you ever watched a toddler "read" a book upside down? One day when my younger daughter, Gillian, was almost 2 years old, she picked up the Eric Carle picture book *Brown Bear, Brown Bear, What Do You See?* placed it on her lap upside down and proceeded to point to and name several of the animals. I remember thinking, "How odd. It's like she doesn't even notice that the animals are not right-side-up." DeLoache and her colleagues have documented that this insensitivity to picture orientation happens all the time with children until the age of 2½. Children at 30 months of age show some desire for books to be right-side-up, but at 18 months and 24 months, they just don't care.[16] "And not only do they not care," DeLoache said, "they can perceive it just as well upside down. This is I think an amazing phenomenon."

DeLoache has observed other surprising behaviors in children relating to pictures. Although babies can tell that there is something different between, say, a photograph of a doll and a physically present doll, DeLoache and her colleagues heard amusing anecdotes from people about how babies interact with pictures. Some stories described babies who picked and scratched at images in board books, as if they wanted to pull the images off the page. One researcher spoke of his 16-month-old son who tried to step into a picture of a shoe, as if trying it on for size. An acquaintance described a moment when her 14-month-old saw a milk bottle on a television commercial and tried to pry it off the screen, screaming "baba!"[17]

DeLoache and her colleagues believed these stories were probably aberrations. Yet what they discovered was exactly the reverse. In 1998, she and her fellow researchers brought ten 9-month-old babies into a psychology laboratory to see what they would do when shown color, life-sized photographs of objects like bottles and rattles. "To our surprise, every child in the initial study and most in our subsequent studies reached out to feel, rub, pat or scratch the pictures," DeLoache wrote. "Sometimes the infants even grasped at the depicted objects as if trying to pick them up off the page."[18]

DeLoache documented the experiment with a video recording. While watching it you cannot help but smile. The kids are absolutely determined to get at these images. The fact that they are having no luck doesn't seem to faze them. As DeLoache puts it, "Even the most persistent infants, who repeatedly tried to grasp picture after picture, were relatively matter of fact about their failure."[19]

Would video images have the same effect? Two psychologists who were DeLoache's graduate students—Georgene Troseth and Sophia Pierroutsakos—wanted to know. They created a videotape

for babies that showed eight toys being placed upon a table, one after the other, for fifteen seconds at a time. A narrator issued multiple prompts, like "Look at the TV!" and, "Wow, look at that."

The babies' reactions were similar to the way the children had
responded to still photographs, if not more animated.[20] The infants would pat the screen, pluck at the toys shown, or even try to
grab them off the screen. One of the toys was a mechanical snail
that moved from one side of the screen to the other. "I remember
one baby tracking the snail the whole way as if trying to catch it
before it falls off the table," Troseth said.

The babies' responses, however, differed with age. Nine-month-
old babies were the most persistent and animated in trying to ma-
nipulate the objects. By 14 months, they still grabbed at the screen,
but not to the same degree. By 19 months, the children had, by and
large, stopped trying to touch the screen. Instead, they pointed to it,
often trying to verbalize what they saw. Something had started to
"click." They had learned that, though a video has some of the same
attributes of the object it depicts, it really is a whole different ball of
wax. Imagine the babies finally realizing, "Okay, I get it. This is
something to look at, to label, to talk about. But if I want to feel the
soft, warm fur of a kitten, I'll have more luck petting our cat."

Beyond the toddler years, children have been witnessed doing
some amusing things with images. John Flavell of Stanford University once showed 3-year-olds a video image of a bowl of popcorn. When he asked them whether the popcorn would spill if he
turned the TV set upside down, they answered, yes.[21] You can find
the same delightful confusion in letters to Mister Rogers from 4-
and 5-year-olds:

> Dear Mr. Rogers, I would like to know how you get into the TV.
> (Robby, age 4)
> Dear Mr. Rogers, I wish you accidentally stepped out of the TV
> into my house so I could play with you. (Josiah, age 5)[22]

My older daughter, Janelle, had a thing for *JoJo's Circus* when she was about 2½ years old. The show ran in the morning, during the Playhouse Disney time block on the Disney channel. Almost daily, Janelle would ask for JoJo, the claymation clown with striped pants, big feet, red hair and a button nose. At the opening credits, viewers were treated to a bird's-eye view of the world JoJo lived in, with paths leading between brightly colored circus tents. In JoJo's world, every day was like a carnival, with jumping and twirling contests, popcorn, cotton candy, and friends around to make you laugh.

I could understand Janelle's enthusiasm for the show. The place looked like fun. But I realize now that I wasn't seeing it quite the way she was. I knew this wasn't real. Janelle, however, may have thought otherwise. One morning, as I turned off the TV, Janelle asked, "May I go in later?"

"Go in?" I asked. "Go in what?"

"In JoJo," she said.

I grinned. "To play?" I asked.

"Yeah!"

~~~

It is becoming clear that children have a lot of growing and learning to do before they see symbolic information the way we do. DeLoache believes that children have trouble making sense of something that represents something else. To understand symbols, they need to hold two thoughts in their heads at one time—one thought about the image in front of them, and another about what the image symbolizes. DeLoache calls this dual representation, a skill very young children may not be equipped to perform.

DeLoache arrived at this theory after one of her studies showed that young children did not seem to understand the concept of scale models. They didn't get the idea that a small model of, say, a living room could be a symbol of a larger one. She discovered this through a series of find-the-toy games she played with children. First, she would show the children a model of a room displayed on a table, complete with miniature furniture. She would show them a plastic dog—Little Snoopy—and ask them to watch as she placed the little dog behind, say, the miniature couch. She would then lead the children to a room with exactly the same layout and the same furniture, scaled at full size. She would tell them that another dog named Big Snoopy was hiding in the same place as Little Snoopy. "Can you find him?" she would ask. The 3-year-olds got it. The 2½-year-olds had no clue. As DeLoache wrote in one of her articles, the children "cheerfully ran into the room to retrieve the larger toy, but most of them had no idea where to look, even though they remembered where the tiny toy was hidden in the miniature room and could readily find it there."[23]

"It was quite stunning when we first started doing that research," DeLoache told me. "No one expected that result. No one." The reason the children could not locate the toy, she hypothesized, was that they just couldn't grasp the fact that one room was supposed to represent another. They didn't get that the model they were seeing was a symbol or map of the other room. To find out if her theory was right, she had to trick the children—with the consent of their parents, of course—into thinking that the rooms weren't two separate things at all. She had to create a "shrinking machine." She first demonstrated the power of the shrinking machine to the children by showing them a Troll doll with purple hair, putting it in front of the "machine" (a shiny metal box with knobs), and asking them to step outside for a minute while the machine did its magic. When they returned, a tiny Troll doll sat where the big one had been. (This seemed perfectly plausible to the kids, DeLoache reported.) Once the children understood how the machine worked, the researchers used it again, "shrinking" not only the Troll but also a full-sized tent it was hiding within. The children got a good look at where the big Troll was hiding in the big tent, and then—after the "shrinking" occurred—the children were asked to find the small Troll in the small model tent. This time, the 2½-year-old children had no problem. "Unlike in our scale model experiment, they had no dual representation to master," DeLoache said. "In the child's mind, the small tent was the same as the big tent, and thus the toy was where it should be."

This experiment may sound far afield of explaining what is happening in a baby's brain when he views a video. But it set up yet another "trick" that Troseth and DeLoache designed. This one, again, involved a game of find-the-toy. And it, too, was designed to get to the bottom of what children understand of symbols—and what they can learn from them. For this study, the question was, Can children find a toy if they first watch it being hidden on live video?

The study involved two groups of children, twelve 2-year-olds and twelve 2½-year olds. Each group was first shown a room with a video camera and monitor. They got a demonstration of how live video worked, with researchers pointing out that the children could see themselves, the chairs, the tables, and the toy—Snoopy—on the screen. The children were then sent back to a viewing room. They were told to watch the video screen to see where the experimenter hid the toy. Then they had to find it in the corresponding room.

This time, the older kids aced the task, but the vast majority of 2-year-olds failed. Was it because they couldn't process the idea that the video could represent a real event happening in the room? There was only one way to find out: fool the children into thinking that what they were seeing on screen was unmediated real life. To do so, the researchers asked the children to look through a "window" with curtains to see where Snoopy was being hidden. Except that the window wasn't a window at all; it was an opening in a wall fitted with a video monitor.

The trick seemed to work. "More than half of the children who were actually watching video, but were told they were looking through a window, performed perfectly," they wrote.[24] The conclusion matched what DeLoache had sensed was happening in the children's minds. As long as the toddlers did not have to think about the video as a video, they could make sense of what they saw. Taking that extra step, leaping to the realization that a video represents something else, was the hard part. This is what DeLoache calls becoming "symbol-minded," becoming sensitive to the meaning of pictorial representation. "All throughout the first few years of life, children are, step by step, working out what symbolic media are and how they are used," she said.

~~~

Let's consider another test of whether babies are learning from the screen: their ability to imitate what they see on it. If the TV shows toddlers building a tower with blocks, will a youngster try it at home, too? If a video depicts someone locking a door, writing with a pen or punching numbers into a phone, will a child try the same in real life?

Because children today have already seen such activities in person, researchers have built experiments using never-before-seen tasks. Andrew Meltzoff of the University of Washington designed one of the first of these experiments to be applied to TV. He fashioned a toy dumbbell from two wooden cubes and a couple of pieces of plastic tubing. The test was whether children, at age 14 months and 24 months, after watching video of someone taking the dumbbell apart, would be able to imitate the action when given the toy.

Meltzoff's results were surprising to many. They showed that even 14-month-olds could retain what they saw on screen and imitate it twenty-four hours later. As Meltzoff wrote in 1988 when the results were published, "It is sobering to realize that, at least under the laboratory conditions described here, infants early in the second year of life can incorporate and repeat behaviors they see presented on TV."[25] Reflecting on the experiment a decade later, he wrote, "It is relevant to the debate of whether we should show young children television depicting violent uses of knives, guns or other weapons that may be around the house. At least under ideal viewing conditions such as those used in the laboratory experiment, infants can learn from TV and will repeat what they see there."[26]

Meltzoff did not, however, compare TV imitation to real-life imitation. His experiment made me wonder if there was any chance that babies could learn as quickly by video observation as they do when observing something that is physically present.

Rachel Barr, a psychologist at Georgetown University, has been chipping away at that question for several years with a series of tests performed in homes and laboratories. In one of her experiments with 1-year-olds and toddlers, the children sit on a parent's lap and watch a little show. Some watch the show live, with the performer physically present. Others watch it on video. In one show, for example, babies watch a woman put on a hand puppet that looks like a fuzzy pink rabbit. Then they watch as she puts a tiny felt mitten on the rabbit's paw, displays the mitten-covered paw, and then takes the mitten off. In both the video and the live situation, the show is exactly the same, with exactly the same movements and timing.

Now comes the test. Can the children imitate what they saw? When presented with the puppet, will they try to do the same thing, given what they have seen? Can they do the same twenty-four hours later? And how does their performance compare between video and live conditions? Is there something about watching that action on a screen that makes it more difficult to comprehend, memorize and recall what they are seeing?

Barr's research has shown in repeated studies that the children are slower to imitate what they see on screen.[27] In some cases, they need to see the show twice as many times on screen before they can match the performance as opposed to watching the task live. The phenomenon, found in study after study in children from 12 to 36 months of age by researchers around the world, is called the "video

In a memory experiment, babies are placed in front of a video showing a pink puppet, a little mitten that can be removed from the puppet, and a bell hidden in the mitten that rings when shaken. To test
babies' ability to imitate what they have seen on screen, the children
are given the opportunity to do the same thing with the puppet
when it is put within their reach. Unlike with real-life demonstrations, the babies need repeated video viewings before they can do so.
(Reprinted with permission by Rachel Barr, Georgetown University)

deficit."[28] This deficit doesn't apply solely to imitation tasks; evidence for it has popped up in experiments on word learning and
problem solving, too.[29] Even when the material on the screen is
designed to look, feel and sound exactly the same as if a person
is standing there in the room, live observances stick with children
at a higher rate. It is as if something about the information on the

video screen is impoverished, lacking in the richness children need to retain and recall what they see.

But, as Barr also points out, the children in her experiments do eventually imitate the on-screen action. It's just that they need to see it over and over and over again. To many parents who have exposed their toddlers to television, the research rings true. I have heard stories of children performing little dances that seemingly imitate what they have seen on *The Wiggles* countless mornings in a row. One mother told me how her 1-year-old son would swing his arms back and forth like Steve during the *Blue's Clues* theme song. He watched the show daily.

Barr and other researchers are now trying to figure out exactly what about the screen is causing the video deficit, why children seem to need more repetition to learn from video as opposed to in-person demonstrations. "It's definitely a puzzle," she told me. Are the limited capabilities of a young child's memory having an effect? Is the symbolic nature of media to blame? Could the two-dimensional nature of the experience play a role? A recent experiment measuring processing speeds in the brain, for example, showed that 18-month-old children are slower at differentiating objects when they were shown as pictures instead of real three-dimensional objects.[30]

The answers, Barr said, could have practical implications for using books, computers or video to teach and expose young children to new things. She is not averse to the idea that multimedia of all kinds, if designed right, could play a role in teaching young children. In fact, Barr consulted for Nick Jr. in the production of its *Curious Buddies* videotapes. "We could enhance learning or decrease potential harm" by using research-based methods on how to best approach pictorial material with children, Barr told me. She added, "Understanding how children process 2D information has implications for a lot of different platforms, not just television."

⁓

For parents who simply want to know whether certain videos live up to the promises of their packaging, the sum of evidence uncovered so far can at least tell us this much: If your baby is not yet 6 months old, he may not be seeing what is on screen with much precision in the first place. If he is younger than 12 months old— well, the research on this age group doesn't yet offer more than a fleeting glimpse into whether much learning can happen. It may be, as some researchers predict, that the type of content displayed on the screen can make a difference, although, remember the experiment led by Dan Anderson at the University of Massachusetts that involved *Teletubbies*. It showed that children this young cannot differentiate between scrambled and regular versions of the program, let alone comprehend any narrative the videos might be delivering.[31] But a recent experiment, by Barr at Georgetown, has demonstrated that 6-month-olds can imitate short, simple videotaped actions twenty-four hours after viewing them.[32] Clearly there are many gaps that researchers have yet to fill in our understanding of video learning with babies younger than 1.

After 12 months of age, it appears more likely that a child will be able to recall what he sees on video and perform it himself—if the video is designed like the ones in these laboratory experiments, with slow, simple actions, lots of repetition and words uttered precisely to coincide with what appears on screen. Some research (as you'll see in the chapters on language and vocabulary) shows that even a 1-year-old can recognize words he has heard on video. But if the video tries to tell a story with film cuts between scenes, it is probably going right over his head. If the video asks him to take information he has viewed on screen and use it to find things or solve other problems in his immediate surroundings, he won't yet have the symbol-mindedness to know what to do; he most likely won't be able to recognize that what is on screen is a representation of real life. And until he is about 19 months of age, he just may try to touch and grab at what he sees on screen—a sign that he may be still trying to make sense of the media itself, let alone the content it offers.

Most of all, the research prompts us to remember the value of exposing babies to plain old real life. I didn't come to any concrete understanding about these points until a few years after my second daughter, Gillian, was born, so I can't claim that they caused me to make any major changes in the way I used videos with my children. Unlike my first child, Gillian was not a terribly fussy baby, so I did not have as many moments when I resorted to baby videos. Instead, by virtue of her toddler sister's choices, her babyhood included Elmo videos, *JoJo's Circus* and *Dora the Explorer*—and in those cases, it was my need for a break, not my desire to fill my baby with video-mediated knowledge, that drove her TV watching. Still, if I had a baby today, the video deficit would be in the back of my mind. It is hard to ignore the research showing that, for children up to age 3, actions observed in real life are easier to understand than what is shown on a video screen. In other words, at these ages, something as simple as watching laundry being folded could have educational merit that a video doesn't.

As for claims of cognitive stimulation that might come from exposure to videotapes, those deserve to be taken with a grain of salt. I asked William T. Greenough, the neurobiologist who has researched how brains develop, what he thought of the promotional statements that come with videos marketed to babies. "Any claim of cognitive stimulation has to be backed up with data," he said, referring to research comparing viewers to a control group. "If the toy manufacturer or seller hasn't done that, they really can't make a legitimate claim to cognitive stimulation and would know nothing about its generalizability." Rather than turning to a DVD to provide an enriching experience for a child, Greenough's advice is to "make yourself the ultimate agent of enrichment." Take heart, as a parent, that your child will learn just what he needs by watching, listening to, and interacting with you.

NOTES

1. This history of Baby Einstein was adapted from the Baby Einstein Web site, http://www.babyeinstein.com/about/01–02_history.asp, which includes a short biography of Julie Aigner-Clark made available to the press by the Disney company; and an interview from CBS News's *The Early Show*, June 24, 2005, http://www.cbsnews.com/stories/2005/06/23/earlyshow/living/money/main703820_page2.shtml.

2. Based on The Walt Disney Company Annual Report 2006, p. 29; The Walt Disney Company Annual Report 2005, p. 33; and correspondence with a Disney public relations officer.

3. Hirsh-Pasek and Golinkoff, 2003, pp. 17–18. See also Linton, 1999.

4. "Brainy Baby . . . a little genius in the making," 2005 Product Catalog, p. 3.

5. These examples are cited by Garrison and Christakis, 2005, p. 54.

6. See the video company's Web site, www.infantlearning.com.

7. Web pages cached by Campaign for a Commercial-Free Childhood, http://www.commercialfreechildhood.org/babyvideos/attachments/Attachment %204%20-%20BE%20testimonial%20headings.pdf.

8. Garrison and Christakis, 2005, p. 27.

9. Two-photon microscopes at the Massachusetts Institute of Technology, for example, have enabled scientists to watch how neurons change in live adult mice. For more on this, see E. Singer, 2006.

10. Anderson et al., 2006.

11. Personal interviews with Anderson, January and February 2006.

12. Eliot, 1999, p. 245.

13. For a description of infants' auditory development, see Hollich et al., 2005, p. 599.

14. Eliot, 1999, p. 210.

15. Ibid., pp. 215–218.

16. DeLoache, Uttal, and Pierroutsakos, 2000, pp. 81–95.

17. Pierroutsakos and Troseth, 2003, p. 185.

18. DeLoache, 2005, p. 74. In a 2005 article for the journal *Infancy*, Albert Yonas, a psychologist at the University of Minnesota, questioned De-Loache's data, stating that when he set up a similar experiment, he found no evidence of children grasping at photographs; he has only witnessed them touching and patting. I have seen the video from DeLoache's experiments, and it looks like grasping to me, but the cases of actual grasping are rare.

Patting and rubbing are more common. Either way, DeLoache argues, this evidence shows that children are trying to figure out what pictures and photographs are.

19. DeLoache et al., 1998, p. 209.

20. Pierroutsakos and Troseth, 2003, pp. 189–190.

21. Troseth and DeLoache described Flavell's work in their 1998 article for *Child Development*, noting not only the popcorn study but also an experiment with a photograph of a glass of juice, which children believed would spill if inverted. "Thus," they wrote on page 951, "the children appeared to be thinking about the referent of the image—a real bowl of popcorn or a real glass of juice—while answering, even though Flavell et al. made valiant attempts to get them to center their attention on the image itself." Other references to the Flavell study are on DeLoache et al., 1998, p. 210, and DeLoache, 2005, p. 74.

22. Siegler, DeLoache, and Eisenberg, 2003, p. 15.

23. Troseth and DeLoache, 1998, pp. 959–960.

24. DeLoache, 2005, p. 73.

25. Meltzoff, 1988, p. 1226.

26. Meltzoff, 1999, p. 6.

27. Barr and Hayne, 1999; and Barr, in press.

28. Coined by Daniel Anderson and Tiffany Pempek in an article in the January 2005 issue of *American Behavioral Scientist.*

29. See Troseth, Saylor, and Archer, 2006, for a review of other "video deficit" experiments.

30. Barr, in press, referring to research published in 2006 in *Developmental Science* by Carver, Meltzoff, and Dawson.

31. See Anderson and Pempek's research on *Teletubbies*, described in chapter 2.

32. Barr, in press.

Chapter Four

My Toddler Doesn't
Seem to Notice When the
TV Is On—or Does He?

I t was a cool spring morning when I met Sara, the mother of a 7-month-old baby named Anna Marie.[1] Sara is a young immigrant from Bolivia who lives in Arlington, Virginia, in her parents' small, two-bedroom apartment. Their building faces a busy boulevard lined with fast food joints, check-cashing centers and diners advertising "el pollo" Peruvian-style. As a single mother, Sara struggles, but she is fortunate to have the shelter and support of her parents, and she stays home with her baby every day.

My visit to Sara's apartment was one of a few trips I took with social workers in northern Virginia to gain a broader sense of how electronic media is integrated into the lives of families of all shapes, sizes and income levels. Before we arrived, the social worker told me that she was often annoyed by the drone of the television set at Sara's apartment during their visits. "The TV is always on," she told me. "It will be on the whole time we are there."

A few days earlier, the social worker had asked Sara if she would mind having a reporter attend one of their monthly sessions at her home, and Sara had consented. She had been told that I would be asking about television use, and so I wasn't surprised when she opened the apartment door that deposited us into her living room that the television was off. As Sara turned to collect her baby, the social worker widened her eyes in disbelief and nodded to the Toshiba, dark and quiet. We followed Sara into the kitchen, where she unstrapped her smiling baby from a high chair and gave her a nuzzle. The child had been facing another television, much smaller, that was sitting next to the sink. This one was on and tuned to Univision, a Spanish-language channel known for its soap operas, or telenovelas.

Down the short hall, in the bedroom Sara shared with her daughter, another television was on, tuned to the same station and nearly as large as the one in the living room. It was on the dresser a few feet from Anna Marie's crib. Sara told me that her parents' bedroom held a TV, too. That was four televisions in less than 800 square feet.

That day, Sara and the social worker talked about Anna Marie's progress. She wasn't yet crawling but kicked her feet energetically when she lay on her tummy. She was especially fond of her activity table with its toy piano. She had grown two new front teeth. The baby seemed happy and well cared for.

The entire conversation was accompanied by the sounds of that morning's telenovela emanating from the kitchen and bedroom. I heard television voices hot with anger, tightened to whispers, and sometimes sobbing. I heard ominous organ music, what sounded like a mariachi band, and the lively jingles of commercials. By the end of the hour, when we talked briefly about how she uses media in her home, she admitted that the TV was on almost all the time: "I prefer noise," she said simply. "I don't like quiet."

Of course, we've known for years that television is omnipresent in many households. And the above example probably reaffirms a myth that educated people have held onto for years—namely, that the heaviest television users are the poor, the people in our society with the least education and fewest resources. But it's not only low-income families who live and breathe by the flicker of the screen.

Let me paint another picture. This time I was spending several days visiting the home of a family I know well, whom I will call the Smiths. They are relatively affluent and white. They have a young boy. Their house has four bedrooms, a spacious basement and an ample backyard with a jungle gym in a comfortable suburban neighborhood. There is a TV set in the boy's room, the parents' room, the living room, the basement and the kitchen. I walked between the rooms in the morning and didn't miss a beat of the *Today* show. A few hours later, the living room TV was tuned to Nickelodeon. The one in the bedroom, which was by then empty, was still broadcasting NBC. By afternoon, the TV in the kitchen was on instead. And on the occasions when the television was off, I could hear the radio bringing in a steady drumbeat of talk and news.

A recent study blows apart some of the most strongly held assumptions about who is going about life with "always-on" television. Elizabeth Vandewater at the University of Texas and several of her colleagues probed the results of a survey about television use to find out which characteristics are most closely associated with background TV. The survey was conducted as a telephone interview of 1,000 families selected at random. Not surprisingly, background television turned up frequently. About 39 percent of families with babies, infants and preschoolers up to 4 years old said that the television was on most or all of the time.[2] In other words, two in five American families acknowledged raising their children against the constant conversations and continually changing images of an audio-visual display.

Were these the poorest families? The least educated? Not necessarily. In fact, neither of those demographic characteristics were significant predictors of heavy television use. Instead, the factor most strongly associated with heavy television use among families with infants and toddlers was parental attitude toward TV. If the primary caregiver in the family rated educational TV as a "very important" contributor to intellectual development, that family was twice as likely to have the TV on most or all of the time.

Vandewater's survey also revealed predictors of always-on television families that do fit the stereotypes. If respondents said that the television was used as a babysitter, if they were single parents, or if they kept a television in their child's bedroom, the odds were high that they were heavy television users. Families who don't have the television on all the time are not necessarily the most educated or well off financially. Instead, they are simply the families who think that television may hurt their child's development. My guess is that many of these respondents may believe that, as debunked earlier, television will turn their children into unthinking zombies. Or, despite the dearth of any causal data, they have a fear of attention deficit disorders.

It turns out, however, that these families are right to be worried—but not for those reasons. There is plenty of hand-wringing about foreground television use that has no basis in science. But background television, which on the contrary gets very little attention, has been shown in recent scientific studies to have the potential to do harm to very young children. The repercussions have nothing to do with attention deficits or "zoning out." Instead, they hinge on three critical elements of children's growth in their youngest years: their ability to engage in pretend play, their interactions with their parents, and their efforts to learn language.

On April 19, 1993, people around the country were glued to their televisions. On that day, the U.S. government's siege against the Branch Davidian sect near Waco, Texas, ended in a fire engulfing the group's compound and killing dozens of men, women and children. Daniel Anderson of the University of Massachusetts was at home caring for his 1-year-old daughter, watching breaking news of the story. "I had CNN on all day and my daughter was playing in front of the television," he said. He knew that she was not old

enough to understand the events unfolding. She wasn't even looking at the TV set. But Anderson, who had already spent a decade
researching television and preschoolers, started to feel uneasy. "Is
this having some effect on her?" he asked himself. "Is this disrupt-
ing her play patterns? Is it having a disruptive effect?"

As a developmental psychologist, Anderson already knew about
the importance of play for very young children. Through pretend
play, for example, children learn initiative and how to create things
themselves. (Deciding to go on a "trip," they might turn a grocery
bag into a suitcase.) They learn how to solve problems. (Discovering
that their big teddy bear doesn't fit in the "suitcase," they may prop
him up in a toy stroller instead.) They are given a sense of power;
they are setting the agenda. ("I'm off to Boston, Mommy! But I'll
come back, don't worry.") In a life in which they have very little say
in their own daily routines, play is one way children can be trans-
ported to a space and time wherein they have complete control.

"It is play, plain and simple play, that affords many of the most
essential intellectual and social advantages for children," wrote
Hirsh-Pasek and Golinkoff in *Einstein Never Used Flashcards*.[3] On
the flip side, they wrote, not being afforded much time to play can
have ill effects. Studies on young rats have shown that, when researchers withhold playtime (like the chance to tumble and wres-
tle), brain growth is delayed. At a 2006 lecture in Washington DC,
David Elkind drove home the point: "Play is not an extravagance;
play is not a luxury," said the renowned author of *The Hurried
Child*. "Play is a necessity. Play is basic to learning."[4] A few months
later, the American Academy of Pediatrics reported that some children were not getting enough time to play and issued a clinical
report stressing its importance.[5]

For many of us, this sounds like a no-brainer. Of course children
need playtime. Infants don't need to be prodded into shaking, rat-
tling, twisting, bouncing, grabbing and dropping anything they
come in contact with. Toddlers can lapse into pretend play regardless of what is happening around them. There was no question,

Anderson said, that his daughter was, indeed, playing while he tuned into the talking heads on CNN. The question was, was there something different about the nature of her play when the television was on in the background? Was it being invisibly shaped by the sounds in her ears and the scenes in her peripheral vision? Was it somehow less than it might have been without that distraction? It would take another decade for him to delve into the question deeply enough to come up with his troubling answer: yes.

Ten years after Waco, Marie Evans, a doctoral student under Anderson, set up an experiment to determine scientifically whether the existence of background television disrupted children's playtimes. She and her colleagues identified a random set of fifty mothers with children 1, 2 or 3 years old and recruited them to come to their laboratory in Springfield, Massachusetts. The families were led to a simply furnished room with a couch, chair, side table, coffee table, several shelves of toys, and a television. A camera hidden behind a one-way mirror recorded their movements for a full hour. Half of the time, the television showed *Jeopardy*. During the other thirty minutes, it was turned off. Parents were told they could read magazines as well as watch the television, and they were instructed not to initiate activities with their children but instead to let them play on their own. Parents would sometimes make casual comments about how sure they were that the TV was having no effect on their kids before the experiments got underway. They would tell Evans and Anderson, "We watch the evening news, and I know they don't watch it. They're not paying attention."

Their remarks reminded me of my own view of background television before I started asking questions. We're not an "always-on" TV family, but there were plenty of times I recalled having the television tuned to CNN's *Headline News* when my first daughter was about a year old. She would be toddling around the family room, barely even acknowledging the TV. In fact, I felt proud whenever I observed her playing with her blocks or pushing her plastic shopping cart around. See, I would tell myself. She's not lured in the least.

But could the impact be so subtle as to be nearly invisible? That's what the Massachusetts researchers wanted to know. After a few months of collecting data for their study, they came away with dozens of videotapes holding hours of recordings. To analyze what was on them, trained assistants sat at a computer, watching every hour—usually in slow motion—to take note of the tiniest details about how the children played. They marked the onset and offset of focused attention. They coded the beginning and end of every "play episode"—such as a child picking up a miniature broom, sweeping it back and forth, and then dropping the broom to the floor. And they rated each of these episodes on a scale for "maturity of play." A rating of 1 meant that the child was performing simple indiscriminate actions, like banging a block against the floor. The top level, 14, meant that children were playing pretend with imaginary objects that didn't exist, like feeding imaginary food to a baby doll.

During a visit to Amherst, I got a look at these coded files. Tiffany Pempek, another of Anderson's doctoral students, clicked open a page of nothing but rows and columns of numbers denoting start times, stop times, the maturity of play, and how the maturity levels went up or down with each passing second.

When the results for every participant were analyzed and compared, the impact of *Jeopardy* was clear. When the TV was on, there was a pronounced decrease in the length of play episodes. At each age—1, 2 and 3 years old—playtime fell significantly in the presence of television. One-year-olds, for example, had play episodes that lasted over eighty seconds on average without the TV on. With background television, those episodes lasted less than sixty seconds. Toddlers are already famous for their short attention spans—at a minute per toy, it's no wonder that some parents think they need to buy more and more stuff—but with the addition of background television, those spans were even shorter. The children behaved as though something was distracting them, causing them to bounce from one toy to another. Even when they weren't looking at the television, they still acted like something was keeping them from focusing on what was in front of them.[6]

The results have caused Pempek, who started her career focusing on foreground television, to become a big believer in the harm that may come from too much background television. Parents may think that an always-on television is not making much of a difference in the way their children play, but she can point to proof that children are worse off. "I'm passionate about this now," she said.

～〇

The study, however, left one question unanswered. The experiments showed no significant effect of background television on the maturity of children's play. Why not? Could it be that television had no distracting effect on children who were already playing at the level of pretend tea parties? The researchers weren't ready to make that call. Instead, they hypothesized that, because parents were instructed not to play with their kids, evidence related to elaborate pretend play may have been suppressed. Child-development research has shown that, when parents get on the floor and play jointly with their children, the maturity level of the child's play automatically rises. But in the above study, parents were instructed not to initiate play with their children (although they were allowed to interact with them in general, by, say, answering their questions or retying their shoelaces). It was time to do another study—one that emphasized a parent's interactions with his or her child. Could background television be interfering with that, too?

The results were not obvious at first. Heather Kirkorian, a graduate student working with Anderson and Pempek, videotaped parents and young children in the same room in Springfield, Massachusetts, with the television on for half an hour and off the other half-hour. But these parents were given a different set of instructions. They were told to act as normally as possible, behaving as they would when at home. They were also told they could choose among several pre-recorded television programs for the "TV on" segment of the experiment—again attempting to replicate a scenario more like home. The point was to see if the parents interacted differently with their children when the television was off.

Kirkorian showed me a clip from one of the videotapes. The sitcom *Raymond* is on the television. Mom has a magazine in her lap. Her little boy, age 2 and wearing a T-shirt emblazoned with Tigger, is bopping around the room, investigating several toys. He plays with the Playskool school bus, opening and closing its doors. She glances at the show, then starts reading the magazine. Her son presses buttons on a toy telephone and dances, swaying his hips to the music it makes. She laughs and encourages him. She notices that his nose is dripping, fishes for a tissue, corrals him for a moment, wipes him clean, and goes back to her magazine. A few minutes later, she notices her son touching a doll lying against the shelf. "Playing with the dolly now?" she asks. "Has the dolly been fed?" An orange juice commercial can be heard on the TV.

Before analyzing these recordings, Kirkorian had started to wonder if her hypothesis was wrong. She had observed several sessions, and in many of them the mothers seemed to be quite attentive to their children even in the face of television. The mother on this particular video was one of them. "This is one of those videos where we said, 'Oh, there's no effect. She's still talking to him; she's not just passive.'"

Just as *Raymond* ends, the mother discovers that her child needs a diaper change. These few moments are not recorded, but when the recording resumes, the mother stays on the floor where she had just finished changing her son and brings him to her lap, rocking him playfully. The room is silent. Soon she grabs a wooden peg puzzle about animals. "Look, look at the kitty. And the doggy." The boy manipulates a few of the pieces. "And see, the barn doors go here." Now her interactions seem to have a greater depth to them. They are longer and more focused on her child.

When the final results of the quantity and quality of her interactions were tallied, the difference was clear. When the TV was off, she interacted with her son 88 percent of the time. When the TV was on, the number was 38 percent. How did her interaction rate in terms of quality? Without the presence of *Raymond*, she was actively engaged with her child 78 percent of the time. With *Raymond*, 19 percent.

Other recordings of participants in the research, Kirkorian said, do not demonstrate such obvious distinctions in interaction time—at least not to a casual observer. The effect is usually more subtle. But when the numbers are tallied and crunched, the impact adds up. With the TV on, there was a 21 percent decrease in the amount of time that parents spent interacting with their children.[7] Put another way, parents were actively involved with their children 66 percent of the time with no TV versus 54 percent of the time with the TV on. The way they played with their children was affected to an even greater extent. With no TV, 74 percent of their play with their children was active. With the background television, that declined to 59 percent.[8] "Not only did the quantity drop, but the overall quality did, too," Kirkorian said.

Kirkorian recognizes, however, that it's not always easy to keep young children away from background television. "The point is not to say, don't ever do this," she said. "It's an awareness thing. The effects are small. Keep this in mind."

Another point to keep in mind, however, is that both of these studies were done in laboratories, in artificial environments that could not possibly mimic all that happens at home. Anderson and his colleagues are eager to do more home-based studies, which are typically much more expensive and time-consuming. They require more equipment, more set-up time, and the availability of subjects willing to be videotaped in their homes.

But I found something convincing about these studies, none-theless. Agreed, the mothers were probably on their best behavior. And, yes, the simple act of being there for sixty minutes was probably an anomaly in their daily lives. Here, they were in a relatively contained space in which their children were allowed to explore shelves of new toys. The mothers could sit on the couch in peace, without phone calls to make or laundry to fold or dishes to unload. But the studies showed what might happen in those sixty minutes of peace both with and without television. Even assuming that these parents were being more attentive than normal, there was still a significant difference between the two states. I suspect that in real life—where toys get boring and caregivers may feel desperate for a taste of the outside, grownup world—the presence of background television could have an even larger effect on play episodes and parent-child interactions.

～〇

Whenever I interviewed social workers about background television, one exasperated phrase always popped up: "the noise." House-holds with televisions droning all day are not quiet places, and many families cannot afford spacious living quarters, so there's no getting away from the sounds of the screen. Sometimes the volume is loud enough to be heard through apartment walls, and certain programs and commercials seem to be set at already high decibels. "On these Spanish talk shows, they are just screaming," said one social worker, who is a Spanish-speaking immigrant herself. Another social worker told me, "The noise gets to me. I can't have a conversation."

Now think for a minute of the babies and toddlers who may be immersed in these always-on multimedia environments. They are trying to learn a language, trying to differentiate sounds from one another, trying to pick words out of streams of speech, trying to attach specific sounds to specific meanings. Roberta Michnick Golinkoff and Kathy Hirsh-Pasek, the authors of *How Babies Talk*, liken this to being in a foreign country with people speaking in an undecipherable language all around you. You feel "as though the new language is flooding over you and offering you no anchor point."[9] There are no spaces between words as they are spoken, no periods or commas or capitalized letters hanging in the air. That is what an infant hears, too. Imagine it as a bunch of words all running together: "Comehereyoumunchkin!Doyouneedanewdiaper?"

Add to this other challenges unique to infants. They are not great, for example, at localizing sound. A 7-month-old cannot differentiate between one sound and another if they are coming from two places less than nineteen degrees apart. And even in quiet conditions, they require greater intensity levels than adults do to discriminate speech sounds.[10]

The auditory challenges of babies led Rochelle Newman, now a professor of speech development at the University of Maryland, to wonder how babies make sense of language in less-than-quiet conditions. Decades of research exist on how adults deal with what is known as the "cocktail party effect," where people force themselves to follow a conversation when many people are speaking at the same time. But nothing had been done on infants. It was time.

In the 1990s, Newman heard about an interesting technique that had been used to test whether infants could pick words out of a spoken sentence. Called the "head-turn preference" procedure, it was designed by the late Peter W. Jusczyk, a psychologist at Johns Hopkins University. In his first study using the procedure, Jusczyk had determined that, while 6-month-old babies could not recognize words in a fluent stream of speech, babies just a month and a half older could do so.[11]

Newman asked to collaborate on a project in Jusczyk's lab testing whether infants could pick words out of sentences in the presence of background speech. He was game. The experiments went like this: A 7½-month-old baby and his mother or father came into a three-sided testing booth. The baby was placed on his parent's lap, facing a green light bulb in the front of the booth. On the walls to the right and left were two more light bulbs. These were red, and the baby had to turn his head to see them. Below each light bulb was an audio speaker.

At the beginning of each experiment, the baby was trained to understand the procedure. First, his attention was captured by the green light in front of him, which flashed brightly. Then it would stop flashing, and one of the red side lights would blink. The baby would notice the red light peripherally and turn to face it, at which point the light would stop flashing and an audio recording would start to emanate from the speaker below it. If the baby turned away from the light for more than two seconds, the audio would stop. If he looked back at the red light, the audio would start again.

That was the "head-turn" part. Now for the "preference" part. In earlier research by Jusczyk, babies kept their heads turned toward some recordings, listening until they were over. With other recordings, the babies seemed to take little interest and looked away, prompting the sounds to end. In other words, the babies seemed to show a preference for one recording over another. Jusczyk found that babies maintained an interest in recordings that contained words they had heard a few minutes earlier, as if they realized that they contained the same words and that it might be worth their while to remember, process, and figure them out. For instance, if a baby heard the word "cup" over and over and then heard a sentence that contained the word "cup," the baby had a preference for that sentence over one that didn't include the word cup. The baby, he reasoned, must have picked out the word "cup" from the cup-containing sentence. The baby was segmenting speech.

In their study on how babies cope with the "cocktail party effect," Newman and Jusczyk upped the ante. They wanted to find out if a baby could pick out the word "cup" from a sentence while also hearing a background voice talking about something entirely different. They knew it would be a tough task, so they tried to make it relatively easy. They used a pleasant female voice for the primary-sentence speaker and a made sure that the distracting voice, which was male and monotone, was dictating words that would be dull and meaningless to the baby. They also intensified the voice of the primary speaker, increasing the signal-to-noise ratio progressively from 0, to 5, to 10 decibels.

The result was that most children could, in fact, separate the two streams of speech when the female voice was 10 decibels higher than that of the distracting voice. At a signal-to-noise ratio of 5 decibels, some infants could still manage the task. But if the distracting and female voices were at the same level, there was no evidence that babies could make heads or tails of what the female voice was saying.[12] They showed no ability to segment speech.

Do parents typically speak to their children at levels 10 decibels higher than the sound of their TV sets? It's an impossible question to answer without equipping children with noise meters and capturing everyday conversations in the presence of televisions. The volume of the TVs and their proximity to the kids would make all the difference. (To sense what a 10-decibel difference might be, think of raising your voice when speaking to a friend in a busy but not boisterous restaurant.)

A few recent studies have shown that infants do find ways to get around the distraction of background noise. George Hollich, director of the Infant Language Lab at Purdue University, has determined that babies can segment speech in noisy conditions when they are able to use visual cues. He found that babies, for example, overcame the noise hurdle when they could see Mom's face—or anyone's face for that matter—and watch her mouth moving. They could even overcome the noise problem when watching a computer monitor that showed an oscillating graphic synchronized with the speech they were trying to hear.[13]

In many households with an always-on television, however, I would venture to guess that infants are not catching everything Mom and Dad are saying. And if their ability to segment speech is slowed, their ability to learn language could be delayed. Think about it: if you were given the choice of learning a foreign language in a classroom where people speak one at a time versus one in which each speaker must compete with background television, which would you choose?

~⁓

Studies on older children have shown that the impact of noise can be alarmingly negative. Studies by Theodore Wachs at Purdue, for example, have shown that a child's cognitive growth and language skills are tied to the level of chaos in their homes. Children suffer in households that lack routines, with multiple people and siblings coming and going, with more than the usual everyday stresses, and against a backdrop of constant noise, including that from the television.[14] Gary Evans, a professor of human development at Cornell, has studied how elementary schoolchildren in Queens, New York, fared when they were living and being taught within the flight path of an airport. He compared them to children of the same socioeconomic status who lived and went to school in a quieter town. The children who had experienced chronic airport noise had problems their counterparts didn't, even when both were tested in equally quiet rooms. The airport children could not perceive and differentiate between spoken words. They also had significant deficits in reading found to be related to their speech perception problems.[15] Their ability to learn had been hampered by growing up surrounded by noise.

What are the effects of background noise on speech and language development among children 0 to 4? Studies on the very young are just now starting to be done. Hollich and his colleagues at Purdue, for example, have been running a few experiments that shed light on how babies learn amid background noise. His results are distressing. "Devastatingly impaired" is how he described children trying to learn the meaning of words in the presence of noise.

His experiments have so far used only white noise, like the low roar of an air conditioner. In one study, for example, toddlers of varying ages were tested to see if they could learn the meaning of words completely new to them when taught in white noise conditions. The tests used never-before-seen objects (strange, three-dimensional things concocted using a computer graphics program) that were labeled with "words" that are not part of the English language. Experimenters would display the strange three-dimensional object and say, for example, "See the turb? It's a nice little turb. Isn't it a nice turb?" Other objects included a "turch" and a "plotch."

The children were then tested, using habituation techniques, to determine if they recognized the difference between two words and knew which word went with which object. With no noise, the toddlers did fine. They were able to match the words to the objects. But with noise, the results were dismal. Not only did the children have difficulty hearing the difference between the sounds "b" and "ch" at the ends of the words "turb" and "torch," but they didn't seem able to learn about words that sound quite different, like "plotch." They showed no retention of what they had been taught about the objects and their names.[16] "They didn't learn at all," Hollich said. He and his colleagues were stunned. Background noise was not just a problem of acoustics. It seemed to have an impact on the toddlers' ability to pay attention and retain what they learned as much as on their ability to simply hear.

For me, these studies were a wake-up call. I started to think about not only television noise but radio, which I listened to religiously during Janelle's first year. Back then, there was little chance of sitting down to read the newspaper in any depth, but at least I could get beyond the headlines by listening to Diane Rehm and Kojo Nnamdi on National Public Radio while folding clothes, putting dishes away, and carrying my fussy baby around on my hip for hours.

My need for an almost constant stream of radio and television news was a hard habit to break. I imagine that reducing background television will be equally difficult for Sara or the Smiths or the 39 percent of young families in the United States who have the television on all or most of the time. Even the social workers I interviewed who complained about the background television at their clients' apartments admitted that they turned on their own TVs the minute they came home from work and didn't turn them off until bedtime. Background television and radio have become companions, ways to fill a lonely house, resources for staying on top of the news, channels to connect with American and immigrant cultures. For many of today's parents, this background noise has been an integral part of their existence since they were children themselves. Their daily routines have been turned upside down since the arrival of baby, and the last thing they want to hear is that the hum of the TV or radio has to go, too.

Still, I began to think twice about having the radio on during the mornings I spent with my daughters. My husband and I started making a concerted effort to make sure that TV time around our kids became foreground television for our kids. I managed to stop turning on *Headline News* in the afternoons, partly because I was fortunate enough to be able to hire a babysitter and start working from my home office a few days a week, where I would feast on online news. It was getting to be time to turn off the televised news around the kids, anyway; when Janelle hit age 3, she started to understand some of what flashed on the screen, and until she could understand the larger context, I wanted to keep her from images of torture, warring soldiers, starving children, and deadly hurricanes.

That is not to say that our children are completely free of radio and background TV. There are moments—sometimes full hours—when it happens. We'll watch college basketball on a cold Saturday.

We'll tune into the Weather Channel before a storm. Having children of different ages makes things complicated, too. What is good, appropriate programming for a 3-year-old is background TV for a 1-year-old. There is no doubt that our younger daughter's playtime is affected when her older sister gets to watch *Blue's Clues*. I'm now woefully aware that these are the moments when my kids are not getting good Mommy time, when their playtimes are shortened, when they are straining to hear and learn the words we speak.

But moderation is the key, and most parents recognize that a little bit of background television a few hours a week is not the same as a television turned on nearly all the time, every day of every week. Much can be gained for today's children if adults are proactive in turning off the television whenever a show is over. Make a concerted effort not to have it droning away in the background when children are playing. Keep the house relatively quiet when you are talking with them one on one. If you're worried that the house will be too quiet without the sound of the TV, just think of the noises that will arrive instead: the sounds of babies learning to talk, toddlers trying out sentences as they start to play pretend, and preschoolers chatting it up in elaborate, creative, make-believe worlds.

NOTES

1. Names have been changed to protect the family's privacy.

2. Vandewater et al., 2005, p. 564.

3. Hirsh-Pasek and Golinkoff, 2003, p. 213.

4. Elkind was featured at the Beauvoir School lecture series, National Cathedral, April 27, 2006.

5. Ginsburg and the AAP Committee on Communications and the Committee on Psychosocial Aspects of Child and Family Health, 2006, pp. 1–32.

6. Evans et al., 2004, p. 1.

7. Kirkorian et al., 2005, p.1.

8. Data presented to me during an interview with Kirkorian at the University of Massachusetts at Amherst on January 12, 2006.

9. Golinkoff and Hirsh-Pasek, 1999, pp. 48–49.

10. Hollich, Newman, and Jusczyk, 2005, p. 600.

11. Jusczyk and Aslin, 1995, p. 1.

12. Newman and Jusczyk, 1996, p. 1145.

13. Hollich, Newman, and Jusczyk, 2005, p. 598.

14. Purdue News Service, 1997, p.1.

15. Evans and Maxwell, 1997, p. 638.

16. Rashad and Hollich, 2005, p. 1.

Chapter Five

Which Videos Are Too Scary for My Child?

Wendee Goles, a mother of two in Villa Park, Illinois, loves movies of all kinds, horror flicks and psychodramas among them. So one evening during a summer vacation in 2005, she decided to see *Hostel*, a film produced by Quentin Tarantino, a director known for disturbing and violent work. Her reaction? "I was shaking," she said. "I was so upset."

It wasn't the story on the screen that affected her. It was the audience. Surrounding her that evening, at the 10 o'clock show, were infants, toddlers and preschoolers. A few sat next to her, two were a few rows behind her, and another couple of children were nearby in the center aisle. Parents had brought in car seats and had propped them up in the row. A few seats below, a boy was being shushed by his mother. He was pointing to the screen, screaming, "Mommy, what's that?" In the very back, a child was crying.

It wasn't the first time that Goles had found herself sitting next to children still in diapers while watching violence on screen. For more than a year, the sight of youngsters at these movies had bothered her. But that evening she resolved to do something about it. She sought out the manager and the next day asked the owner of the theater, did she realize that young children were being brought to these shows? Did she realize what these images might do to these kids? Did she know this was ruining the movie experience for adults? The owner, who had two kids of her own, said she sympathized but that her hands were tied. Those were the rules; parents were allowed to bring their children to these shows if they wanted to.

Undeterred, Goles started a campaign to bring awareness to the issue. On a site called BoxOfficeOffenders.com, she encourages anyone who is similarly outraged to lobby their local theaters and lawmakers to post restrictions or pass laws to keep young children out of R and NC–17 movies. "My goal is to stop this madness," she said.

Goles is likely to find other parents disturbed by the idea of toddlers watching Quentin Tarantino movies. But not all parents see scary media as a cause for concern. Some have no qualms about putting their toddlers in front of DVDs like *Star Wars* or *Indiana Jones*. Many of these parents are college educated, well-off financially, and normally protective of their children, but they don't see much harm in them being frightened by adult media once in a while. "She's scared, yes," one mother told me about her 3-year-old daughter who watches *The Chronicles of Narnia*. "But she loves it. She asks for it." In a focus group conducted by the Henry J. Kaiser Family Foundation, the mother of a 3-year-old girl said, "I watch *CSI*. . . . She will sit down and watch with me. I don't know how harmful it is to her. It's sometimes gory, but it doesn't seem to bother her. She hasn't had any nightmares from it."[1]

The varying reactions of adults toward exposing young kids to scary media left me puzzled. Is this madness, or is Goles raising much ado about nothing? How much do young children absorb of the images and sounds of foreboding places, imperiled characters and brutal killings? Does it matter as long as the good guys win in the end? Would the age of the child make a difference? Would a baby be too young to take any of it in and therefore be protected from the emotional impact? Would a 4-year-old who could understand some vague outline of the plot be worse off than a 2-year-old? What about seemingly benign children's shows and movies that include moments of peril, disaster and death? Could they be harmful? Or could it be that some amount of violent fantasy is actually good for preschoolers, helping them see their fears played out to happy endings?

For a glimpse inside the psyche of children, I sought out Michael Brody, a child psychiatrist in Bethesda, Maryland, who is chairperson of the television and media committee of the American Academy of Child and Adolescent Psychiatry. He thinks that Goles is on the right track. He has been taking mental notes on the types of movies to which parents bring their children, and several examples recently, he said, seem particularly egregious. Some are movies that parents have subjected their children to on purpose, like *The Passion of the Christ.* "I couldn't believe that these people brought these children to see that movie," he told me. "It was horrifying. Horrifying. Kids were literally screaming in the movie theaters."

At the risk of sounding like an idiot, I asked Brody why the idea of children watching this movie was so horrifying. What, I asked, is going on inside a child's little mind when she sees a crucifixion? He answered that we cannot know for sure. But he instructed me to take a look at classic theories of child development and at the latest research on how much children need to be surrounded by feelings of love and security in their earliest years of life. Those ideas, coupled with recent research on memory and emotion, brought me to think more deeply not only about how children make sense of what they see but how much their reaction to a scary movie depends on other things, like their capacity to remember it, whether it evokes and therefore exacerbates real-life anxieties they already face, the number of times they see it, and the emotional reactions of Mom, Dad, and other viewers around them. As a mother, I have begun to take my role as video selector for my children more seriously, and I have changed my strategies for calming their fears because, as I discovered, you can remind your children over and over that the bad guys aren't real, but they just may not be persuaded.

Let's first consider the theories of Jean Piaget, the psychologist of the early twentieth century who conducted myriad experiments to test how children understand their worlds. A few of Piaget's theories have not been borne out in current research,[2] but the backbone of his ideas—the idea of children progressing through increasingly complex stages of understanding—is still considered vitally important. Until the age of 2, Piaget said, babies are living in the here and now, with little sense of past or future. Their cognitive growth comes from what they see, hear, smell, taste, sense, touch and reach for. They move into a second stage when they pass age 2. Then, and until about 7 years old, they are what Piaget called "preoperational." Think of this stage as one in which children are not yet capable of performing mental operations that take in information from different points of view. There is a famous experiment often recounted when describing this level: When water from a short, stout glass is poured into a tall, narrow one, children at this stage are sure that the tall glass contains more water than the short one did. It doesn't matter that the pouring happened right in front of their eyes. They still don't believe that the tall glass could possibly contain the same amount of water as the short one.

Put simply, young children don't think logically. It's the charm of childhood—the ability of toddlers and preschoolers to think of things as magical, to delight in fantasy, to play pretend, to think that the animals know their names, to figure that the moon moves because it wants to. Erik H. Erikson, another intellectual giant among psychologists, put it this way in 1950: "The child, because of his immature equipment, has no way of differentiating between inner and outer, real and imagined, dangers: he has yet to learn this."[3]

What did Erikson mean by immature equipment? Today, with advances in brain science, we can elaborate in ways he couldn't about which parts of the brain help make sense of dramatic and upsetting stories. At birth, children are born with a functioning amygdala, the region of the brain that reflexively reacts to dangers, raising our heart rates, seizing our breath, and telling us to flee. But the cerebral cortex—the hub of brain power that allows us to think abstractly—does not develop fully until the teenage years. It is the last part of the brain to develop.[4]

Without logic and without the abstract thinking required to understand themes of love, history, religion, hatred, betrayal, revenge, and forgiveness, children take away far different ideas from media than adults do. Brody said that, after the terrorist attacks of September 11, he saw many young children in his office who didn't believe that only two planes flew into the World Trade Center. They were convinced that the attack was the force of many planes with many explosions. Why? Because when they watched the events unfolding on their television screens, they saw planes flying into buildings over and over again. They didn't understand that they were seeing a recording being replayed.

If that's the case with news coverage of a real event, what are children thinking when they see fantasy? What do they comprehend about deceivingly real-looking images of elves, hobbits and goths, talking lions, and men with black masks and light sabers? Is it doing any good when we tell our children, "Don't worry; it's not real"?

Many years ago, two psychologists named Patricia Morison and Howard Gardner published an academic study titled *Dragons and Dinosaurs: The Child's Capacity to Differentiate Fantasy from Reality*.[5] They didn't simply ask children, "Are dragons real?" since that question wouldn't necessarily have helped them determine whether children really know what "pretend" and "real" mean. They noted, for example, that a young viewer of *Sesame Street* once said: "I know that Big Bird isn't real. That's just a costume. There's just a plain bird inside." So they tried something else. They gave children a stack of cards with pictures of fantastical and real figures. In one test, they asked the participants to pair the cards however they wished (putting, say, a witch with a bird, since both can fly). In another, the children were asked to sort the cards into two piles, with "real" figures in one and "pretend" in the other. While the children matched and sorted, observers asked questions like, "Why do these two go together?" and recorded the answers.

The results showed what one might expect. The oldest children in the group were more likely to explain their work with statements like "both are fake," or "they are not real." Younger children usually gave more ambiguous explanations, like "because you don't see them roaming around every day" and often didn't categorize them correctly in the first place. In the final analysis, the authors concluded that young children assign figures to "real" or "unreal" categories indiscriminately. When they get older, a category of "unreal things" gradually forms, enabling them to pull figures out of the undifferentiated mass of seemingly "real" things and call them "unreal" instead.

But here's the zinger. The children in this study were school-aged, from kindergarten to sixth grade. Even sixth graders—11- and 12-year-olds—did not seem to have full command of the categories of real and unreal when they were asked to pair cards. Figures like dinosaurs, knights, and Indians were sometimes mistakenly put into the "unreal" category.

If children in elementary school are still coming to terms with what make-believe means, toddlers and preschoolers must be even more in the dark. They must not have a clue about the difference between real and fantasy, I thought to myself. But I was still a little perplexed. After all, children as young as 18 months old are starting to play pretend, sipping imaginary tea and driving invisible cars. In our house on a regular basis I'm given very explicit orders by my 2-year-old: "You be baby, and I'll be Mommy." Surely there is some realm of unreality that children do understand at very young ages, I thought. If I could figure out exactly what they comprehend at what age, I could get a grasp on how to have a conversation on their level about what is real and what is not, on and off the screen.

Jacqueline Woolley, a psychologist at the University of Texas, has done some work that can help. Based on her studies, she has found that children as young as 3 do make some important distinctions between reality and unreality. In one of her studies, she and colleague Henry M. Wellman looked at a database of children's everyday conversations and analyzed how they talked about what is "real." They found that, by age 3, children are perfectly capable of understanding, for example, that stuffed animals are not real animals, and that toy trains are not the same as trains people ride to work. They consistently and appropriately categorized them as not real.

The problems, Woolley and Wellman found, appear when 3-year-olds are faced with illusions, with objects designed to deceive people into thinking they are something else. In one of their studies, they tested how children responded to a sponge that looked almost exactly like a rock. The 4-year-olds got it. They could see that the rock was really a sponge made to look like a rock. The 3-year-olds didn't. They thought the sponge was indeed a rock or were otherwise confused about just what they were seeing.[6]

If illusions like fake rocks are able to throw children off, what about the illusory world created on stage, on screen, or in fiction books? At what age do children understand that an event they see on screen or in a book might not occur in real life? Probably not until after age 4, according to psychologists Adrienne Samuels and Marjorie Taylor. They questioned children about illustrations in storybooks and asked if the events in the picture could happen in real life. Three-year-old and young 4-year-old children were as likely to report that a fantasy event could happen in real life as they were to say that it could happen in a dream.[7] What's more, they found that children were most confused when what they saw was frightening.

All of this research undermines a strategy that people routinely employ to comfort young children. Saying, "Don't worry, it's not real," just doesn't mean much to the very young. If, for example, they are faced with a person disguised to look like a monstrous beast, it may be very difficult to convince them that the beast isn't what it seems to be. If that beast is on a screen, it may be equally difficult to convince them that what is depicted is make-believe and not an image of something from real life.

Any hope that viewing fantasy violence can be helpful to very young children is thrown into question with these findings, too. In fact, media scholars tell me, most studies give no evidence that this violence can be beneficial. I did read about one psychiatrist who has seen 10-year-old boys cope best with their fears by playing violent videogames or acting as superheroes killing bad guys.[8] But those boys are at an age when they have a much better comprehension of what they are seeing and how it may relate to their lives. Children at age 2, 3 and 4, psychologists say, aren't there yet. What is there, however, is the amygdala in their brains, firing away, causing the heartbeat to race and the body to tense. Those fear reactions may feel short-lived for adults. Our heart pounds, but we remind ourselves that it is not real, and in a few minutes, we're fine again. The heart-pounding of scared children may subside relatively quickly, too. But, as I soon learned, those minutes of fear might be leaving traces of anxiety that are hard to erase.

Think back to your own early experiences of being frightened by something on the screen. Was there a show or movie that had you hiding behind the couch? I still remember the horror that rocked me when I first heard the screeching voice of the Wicked Witch of the West on the *Wizard of Oz*. My husband remembers being terrified by the flying monkeys. Even Dorothy's walk through the woods before meeting the Cowardly Lion was enough to send me and several people I've interviewed fleeing from the family room.

Reports like those are anecdotal and unscientific. And you may be thinking, yeah, so I was scared. So what?

In the 1980s and 1990s, a communications professor at the University of Wisconsin named Joanne Cantor decided to collect similar reports and apply a more rigorous science to them, trying to learn whether irrational fears persist long after a child views something scary. In one study, she and Kristen Harrison, now a communication professor at the University of Illinois at Urbana-Champaign, asked more than 150 college students to take home a questionnaire on whether they had ever had the experience of "intense and enduring fright" caused by mass media at any age. If yes, they were asked to write several paragraphs about the incident and then answer a few more questions about the emotional effects of the show and their age at the time of viewing. If they had never had a frightful experience, they didn't have to write a thing. Either way, they would get extra credit for responding.

You might think that the students would have opted for the easy way out. But the vast majority turned in detailed reports. More than half said that they had had trouble sleeping or eating after watching the shows. More than a quarter of respondents said that the effects lasted for more than a year and were still persisting.[9]

Cantor writes persuasively about what she's learned from these self-reports in her 1998 book, *Mommy, I'm Scared*. It is peppered with excerpts from respondents describing the recurring sleep problems or phobias that came from movies as varied as *Friday the Thirteenth* and *Willy Wonka and the Chocolate Factory*. In most cases, the movies were seen in elementary, middle or high school. But a few people recalled the way media affected them as preschoolers. One student wrote about the impact of watching, at age 4, an episode of *Star Trek* that featured a creature with "salt suckers"—suction cups on its fingers for extracting salt from its victims' faces. "The image of this grotesquely hideous creature kept me awake the entire night," he wrote. "I had this fear that the salt vampire was going to grab me from underneath my bed, suck out my face and end my life."[10]

What about memories of viewing before the age of 4? Has Cantor found many students who have written coherently about being scared by the screen at age 1, 2 or 3? No—and there's a good reason. Think back to your earliest memory. Chances are, you are like the vast majority of people who can only recall experiences that happened around age 3. Very few memories remain from the years before that age. Most people do not have memories of sleeping, crying, crawling or, mercifully, having their diaper changed.

It might be tempting, therefore, to assume that 1-, 2- and 3-year-old children will not remember something they see on a video screen. Evidence does show that, when children experience an event directly, their memory of it is much more elaborate and complete than if they simply watched it happen. And the experience of watching via a screen versus watching in "real life" may be yet harder to catch in the memory net. I contacted Robyn Fivush, a psychologist who specializes in children's memory at Emory University, to try to learn more. "We know that 2- to 3-year-old children retain memories for many years," Fivush told me in an email interview, "but we also know that MANY memories are forgotten, that memories that are not talked about are significantly MORE likely to be forgotten, and that memories that are less elaborated (i.e., seen versus experienced events) are less stable and more easily forgotten memories."

I wondered if, given that their memories are more easily forgotten, very young children are simply immune, unaffected by what they are watching. But then I remembered the research of Rachel Barr, an infant-memory specialist at Georgetown. She has evidence that children as young as 6 months can imitate something they see on a video screen a day later. Experiments by Anderson and Richards have shown that very young children are attentive to television, with physiological signs of being cognitively engaged and aroused by it. Word-learning research has shown that toddlers can be trained to match words to objects or movements that are labeled in videos. Much more research needs to be done on how children use memories of video in the short and long term, but it is not inconceivable that they tuck things away for later recall.

~~~~⌒

One day, when I was knee-deep in research on "scary" media, I got a phone call from a close friend. "My son is having nightmares about Swiper," she said. At 3¹/₂, her son had started waking up in the middle of the night screaming about Swiper, the sneaky fox in *Dora the Explorer* who steals things from Dora and her cohorts and then tosses them out of reach. Could there be something about the show—which was viewed frequently at her house months before—that was triggering bad dreams?

It certainly sounded plausible, and I promised her I would find out. What I learned, however, deepened the mystery of the Swiper shrieks. I could find no scientific research showing a connection between what a very young child sees on screen and what a child experiences when asleep. In fact, I found that gleaning anything about dreams in young children is a dicey endeavor. As you'll see in the following chapters on educational television and language development, not until sometime between 2 and 3 years old can most children really follow a narrative, a linear story of "this happened, then this happened, and so on." And yet it would seem that perceiving and then retelling a narrative is critical to dreaming. Could it be that infants and toddlers just don't have the mental equipment to really dream in the first place?

David Foulkes thinks so. Foulkes is a retired psychologist in Florence, Oregon, who spent the majority of his career studying the dreaming of children. He has conducted some of the most extensive sleep-laboratory projects ever conducted, including a study at the University of Wyoming that collected and analyzed reports of dreams from children as they grew from age 3 to age 8. He and his staff conducted more than 2,700 dream interviews. In a book summarizing his research titled *Children's Dreaming and the Development of Consciousness*, he wrote: "The received wisdom that human infants (and other animals) dream stands on very shaky ground."[11]

Foulkes believes, and several sleep scientists concur, that true dreaming in children does not begin until somewhere between the ages of 7 to 9 years old and that, before the age of 3, children most likely don't dream at all. Yes, children at very young ages experience a lot of REM sleep, and REM sleep is often equated with dreaming, but Foulkes isn't so sure that the connection between REM sleep and dreaming is as tight as we might think. To dream, Foulkes explains, a person must have a certain level of consciousness, an awareness of the state of their minds, an understanding that they are "in an imagined world in which things happen."[12] In the earliest years of life, children give no signs of being aware of the state of their minds. You don't hear 2-year-olds saying, "let's see, the last time I was holding my blankie I was thinking about what I might like to eat, so maybe I brought blankie into the kitchen." They aren't old enough yet to be thinking about thinking.

When Foulkes tried to take reports on the dreams of children as young as 3, his main finding was the absence of them. The vast majority of the time, there was just nothing there. If a preschool-aged child did report a dream, it was often emotionless and static, like a photo instead of a video. It did not include the child in any way. Indeed, in many reports children used just a few words and described an animal, like a calf in a barn or a chicken eating corn. Moreover, Foulkes found many reasons to suspect that the reports he received from the very youngest of that group were inaccurate, either because the children did not understand exactly what they were being asked or because they were talkative by nature and acting on a desire to amuse or please the interviewer. It is not until around age 5, Foulkes reported in his book, that a child's description of a dream becomes generally credible.[13]

According to Foulkes and other sleep researchers, many parents may be confusing nightmares with night terrors, which manifest as shrieks in the night yet have been found to be devoid of any content at all. Parents understandably want to attach meaning to these terrors, which can scare the bejesus out of anyone, but they may have no correlation to a child's emotional or mental state. If not night terrors, an equally plausible cause of children's presumed nightmares are noises or discomforts that awaken the child, who then finds himself alone in the dark. It's a circumstance that could be scary enough for a young child to induce screaming, not to mention trigger panic about what might be lurking beneath the bed.

In sum, there is no way to know exactly what led my friend's son to scream about Swiper in the dark of the night. In fact, as you'll soon see, the creators of *Dora* have had some heated debates about Swiper's influence on kids. And it's not out of the realm of possibility that her son did, indeed, see Swiper in a dream. But until much more is understood about children's dreaming, nightmares, and the interplay of media content, parents may just have to trust their instincts, doing their best to keep an eye on just how much the characters on screen—or in any story for that matter—are affecting the way their children sleep.

Now let's step for a minute into territory that has been even less explored. What about the media's impact on children younger than 2? What about tiny babies? I have yet to find a study, for example, that examines the impact of watching *The Sopranos* while cuddling up with a 9-month-old. If an infant is snoozing nearby while his parents have finally managed to get some couple time in front of the TV, I'd be willing to bet that no harm is done. But when awake, infants are taking in emotional information from all around. They have limited ability to modulate their own emotions, but they are starting to sense distinctions in how other people feel.[14] Newborn infants cry when another newborn is crying. Three-month-old babies can recognize a smile well enough to smile back. Four-month-olds can make distinctions between sad, happy, fearful or angry faces when playing peek-a-boo.[15] And when Mom is anxious, babies of all ages become anxious, too.

So the question is, can babies be affected by people who aren't actually in the room but are on the screen? And, if so, at what age do those responses kick in? Donna Mumme and Anne Fernald, two developmental psychologists, created a laboratory experiment to find the answers. They brought infants of 10 and 12 months of age into a room and sat them in a high chair in front of a table and video monitor (with Mom or Dad sitting nearby). Videos had been prepared ahead of time that featured an actress pointing at and talking about various three-dimensional objects that the babies had never seen before. One object, for example, was a red spiral letter holder. "Look at that!" the actress would say, "It's plastic. It has four legs. It has lots of hoops. It's a cylinder. It's bright red. Look at that." The actress spoke the same words in each video, but her tone and facial expressions differed sharply. In one video, she used a fearful, anxious voice. In another, she spoke in positive, happy tones, and in the third, she stayed neutral.

While the babies watched, the same object and a distracting object were sitting on the table in front of them, both of which were pushed within their reach when the video ended. The researchers wanted to know if the babies would reach for the red letter holder if the person on the TV screen seemed fearful of it. Or, would they hold back, accurately reading the tone and expressions of the woman on the screen?

The answer, it turned out, depended on the age of the child and the type of emotion. Ten-month-old babies did not demonstrate any connection to the emotions, whether they were good or bad. But 12-month-olds were clearly affected. When the actress expressed fear, they held back, avoiding any interaction with the object. It was as if they were saying, "No way. If she doesn't like it, I'm not touching that thing either." These results jibe with other research on babies that shows that the latter part of a child's first year is a turning point in processing and understanding emotions.

But this result wasn't all they discovered. The psychologists also witnessed signs of what is called "emotional contagion." The 12-month-olds who watched the fearful actress started to show signs of being fearful themselves, with furrowed brows, frowns, worried expressions and crying.[16] Clearly, what they saw on the screen had had a negative impact.

These results surprised Mumme and led her to believe that even 12-month-olds can, as she told me, "pick up on the emotional energy" of something like a horror movie. They are likely to become fearful or upset as a direct response to what they are seeing and hearing. Whether those responses have lasting impact, however, is less understood. In another set of experiments, Mumme tried to find out whether 1-year-olds would retain their fear of an object twenty minutes later. So far she has found no evidence that they do. She hypothesizes that either the design of her experiment or the lack of repetition are the culprits. Children in all sorts of settings have shown the need for continuous and repeated exposure to retain what they are seeing and hearing, and emotional learning, she said, is probably no different.

Mumme points out, however, that a 3-month-old who doesn't pick up on the emotion from a movie is still capable of picking up on her parent's response to that movie. And scientists in psychology and neuroscience have already debunked the once-conventional wisdom that babies and toddlers are simply too young to be affected by stresses in their environments.[17] Mumme makes a compelling argument for erring on the side of caution. Years ago, she argues, people were convinced that babies could not feel pain the way adults do, and anesthesia was not used in common procedures like

circumcisions. New research has shown otherwise. "I wouldn't want
to make that mistake again," she said.

꩜

I know there are readers saying, but that's not me. There's no way I
would expose my children to movies that I find scary. They only
watch what's made for children.

If only it were so simple. Children's programming that is appropriate for an 8-year-old is far different from that made for a 4-year-
old, and as research on the very youngest years has shown us,
programming for a 4-year-old may be inappropriate for a 3-year-
old, which may be inappropriate for a 2-year-old. A lot of cognitive
and social-emotional development is happening in those short
twelve-month spans. But the typical dialogue about children's programming doesn't seem to take that factor into account. Consider
these comments from three different people, posted on a Parent-
Center.com bulletin board:[18]

> I could see a 3 and 4 year old watching *Harry Potter*. There is noth-
> ing wrong with that as long as the PARENTS are responsible
> enough to EXPLAIN to their kids what is happening. . . . Kids get
> more violence off of cartoon network than they would get off of
> another kids movie.
>
> My 2½ year old and I just watched *Toy Story* together . . . and
> with some editing (which is very easy with DVDs), he and his
> daddy have enjoyed the original *Star Wars Trilogy* and the first and
> last *Indiana Jones* movies.
>
> My 4 year old son was horrified by *Harry Potter*! and I thought it
> was a kids movie.

These remarks tell us a lot about the state of confusion that
parents—myself included—may be feeling these days. First, there's

the idea that, by talking to children about what they are seeing, they'll understand it the way adults do. From what we know about brain development and preschoolers' understanding of fantasy, that simply is not the case. Then there's the question of Cartoon Network, which provokes two completely different responses from parents I've interviewed. Either it is considered completely innocuous and even appropriate for toddlers and preschoolers, since it is in cartoon format, or it is to be avoided because its shows are made for school-aged children and contain violence. Most developmental psychologists say the latter is closer to the truth, for persuasive evidence has piled up over the years about how on-screen violence can lead some children to act more aggressively. In one famous study in 1971, preschoolers were randomly divided into two groups, one that watched children's cartoons that contained violence and one that watched nonviolent cartoons. Before the groups had been exposed to the programming, they exhibited comparable styles of play. But after several weeks of exposure, the kids watching violent programs were kicking, choking or hitting their classmates more often than were children from the control group.[19]

What about the movies mentioned? *Star Wars*, *Indiana Jones*, and *Harry Potter* are rated PG–13 and contain moments that even adults consider scary. Psychiatrists and psychologists advise parents to simply keep their kids away from this content until they're older. *Toy Story* is rated G, but the G rating simply means that the movie contains no sex, violence or naughty words. It tells us nothing about what might otherwise upset or frighten very young children. Over the past few years, parent-based movie review sites have cropped up on the Web to provide more insight (see appendix I), and they categorize *Toy Story* as appropriate only for children over 4. Why? There are moments of suspense and peril that can be too emotionally charged for 3-year-olds to take.

Parents can be forgiven for feeling befuddled about what movies are emotionally safe for their kids. After all, isn't that our dear friend Buzz from *Toy Story* on the Huggies "pull-ups" being worn by countless 2-year-olds? All it takes is a walk through retail shops—or your local playground—to find dozens of similar examples. Sippy cups are emblazoned with the clownfish from *Finding Nemo*, even though the movie is judged by reviewers to be appropriate for ages 6 and up. Pajamas, size 2T, come covered by *Spider Man*, a movie rated PG–13. In our backyard is a ride-on toy for 2-year-olds featuring all the characters from *The Lion King*, a movie judged appropriate for kids 6 and up. The movies *Madagascar*, *Shrek*, *Aladdin* and *The Incredibles* have been deemed best for kids over 8, but their characters have been licensed to appear on toys and clothing for children as young as 3.

Today the intensity of marketing related to children's entertainment can be overwhelming, and it may be leading many parents to show movies to toddlers who are not ready for them. But the presence of very young children at such movies is not new. Even back in 1937, when Disney released *Snow White and the Seven Dwarfs*, young children were in attendance at the theaters. Nelson Rockefeller once said that he had to reupholster the seats in Radio City Music Hall because "they were wet so often by frightened children" watching the movie.[20] I wouldn't be surprised if watching Snow White fleeing through the woods as the huntsman followed to cut her heart out was the reason.

Indeed, it has become clear to many parents, after spending hours calming their children, that the imprimatur of Disney on a DVD does not automatically mean that the movie is right for 2-, 3- or 4-year-olds (or even 5- and 6-year-olds, for that matter). But how else can parents know whether their children might be disturbed by what they see? What exactly are the features of a film or television show to be avoided—and why?

When Cantor embarked on her research on scary programming, she explored this question in depth. She started by considering Piaget's theories of how children comprehend their worlds. Her

Many parents of young children can relate to this *Cul de Sac* comic strip that ran in *The Washington Post Magazine* on June 4, 2006. (Reprinted with permission by Richard Thompson)

concerns were not only that they have a hard time distinguishing between fantasy and reality but also that they are struck very strongly by the physical appearance of something, by what they see rather than what they are told.[21] Vivid images and sounds matter the most, and they trump all else. "At this age," Cantor said, "seeing is believing."

In one of her experiments, Cantor created specialized videos to show groups of children, the youngest of which was comprised of 3- to 5-year-olds. One video showed an elderly woman made up to look like an ugly witch but, nevertheless, behaving kindly, feeding a cat while speaking affectionately to it. In another video, the same woman was made up to look attractive, but she acted cruelly, throwing the cat down the basement and threatening to starve it. After the children watched, they were asked to rate how nice or mean the woman was. It turned out that the woman's behavior made little impression on the youngest kids. Her appearance was all that mattered. They said they expected the attractive old lady to feed them cookies. The witch, they said, would lock them in a closet.[22]

Sesame Workshop once created a segment that was intended to help children come to grips with their fears of the dark. The segment opened with Ernie being unable to sleep because he kept wondering if monsters might be lurking outside his door. His imagination took over, and suddenly the screen showed furry monsters overrunning *Sesame Street* and invading Bert and Ernie's room. In desperation, Ernie started to sing "Bad things, go away!" Bert awoke, realized what was happening and started to sing a calming song to soothe his friend. The segment ended on a sweet, reassuring note, but Sesame Workshop never aired it. They discovered with test audiences that children were highly attentive to Ernie's fear and the invading monsters, but their attention waned during the soothing song. They never got the message of reassurance. All they could focus on was the scary part, and Sesame Workshop did not want to have any part in unnecessarily upsetting its audience.[23]

The 1999 movie *Elmo in Grouchland* is another case in point. The movie starts with a mean, greedy villain snatching Elmo's blankie. When Sesame Workshop tested the movie with kids, it became clear that this scene was too distressing for its audience. "Children were crying in the theater," said Rosemarie Truglio, vice president of education and research for Sesame Workshop. "I was horrified. We had to do something." But it was too late and too expensive to re-shoot the movie. Instead, the producers decided to stop the action at highly emotional moments and insert new segments showing Bert and Ernie reassuring the audience that Elmo will be okay.

The *Grouchland* experience has colored everything Sesame Workshop has done with Elmo since then. But the lesson wasn't that children should never see Elmo frightened or upset. Instead, Truglio said, "you have to be very careful about how you scare Elmo. Children are very in tune to him." After the terrorist attacks of September 11, Sesame Workshop created a series of programs to help children overcome fears and talk about loss. One of them became the DVD *Elmo Goes to the Firehouse*, in which Elmo is about to have lunch in Hooper's store when a fire breaks out in the kitchen. Elmo shakes with fear for a minute or two, but the rest of the video shows Elmo in rapt fascination learning about firefighters, firehouses and how to stay safe. "You have to make the resolution just as salient as the conflict, or else the resolution is just not going to be remembered," Truglio said. "We struggle with it here all the time."

The creators of *Dora the Explorer* have struggled a bit, too. My friend is not the only one who has questions about the impact of the sneaky fox called Swiper. According to Chris Gifford, *Dora's* executive producer, Swiper was the subject of heated debates. Gifford has argued that Swiper, and the tinge of danger accompanying him, was necessary to give kids a reason to keep watching and become cognitively engaged in the show's puzzles and mini-lessons. "We wanted to show a villain who was harmless but threatening," he said.

But, as Gifford told me, at least a few child-development experts hired by Nickelodeon have been less than enamored of the Swiper character. They didn't like the idea that children may start modeling Swiper's behavior, and they worried about how preschoolers would react to a fox with glinting teeth sneaking up on beloved characters. One compromise was to soften Swiper by reducing the number of times he showed his teeth and making them look dull instead of sharp. Gifford said his creative team has also been careful to give children no reason to think that Swiper would do anything but snatch objects. In the first year of the show's production, for example, the team created an episode about the "three little piggies" that sparked real fear among the test audience when Swiper appeared. The problem was that the pigs did not have anything that could be swiped, leading the kids to believe that Swiper was planning to eat the piggies instead. Gifford said that the creators changed the script, adding a moment in which Dora gave medals to the pigs for good behavior. That, he said, made it clear that Swiper was only after the medals.

In the series as a whole, the periodic chants of "Swiper, no swiping!" are most important for children watching the show, Gifford said. Whenever those words are uttered, Swiper immediately halts in his wicked ways. "Being able to stop him is incredibly empowering to our audience," he said. Today, instead of hearing reports of children being frightened by Swiper, he continued, he hears reports of how much kids love the character. He would never purposefully include a scary character in one of his shows, he told me. "My biggest fear in producing preschool TV is that a kid is going to get scared," he said. "My personal experience is that once a kid is scared, they will never watch it again."

Unquestionably, there is still a lot we don't know about the impact of emotionally charged and scary material for very young children. And if children do seem frightened, it is not entirely clear which elements of context or content might have a lasting impact. It is worth remembering, consequently, that children are amazingly resilient. So far, I can only conclude that parents will do best to consider the needs and personalities of their own children. Some kids are especially sensitive. In our household, we discovered that, in addition to scary sounds and visuals, moments of drama could be too much for our first-born daughter. At age 3, she clung to me, terrified, while watching a *Winnie the Pooh* video that showed Piglet caught in a tree. We left the room. A few days past her fourth birthday, I discovered that she was not ready for the movie *Curious George*. She cowered in fear, feeling the air of foreboding in the scene where the mean-looking bellman sniffed out George, who wasn't allowed in the apartment building. We left the theater. So far, her younger sister, now 2½, is not showing quite the same sensitivities, but given my recent obsession with this topic, my husband and I are also paying more attention to the content of the media she is watching than we did for her sister at this age.

Most experts do note, however, that parents should be especially wary of movies that show characters separated from their friends or loved ones. To be left behind, to be motherless or fatherless—these are a toddler or preschooler's worst fears, said Michael Brody, the practicing psychologist who works on media issues. And factors in a child's real life may already be heightening those anxieties. Yet children's movies are rife with these exact themes. I heard about one mother whose 4-year-old son recoiled in horror at anything related to *Finding Nemo* after seeing the DVD. The movie tells the story of a clownfish who, within moments after losing his mother, becomes separated from his dad. At the time he saw the movie, the boy's father had been away from home for months, stationed in Kuwait.

Cantor suggests that, for children under 5, parents should only choose video media that is "all sweetness and light." The producers of programs specifically made for young preschoolers make a point of not including any troubling music or upsetting scenarios. (*Miffy* and *Barney* come to mind.) The first years of childhood are so short, and children are still too young to understand conversations about death or why upsetting things happen to people. Why rush children into movies that aren't made for them?

But even the most protective parents acknowledge that exposure to scary media is bound to happen sometimes. A child might see the destruction of a tornado when a parent tunes into the nightly news. Or he might be desperate to stay with older siblings who are allowed to watch *The Lion King*. When that child becomes frightened, what is a parent to do? As we now know, repeating the words "it's not real" will do little good. Using comforting language and fast-forwarding through the upsetting parts can help, but simply getting away from the screen entirely may be the best option. Experts suggest bringing the children to the kitchen to get a beverage or snack, grabbing their security blankets, or distracting them by pulling out a favorite game and talking about something happy.

Cantor advises parents to ask their children about what they are thinking about. But keep in mind that it can be very difficult for young children to verbalize their fears. Michael Cohen, a research consultant for educational television producers, told me that his daughter recently recounted how she used to be scared of Cookie Monster, fearing that he would come gobble her up. "Why?" he asked her. She reminded him that his affectionate name for her was "cookie," and so, in her preschool mind she figured she was a prime target. "Just last year, at age 13, she told me this," Cohen said. "I had no idea."

If frightened behavior persists, parents can try some interventions.[24] Sometimes it helps to ask children to draw what is on their minds or what they saw in a movie. Doing a little pretend play may work, too. If a child cries out in the night about a character from a movie, psychologists suggest that a possible salve is for the child to play-act the role of that character, enabling him to exert control over what might be frightening him. But most of all, Cantor said, some children may respond best to simply having a caring person to hug and hold onto. As a mother, that is a role I'll gladly take on.

NOTES

1. Rideout and Hamel, 2006, p. 13.
2. For an example, see Bloom, 2004, pp. 8–10.
3. Erikson, 1950, p. 408.
4. Eliot, 1999, pp. 8, 296–297.
5. Morison and Gardner, 1978, pp. 642–648.
6. Woolley and Wellman, 1990, p. 954.
7. Samuels and Taylor, 1994, p. 417.
8. Lynn Ponton in the Foreword to Jones, 2002, p. vii.
9. Harrison and Cantor, 1999, pp. 97–116.
10. Cantor, 1998, p. 55.
11. Foulkes, 1999, p. 16.
12. Ibid., p. 9.
13. Ibid., p. 59.
14. National Scientific Council on the Developing Child, 2004, p. 1.
15. See the work of Arlene Walker-Andrews, a psychologist at Rutgers University.
16. Mumme and Fernald, 2003, pp. 221–237.
17. National Scientific Council on the Developing Child, 2005, p. 5.
18. ParentCenter.com, from the readers' comments section of "Ask the Experts: How Can I Tell If My Child Is Upset by Something in a Movie or on TV?" accessed May 18, 2006.
19. Siegler, DeLoache, and Eisenberg, 2003, p. 33.
20. Bright, 1967, pp. 299–303.
21. Cantor, 1998, p. 50.
22. Ibid., p. 57.
23. Fisch and Truglio, 2001, p. 11.
24. See Cantor's chapter, "The Media and Children's Fears, Anxieties and Perceptions of Danger," in Singer and Singer, 2001, pp. 207–221; and Cantor, 1998, pp. 71–80.

Chapter Six

What Is Educational About "Educational" TV?

I n 2002, a group of creative executives for Noggin embarked on a tour of New York preschools in search of inspiration. Since Noggin's debut a few years earlier, the commercial-free channel had been broadcasting re-runs of popular shows for children aged 2 to 12 as part of a partnership between Nickelodeon and Sesame Workshop. But Sesame Workshop had just sold its stake to Nick, and it was time to regroup. Ratings showed that school-aged children weren't paying much attention, while the younger kids were enraptured. Could the network fill up the entire daytime block—from 6 am to 6 pm—with shows designed for 2- to 5-year-olds? If so, what might the channel's theme be? Should it center on music? Could it focus on global culture? What about language enrichment?

Amy Friedman, founding creative director of Noggin, was pregnant with her first child at the time. She lumbered in and out of preschools with her colleagues, watching snack time and circle time, dress-up and recess. At a preschool in a synagogue on Park Avenue, they realized they had the answer. "It was one of the most amazing places we've ever been," Friedman said. "The kids were so engaged. And we said, 'it's right in front of us.'" They resolved that Noggin would emulate a well-run preschool. It would only run shows designed with specific learning-based goals in mind. In between shows, the screen would display artwork and craft materials from a child's world, like crayon drawings, buttons and clothespins. The animated host of those in-between moments would be a kind, hands-on teacher—the type who has no qualms about getting into the sandbox to play with the kids. Viewers know him as "Moose." Breaks between shows would riff off of the routine moments of a preschoolers' day, with five-minute shorts on snack time, story time and quiet time. Noggin's new tagline became, "It's like preschool on TV."

My reaction was cynical when I first heard that tagline. I had just enrolled my first daughter in preschool, and I remember thinking, "Her experience is exactly what television isn't." Preschool is about running sand through your hands, learning how to ask for a turn on the tricycle, sitting cross-legged next to your friend without provoking a poke-fest. Television can't replace the thrill of standing at an easel, brush dripping, in front of a white scroll of paper. Isn't this just like American society? I grumbled. We put preschool on TV instead of making it easier for working parents to enroll their kids in the real thing.

But that argument belies the reality that exists in my own house, as well as in others I've visited. Millions of children are watching Noggin in addition to preschool, not in place of it. Moreover, the shows at least appear to be educational.

So, are they truly educational? Families can now choose from a growing list of preschool channels. In our house, we get three PBS stations, Nick Jr., Noggin, The Discovery Channel, and the Disney channel, all of which offer preschool programming for at least some portion of the day. Many of the shows are labeled "educational" on their Web sites, which are brimming with information about the show's curriculum and mission, not to mention all the educational consultants who have signed on to advise the script writers. Yet many discerning parents who read these promotional assurances still have questions. After all, just because a television program has paid for a consultant with an EdD does not mean the show is educational. What does it mean that a program has a curriculum? Do the creators of these programs have any proof that young children can actually learn from what they've seen?

Unfortunately, the answers vary for each program and change with each season, and it can be tempting to just abandon the quest altogether. I talked to one mother who allows her children, at 22 months and 3½ years old, to watch only a couple of *Veggie Tales* and *Richard Scarry* videotapes. She hasn't had the time, she said, to figure out which TV programs might be developmentally appropriate for her children and when they are on. "I do think my kids are missing something of value in not watching any public television," she said, "and I'd be interested in learning about particular programs, . . . but I'm a working mom."

I knew how she felt. Sorting hype from reality was daunting, but digging into the question opened my eyes. *Sesame Street*, I discovered, isn't the only program that can boast about teaching young children. Scientific research has shown children to gain, academically and socially, from a number of shows, including *Blue's Clues*, *Barney*, *Dora the Explorer*, *Dragon Tales*, and *Mister Rogers*, as well as a handful of programs that are no longer on the air. The formal features of a program—how it cuts from one scene to another, for example—have become the subject of academic study. Experiments about how and when children learn from video are underway in infant laboratories around the country. And academic research has shown that, if a program is slow enough, linear enough and repetitive enough, it has a much better chance of helping preschool-aged children learn.

Skepticism is healthy, and parents are right to be watchful, but the good news is that many of the experts guiding today's videos come from the fields of education and psychology, where they built their careers around developing and understanding these finer points. They are purposeful and exacting about creating shows that can be great teaching tools for young children. Better yet, they are willing to discuss what doesn't work. Talking about the way some young children's programming falls short, I soon learned, can provide some of the most valuable insights about how to spot and define educational TV.

~~~

First, let's consider what age groups we're talking about. As we know from research on how babies and toddlers comprehend visual material and symbols, evidence of video-based learning in a child younger than 2 is still spotty. That is one reason, say creators at Noggin and Nick Jr., that they only create or license shows designed for an audience of 2- to 5-year-olds. But something magical happens between 24 months and 30 months. With a 24-month-old, you might see Dad struggling to get his child to sit for a reading of "The Three Bears." At that age, kids often have more pressing things to do, like pulling all the books off the library shelves. But somewhere around 30 months, many parents notice a change: their child seems to follow the story, often sits still to the end, and may ask for it over and over again. This newfound engagement occurs with television, too. "At 2½," said Daniel Anderson of the University of Massachusetts, "there is a real shift in their understanding."

When our younger daughter, Gillian, was just 2 years old, she showed little interest in the *Dora the Explorer* shows that her older sister loved. But in a few months, she was not only watching the whole show, she was talking back to the characters. She asked for the same *Dora* show again and again. (I'm chagrined to report that, at the same time, her older sister decided that *Dora* was not her favorite show anymore.)

The ability to understand simple stories is a skill that usually kicks in between a child's second and third birthdays. Before then, children probably cannot recognize time passing. For them, life is all about the present moment, not the past or the future. For the same reason, they may have a hard time understanding a tale that has a beginning, a middle and an end. The pictures may be fascinating, but the stories hold little draw.

This narrative deficiency alone can be a significant hurdle for the designers of educational television for children who have just turned 2. Often producers want to embed a lesson in a story, but if the story means nothing to the kids viewing the show, it's likely they aren't learning the lesson, either. But that's not the only problem. Remember the phenomenon called the "video deficit?" Something about the screen itself may hamper how easily a 24-month-old can learn from TV. Children that age have no trouble imitating a simple three-step task when demonstrated by an adult sitting across from them. But when the same task is demonstrated by the same adult on videotape, they don't get it at first. Only after repeated viewings do they master the task.

Georgene Troseth, a psychologist at Vanderbilt University, is one of several people trying to solve the mystery of the video deficit. Lately, she and fellow Vanderbilt psychologist Megan Saylor have found what seem like significant clues—clues that are giving producers of educational television some new insights into how their shows should be designed. I visited Troseth on a steamy summer day when most people in Nashville were taking refuge in the air-conditioned indoors. Her infant laboratory, on the third floor of an education building, was not only cool, it was a bastion of information about how and when children may learn from video. Videotapes from past experiments were stacked on television monitors. Small rooms were set up with small chairs and tables, serving as staging grounds for experiments with toddlers and babies. Video cameras were positioned in the corners. Crates were full of toys, puppets and strange-looking handmade objects that the experimenters would use to elicit reactions from children.

Scores of parents, infants and toddlers have been visiting this laboratory over the past several years. They watch video screens and participate in experiments tailored to detect how young children respond differently to even the tiniest variations in how information is portrayed on the screen. During the morning I visited, for example, I had a chance to see how a 12-month-old girl, crawling around in pink booties and a flowered sun dress, responded to a vocabulary test, part of an experiment on whether words can be learned via video.

I had come to Vanderbilt to learn about Troseth and Saylor's study, published a month before, that offered some of the first evidence of the video deficit disappearing under the right conditions. Their experiments compared how 24-month-olds responded to two different video experiences. In one, a group of children were introduced to two-way live video. They could see a person on the screen talking to them, and the person on the screen could see and respond to the children. Like a Web cam, the video allowed both sides to respond to each other in real time.

The other video experience was based on a recording of those live sessions. Instead of a two-way interaction, the children could only see recorded actions that were not contingent on anything they did. This would be like watching *Blue's Clues*, where the actor on screen pauses to simulate a conversation, but back-and-forth interaction between the viewer and actor is impossible.

Why did they set up the experiment this way? They wanted to test a hypothesis. Saylor's work typically focuses on how young children learn language, and recent studies had pointed to the critical influence of social interaction. Toddlers seem primed to learn best by interacting with people who respond personally to their words and movements. "Maybe," Troseth said, "the video deficit existed because the children were not thinking of the people on TV as social partners."

The test hinged on a hiding game. First, the 2-year-olds watched the video—either the prerecorded tape or the live version. Then, the screen showed the person hiding a stuffed animal—Piglet—in a nearby room, often under a table or behind a couch. When the video ended, the children were asked to retrieve Piglet from the room. The results confirmed exactly what the researchers had suspected. The children who saw the recorded video had some trouble. They found Piglet only 35 percent of the time. Children in the live group succeeded about 69 percent of the time, a rate similar to face-to-face interaction.[1]

Does this mean that TV programs that only simulate interaction are doing nothing for kids? Not necessarily, the researchers say. A few of the children who saw the recorded video were especially responsive to the games and pauses, and those were the few children in that group who retrieved the toy. "We found that if children gave evidence of treating the video as a social partner," Troseth told me, "they will use the information." Thus *Blue's Clues*, as the researchers wrote in their study, appeared to be "on the right track." Having repetition built into the show surely helps, too, they added, since the "video deficit" dissipates with repeated viewings.

In sum, their study showed that, under the right conditions, a child as young as 2 can take information offered on screen and apply it to the world around her. A recorded video can teach—if designed to elicit responses from the children who watch it.

The results, not surprisingly, thrilled creators of *Blue's Clues*, who have achieved mild fame for a technique called the "pause."[2] Alice Wilder, the show's director of research, stated that, before an episode is produced, live narrators read the scripts in front of children to see if the questions spark natural responses. One critical element is how long they should wait to allow the children to answer. (The creators say the exact amount of time is an industry secret, but my daughters and I have counted. It averages about two or three seconds.) If the children don't respond or seem bored or confused, the scripts are rewritten.

Blue's Clues, however, was not made for 24-month-old children. Its producers say that 4-year-olds are their "sweet spot." Yet the show

does run in a timeslot that advertises itself as being for children age 2
to 5, and we know it is being watched by children age 2 or even
younger.[3] And herein lies the challenge inherent in creating "educational television." Toddlers and preschoolers undergo major changes
in emotional, social and cognitive development with every passing
month. Designing television for preschoolers is thus not the same as
creating a program for a catchall group of teenagers and adults who
easily understand narratives and have the experience and cognitive
ability to understand, retain and recall what they see.

I talked to Amy B. Jordan, a senior researcher and educational
TV expert at the Annenberg School for Communication, about
this problem. She used *Bill Nye the Science Guy* as an example. She
said she once asked Disney, the company behind the program,
Who is your target audience? The answer was 6- to 12-year-olds,
students in first to seventh grades. But when Jordan asked the same
question of Bill Nye's producer, the answer was far more specific:
fourth graders. "To be truly educational, you have to have a very
narrow audience," Jordan said.

But to focus only on the learning needs of a particular age
group—say 30-month-olds—cuts off the possibility of attracting a
larger audience. That situation doesn't sit well with the cable stations and advertisers, not to mention the video producers who need
lots of eyeballs to justify spending millions of dollars to build a
sound educational program. "In order to do good, you have to do
well," said Iris Sroka, a former director of research for Children's
Television Workshop. Consequently, people who make preschool
videos are trying to find a way to make their content comprehensible and enjoyable for a range of ages. As the brains behind Big Bird
can attest, it's not an easy task.

When *Sesame Street* got its start nearly forty years ago, producers were aiming to entertain and educate an audience of 4-year-olds. But in the late 1990s, new data on viewership showed a surprising and not altogether welcome trend: the peak age of viewing was now 2 to 3 years old, and interest in the show seemed to be trailing off around the time children were 3½. Meanwhile, shows like *Blue's Clues* were offering fierce competition. Sesame Workshop realized that it had to embark on a large-scale rethinking of the program's lessons and format. "We had to shake things up a bit," said Rosemarie Truglio, Sesame Workshop's vice president of education and research.

Senior management called for a week-long meeting with producers, writers, Muppeteers, and Truglio, who represented the workshop's research arm. They talked about the length of the show. *Sesame Street* has always been an hour long, versus the thirty minutes of *Blue's Clues* and *Barney*. They talked about the magazine format, in which viewers were treated to a multitude of different scenes, settings and characters. They discussed how to continue touting their trademark "Letter and Number of the Day" while also simplifying content for the younger kids.

"We met for a week and then we said, we've got to make some changes," Truglio told me. They decided to truncate the show to forty-five minutes, because research showed that children's interest began to wane at that point. But it was also clear that children wanted to get to the end of the show so they could see how the Muppets and other *Street* characters, like Maria or Gordon, resolved their problems. The children seemed to like those stories. "The consensus was to continue to break up the narrative, because we're *Sesame Street* and it's a magazine format," Truglio said. "But we said, we'll try to make it much more themed and cohesive."

The management team at Sesame Workshop decided it would continue to perform a balancing act by offering music, puppets, live action and animation. But it still needed to answer one big question: "What do we do for the last 15 minutes?" The answer was to create "Elmo's World," a show within a show, hosted by 3-year-old Elmo who introduces the world as seen through his eyes. The curriculum would focus on what 2- and 3-year-old children could understand. "Simplicity," Truglio said, "is key."

"Elmo's World" debuted in 1998. At first, Truglio's office was flooded with complaints. Parents grumbled, "How could you change my show?" But, Truglio said, the protests stopped after a few months, and parents now tell her that they see the power of the Elmo segments. Sales of DVDs featuring "Elmo's World" are now going strong. On Amazon.com's hourly rankings of best-selling DVDs for preschool-aged children, *Elmo's World* titles appear regularly in the top 25.

But that wasn't the end of the angst at Sesame Workshop. Unfortunately, the other forty-five minutes of the show were still not working, Truglio said. For years, the Workshop had been compiling data about how well children attended to the pilot versions of its shows. "The data showed that the street stories did not hold the children's attention," she said. "That was the weak point of the show." Truglio and others had a hunch as to why. The magazine format was still too jumpy and cut-up. The story lines kept getting interrupted by brief lapses into songs or animation. A similar complaint had come from Dorothy and Jerome Singer, psychologists at Yale University who conducted research on *Barney* and favored it over *Sesame Street*. They had criticized *Sesame Street* for being too frenetic.

What bothered Truglio even more was that low-income children were less interested than middle-income children. Kids in lower-income daycare centers had their eyes on the show 75 to 85 percent of the time, whereas the numbers for children in the middle-income centers were at 95 percent.[4] "This was not good news," she said. *Sesame Street*, after all, was charged at its genesis with broadening educational opportunities for disadvantaged kids. It was time for more big changes. Truglio said she wanted to structure the show to be more predictable and routine, like preschool with its story time, dramatic playtime and snack time. (This was entirely independent of the similar brainstorming happening at Noggin.) She wanted the letter-of-the-day segments to be grouped together and to happen at exactly the same time in each episode. She also wanted participatory games like those on *Blue's Clues*. And she wanted a full uninterrupted story line at the beginning of the show. "Why can't we give the children a narrative?" she asked.

In 2001, *Sesame Street* came out with its second try, another new-and-improved format. "And lo and behold," Truglio said, "I had low-income kids watching longer." For nearly every full program that Sesame Workshop has since tested with children in low-income daycare centers, almost all the children are now attending to it 90 to 95 percent of the time. Not everything about the show is perfect yet, Truglio acknowledged, but she is heartened to know that the new format is having a positive impact on at-risk families. About the once-frenetic pace of *Sesame Street*, Dorothy Singer recently told Truglio, "I can't make that criticism anymore."

The researchers at Sesame Workshop say they are now following a new mantra: "Hold the 2s, reach the 3s and strive for the 4s." They are continually tweaking and re-scripting the episodes to ensure that they continue to attract 2-year-old viewers, reach the 3-year-olds with content appropriate for them, and still have moments that are challenging enough to engage 4-year-olds and prepare them for kindergarten.

~⌒

In February 2005, a conference in Baltimore brought together experts in education, communication, and psychology, as well as producers of televised and online content for kids. Dan Anderson, the expert on children's programming at the University of Massachusetts, was among the speakers.[5] His comments were a summation of his twenty-five years of research on how young children watch

TV, but if you listened carefully, you could come away with a checklist on how to produce something young children might comprehend. After all, if children aren't able to comprehend what they watch, it's hard to imagine that they are learning from it. Among his remarks were the following:

- You want to find the right level of language, the right level of action, and a context that is potentially understandable to children.
- Dialogue and action must be linked.
- Characters (or actors or puppets) should actually do something that illustrates what the scene is about.
- Cuts and pans do elicit looking, but producers have to make informed judgments about how to use them.

Other experts I talked to offered advice, too. Amy B. Jordan said, "Quick cuts and transitions in space and time are baffling to little kids." Shalom M. Fisch, a consultant who has written a book on how children learn from television, agreed. "A 2-year-old is not going to think that a flashback is a flashback. They are going to think it is happening here and now. . . . The simpler the story, the more linear it is, the more explicit stuff is, that will be very important."

Linda Simensky, senior director of children's programming for PBS, described how every program she selects for her line-up must be fun to watch and yet come with specific educational goals. *The Electric Company*, she said, is her model. Children need time to absorb whatever they are hearing. She said she told the creator of *Big, Big World*, a puppet-based show that takes place in a rainforest, "Go deeper. It's okay to spend a few minutes talking about an animal and its habitat." (By the way, just because a show appears on a PBS channel doesn't mean it was hand-picked by Simensky. PBS stations are independently managed, and many managers choose to run shows that haven't been as carefully vetted for educational value.)

After hearing these ideas, I started to see children's programs and DVDs in a new light—and started to notice where they don't stack up educationally. Take the *Veggie Tales* videotape titled *Lyle the Kindly Viking King*. The point of the first tale is clear to adults: the story is about sharing. The word "sharing" is used over and over again—and surely that repetition helps kids learn the word, right? But the action on the screen cuts to all sorts of scenes, and the dialogue is not always related to the action on screen or the lesson being taught. Let's look at one example.

This scene opens with a talking asparagus sitting by a fireplace; the next minute, a curtain opens, and two peas are on a stage in Shakespearean costumes, talking about eggs. The eggs only appear on the screen for a second or two. Then a squash starts to talk about running out of eggs, but a chef brings in a platter with an omelette. (In case you didn't catch it, this is a word play on Hamlet.) "To share or not to share?" the squash asks. Suddenly peas arrive with what look like laptop computers, offering to share their game of Battleship. This gives the squash an idea. He calls other vegetables around him and tells them about the shortage of eggs and how important it is to share them. A few vegetables realize that they had been playing ping-pong with the eggs, thereby causing the shortage. For a brief moment the screen flashes to show a ping-pong table covered in yolks. Soon the curtains close, and a cucumber and asparagus are shown sitting in theater seats.

"Did you understand any of that?" asks the cucumber.

"Not a word," says the asparagus.

To be fair, *Veggie Tales* does not claim to be aimed at 2-, 3- or 4-year-old children. Its marketing materials do not mention an appropriate age group for its products at all. But many parents assume that, because the show is animated and marketed as a wholesome way to "teach life lessons" and Christian values, it can have a positive impact on their preschoolers.

It is also true that *Veggie Tales* is hardly the only video series that may be hard for very young kids to follow. Dozens of children's programs feature cuts between scenes with no warning of what is to come next or where characters from the previous scene have gone. I could also pick on *Winnie the Pooh*, which often relies on flashbacks, or *Richard Scarry* videos, which were once found in a research study of young children to be so dizzying that they were used as an example of an "incomprehensible" video in comprehensibility experiments.[6]

Fisch, a former vice president of program research at Children's Television Workshop and consultant for programs like *Dragon Tales* and *Cyberchase*, has a theory he calls the "capacity model."[7] It is a way of thinking about how—and whether—children process the information they view. An overly simplified version of the theory might go like this: The brain only has so much capacity for taking in new information. To store and recall what it learns, it needs to be able to assign that information a meaningful label or category. (Imagine, for example, a child's brain saying, "Hmmm, 'sharing.' I'll put that concept here, in a category about how grown-ups want me to act around other people.") But categorizing information may be taking a backseat to the brain's other work—that of simply trying to figure out the narrative line of a story or decipher what the characters are doing on screen. ("What was that? A ping-pong table? Have I seen these pea characters before?") When the brain is preoccupied with those questions, it doesn't have much capacity left for categorizing a concept like "sharing," and the lesson of the story isn't learned at all.

Fisch and other experts believe that educational lessons must be tightly woven into the story line of a show. Sesame Workshop has a phrase for this idea—"content on the plot line." Research with older children has shown that the concept works. A study of an episode of *Square One TV*, a program for schoolchildren that ran on PBS, showed that children could explain the Fibonacci sequence—a sophisticated mathematical concept—after watching the episode.[8]

~~~⌒

Every few years at Yale University, a small band of graduate students led by Dorothy Singer convenes in front of a wide-screen TV and watches three hours of back-to-back *Barney* episodes. Their mission is to count all the on-screen moments that hold the potential to be educational for the show's toddler and preschool audience. They have been trained to see the episodes through a child's eyes, being specific about what they record. With pencils poised and scoring sheets spread out in front of them, they make tick marks in boxes that label types of skills: cognitive, emotional, social, physical, music and multicultural awareness. Only spots that could be called teaching moments are reported. For example, on vocabulary measures (listed under the "cognitive" label), the introduction of the word "caterpillar" doesn't count, Dr. Singer explained, unless the characters on screen talk about what it is and show it on the screen.

Singer's team has found that, so far, most *Barney* episodes feature more than a hundred educational moments each. Some shows rate even higher. An episode titled "It's Raining, It's Pouring," for example, scored 178.[9] When they conclude their observations, Singer's team sends a report to the *Barney* producers, who commissioned the study and who use the ratings to inform future productions and trumpet the show's educational value.

Since perfecting that scoring method in the mid-1990s, Singer has applied it to programs viewed by even younger audiences. How does she know which shows to rate? In 2003, she surveyed parents on the media habits of their toddlers and infants, asking parents to note which shows or videos they used. From that list, Singer selected the five top-mentioned video programs and five top-mentioned television shows. She screened two randomly selected episodes from each one. Just as they had with *Barney*, she and her researchers tallied every potentially educational moment, trying to count only the instances that might be understandable to a toddler. The scores were published in *Zero to Three*, a journal for child-development specialists. A video called *The Best of Elmo* and episodes from *Sesame Street*, *Blue's Clues* and *Barney* were at the top in terms of cognitive moments. The *Teletubbies Go* video received by far the highest scores for its potential for teaching about movement, but scored poorly on cognitive, social, emotional or cultural awareness. Baby Einstein's *Baby Mozart* and *Language Nursery* videos seemed to offer little to nothing in those same areas, with slightly elevated scores for content with the potential to teach about movement.[10]

The precision and tidiness of these rankings thrilled me when I first saw them. At last, I thought, here is a scorecard to help me pin down which shows are most educational. But soon new questions dawned: Is there any evidence these educational lessons stick? Can we really say that these programs are, in fact, enabling children to take the lessons they learn from TV and apply them to the real world?

So far, no one has found a scientific way to succinctly answer those questions for baby videos like *Baby Mozart*. But some programs for preschoolers have a right to boast. *Sesame Street*, as you might imagine, has the largest volume of research to back up its educational claims. From its inception, studies have shown that regular viewers of *Sesame Street* do better on tests of cognitive skills and socio-emotional awareness than children who don't watch the show. A massive study conducted in 2001 showed that even 2-year-olds show gains.[11] This result occurs even when family socioeconomic factors—like parental education level and income or whether there are books at home—are taken into account.

Blue's Clues has some impressive data behind it as well. A study of two groups of otherwise similar children in daycare settings—one group that never saw *Blue's Clues* and another that watched it regularly—showed that 3- to 5-year-old children were better at tests of "flexible thinking" than their nonviewing peers, with gains appearing every few months over the span of two years.[12]

Studies of *Barney*, conducted by the Singers in addition to their scoring exercises, show that children even as young as 27 months old are learning from the show. Their studies compared children in daycare centers who had been assigned a two-week *Barney* regimen to those who didn't see the show at all. When tested on vocabulary, awareness of manners and health education, preschoolers who watched *Barney* scored significantly better than the nonviewers. When watching the program was paired with *Barney*-inspired instruction from the teacher, the achievement was even higher. Although the toddlers weren't tested (it would be too much to ask them to respond to a series of questions), they were observed for signs of imaginative play and civil manners. The toddlers who watched *Barney* trumped their nonwatching peers on both counts.[13]

So, now let's up the ante. Do we know that these television programs make a difference years down the road? Are they leading children to do better in school? To answer this question, researchers would need to track a group of children through more than a decade, keeping tabs on those who watched educational TV as preschoolers and those who didn't, comparing their later school achievements.

Several years ago, a team of researchers from the Universities of Texas, Pennsylvania and Massachusetts did just that. They knew of two groups of 5-year-old children whose media use had been studied in detail in the mid-1980s. Ten years later, they reconnected with most of these children, who were now high school students, to see how they had fared. Of the 655 children who participated in the first studies, they were able to locate and interview 570 of them, retrieving their high school transcripts, too.

The analysis, which came to be known as "the recontact study," put all the data from 1985 and 1995 through a battery of statistical formulas to control for the skewing impact of the participants' background, like whether they were first-born children, where they lived, and their parents' level of education. Its findings are compelling enough to quote verbatim: "Adolescents who often watched *Sesame Street* as preschoolers, compared to those who rarely watched the program, had higher grades in English, mathematics, and science; spent more time reading books outside of school; perceived themselves as more competent in school; placed higher value on achievement in mathematics and science; elected more advanced mathematics courses; and expressed lower levels of aggressive attitudes."[14]

Of course, in a study like this one, we cannot say for sure that *Sesame Street* actually caused these kids to take the right path. We have to consider the reverse, too. Could it have been that children "destined" to grow up with these positive abilities and behaviors were naturally attracted to *Sesame Street*? There is no way to know for sure, and other undetected factors may have played a role in their watching. But it is nonetheless striking that, ten years later, a significant link between success and *Sesame Street* appears at all. The researchers behind the study take this result as evidence that there are no negative long-term effects of viewing the show. And they theorize that something about the program sparked or built upon a desire to learn that stuck with these children throughout their years of schooling.

Studies like the recontact study are rare. They require time and money and hinge on the feasibility of keeping track of families as they move, grow and often split up. A bill in Congress called CAMRA, the Children and Media Research Advancement Act, calls for more funding for such research. In 2006 it passed the Senate but stalled in the House of Representative's Subcommittee on Health.

One bright spot is a series of studies on educational television and interactive media proceeding under the Department of Education's Ready to Learn program. For the next five years, researchers will be evaluating whether and how children from ages 2 to 8 learn from new media programs. One of the new shows to be evaluated was designed by Angela Santomero, the lead creator of *Blue's Clues.* Its tentative title is *The Adventures of Super Why*, and it will debut on PBS in the fall of 2007. "It will be literacy based and founded on a curriculum," Santomero told me. "We've looked at everything that children need," she said, ticking off a list that included research on pre-reading readiness, phonics, sound blending and story comprehension. Deborah Linebarger of the University of Pennsylvania is designing the experiments that will test how viewers and nonviewers compare after watching the show for a set time period. This kind of research is scarce, Santomero said, "because a lot of people are scared of the answer. But I always say, it makes it easier. You know if it works."

By now it's probably clear that to be educational, a preschool program should be tested with real children and tweaked accordingly, designed to get viewers to participate as social partners, and built to point children toward specific goals, like the ability to recognize letters, match sounds with instruments, or simply recognize the importance of physical exercise. It should be vetted by childhood experts to ensure it is developmentally appropriate for 2-, 3- or 4-year-olds. (Although it's a relatively good sign to see an educational expert's name on an advisory board for a particular show, look for evidence that the advisers are actually reviewing the content.) Its stories should be linear and easy to follow. It should refrain from excessive cuts between scenes. The pace should be slow and steady. And if the money and will is there, research should be undertaken after a show goes on the air to find out if children really are learning from it.

But I've forgotten one thing: parents. I don't mean that parents have to be sitting by their child's side, pointing to and labeling what they see together, though I should note that research has shown that this interaction can be a big help.[15] What I mean is that the at-

titude a parent brings to the television can affect whether children
learn from it.

Researchers of educational television like to tell the story of
Gavriel Salomon, a social scientist who studied, among other things,
how Israeli children differed from American children in their response to television. It was 1978, and he had expected to find that
Israeli kids—who had nothing more than one black-and-white
channel to watch—would be far worse than Americans at recalling
and understanding what they had seen on screen. The American
children, after all, were already pros at watching TV, with longer
viewing times, color screens and multiple channels to choose from.

But what he found instead was that the Israeli children outscored
them significantly on tests of literate viewing. The explanation, he
discovered, was that Israeli children took television more seriously.
Their mothers viewed television as a source of news. Their families
watched it with purpose. Therefore the children expended more
mental effort trying to learn from what they saw on screen and were
able to retain what they watched.[16]

Jordan, the educational TV expert at the Annenberg School in
Philadelphia, said she is worried about the way television is used in
American homes these days. She has surveyed scores of parents
and concluded that many of them consider the television everything but a teaching tool. Instead, it's just a source of entertainment, something to flip through, like a magazine at the hair salon,
a way to fill dead space at the dinner table, or a technique for getting toddlers to fall asleep. At daycare centers she has visited, while
books are treated as tools for deliberate learning, televisions are
"place holders" and "time-buying tools," used to smooth the transition from lunchtime to naptime.[17]

As Jordan told me, "We teach our children how to use TV." So let's
teach them that the screen can—under the right conditions—teach.

NOTES

1. Troseth, Saylor and Archer, 2006, p. 792.

2. Malcolm Gladwell's best-selling book *The Tipping Point* (2000), which includes a chapter about *Blue's Clues* and *Sesame Street,* provides an engaging description of how the "pause" works; see pp. 89–132.

3. In a 2002 "Parent Media Survey" conducted by Dorothy G. Singer and Deborah S. Weber, *Blue's Clues* was listed second in a top-five list of programs favored by children under 2 years old. *Sesame Street* came first. See Weber and Singer, 2004.

4. Past and present data on attention to the show was provided by Sesame Workshop.

5. A video recording of his speech is at the Web site for the Ready to Learn Summit 2005, http://www.pbs.org/readytolearn/resources/summit_thursday.html.

6. Richards and Anderson, 2004, p. 178.

7. For a more detailed description, see Fisch's chapter on the capacity model in his book *Children's Learning from Educational Television,* 2004.

8. Fisch, 2004, p. 152. And if you are curious, here's the beginning of the Fibonacci sequence: 0, 1, 1, 2, 3, 5, 8, 13, 21, 34, 55. . . . Add the first two numbers (0 + 1) you get the third number (1). Add the second and third numbers (1 + 1) and you get the fourth (2), and so on.

9. Singer and Singer, 1998, p. 318.

10. Weber and Singer, 2004, p. 35.

11. Wright et al., 2001, pp. 1347–1366.

12. Anderson et al., 2000, pp. 179–194.

13. Singer and Singer, 1998, pp. 328–359.

14. Aletha C. Huston, Daniel R. Anderson, John C. Wright, Deborah L. Linebarger, and Kelly L. Schmitt, "*Sesame Street* Viewers as Adolescents: The Recontact Study," in Fisch and Truglio, 2001, pp. 131–143.

15. See Singer and Singer, 1998.

16. Salomon, 1981.

17. Jordan, 2005, pp. 523–538.

Chapter Seven

Could the Right DVD Teach My Child to Speak, or Better Yet, Become Bilingual?

One day in 1971, a little boy arrived at a speech clinic at the University of Connecticut to be treated for anomalies in the way he talked. He became an immediate subject of fascination. The boy, who was 3 years and 9 months old, had deaf parents, but he could hear normally. His parents had no hearing friends or relatives who lived nearby, and he had no hearing playmates. Only rarely, if ever, had he experienced words being spoken to him. He had quite possibly never been engaged in a conversation—even one using signs—because his parents had purposefully held back from teaching him American Sign Language.

"At the time there was a lot of prejudice against signing," said Jacqueline Sachs, a speech therapy professor who helped to document the case of "Jim," as he came to be called among researchers. "The mother was told that, since the child was hearing, she shouldn't use sign language with him because it would inhibit his ability to learn language when he went to school."

In the months after Jim's arrival at the university clinic, therapists interviewed his mother using written messages. She told them that Jim had a younger brother, 1 year and 10 months old, who could also hear normally. She said she had occasionally used simple gestures with her children, like signaling not to touch something or beckoning them to come to dinner. She had been deaf since birth from maternal rubella. Her only oral communication was "No." The boy's father, according to researchers, "did not participate in childcare." He was a factory worker who lost his hearing as a toddler after a bout of pneumonia.[1]

The brothers did watch television frequently, the mother said. No record exists of what exactly they watched, though Sachs remembers that their mom called them "children's shows" and that she turned on the sound so that the boys could hear them. There were a few children's programs being broadcast back then, like *Mister Roger's Neighborhood* and *Sesame Street*. "She thought he maybe learned some words from those shows," Sachs told me, "but she couldn't be sure because she couldn't hear him." Once, when Jim was about 2½ years old, his mother thought that he might have tried to say "Kool-Aid."

The month before Jim arrived at the clinic, his mother enrolled him in preschool, hoping it would help him learn English. "The nursery school teacher said she didn't know what to do with him," Sachs said. One teacher reported that Jim "was a good child, a very quiet child, but never used language spontaneously." The preschool assumed that he must be mentally retarded. He was soon moved to a school for handicapped children, where a social worker spotted him and called the university.

Initial evaluations showed that Jim's hearing was still fine (one ear was just a little congested) and that his motor skills were on track. But he spoke very softly in a monotone and could not articulate well. Some words were unintelligible. He only spoke when asked, and his answers were comprised of one or two words each. His expressive language—his ability to say words—was well below normal for his age. His comprehension of vocabulary words was below normal, too.

Before embarking on a therapy program, Marie Johnson, a speech-language clinician, recorded some sessions with Jim. She put toy trains and planes on the floor, showed him pictures and tried to coax some language from him. Here is some of what he said, excerpted from the journal *Applied Linguistics*, where his case was reported ten years later:

"Look at all the plane."
"Can open that plane?"
"Where the wheels plane? Take it off."
"Off."
"That wheels."
"This not take off plane. This is how a plane."

The word order was often mixed up—something that doesn't typically happen even during a child's earliest attempts at learning to talk.[2] What's more, the words that normally hold sentences together seemed to be missing, and it was hard to understand what went with what. Here are some more phrases with possible translations:

"I want that make." (Possible meaning: I want to make that.)
    When looking at a picture of apples: "My mommy in house apple." (My mommy in the house got apples.)
    When asked if he liked to play ball: "My mommy my house uh play ball." (I play ball at my house with my mommy.)

As Sachs said, "It was clear that his language was lagging behind by almost two years, and that he was absorbing words but not necessarily picking them up in the order that they were used." The average length of his utterances was shorter than those of most kids his age, and his grammar was skewed. But it was clear, Sachs said, that his level of intelligence was otherwise normal. It was as if he was aching to communicate and just didn't know how.

I haven't been able to get Jim's story out of my head. It's not only that I'm riveted by the troubling vision of two kids with well-meaning parents who were nevertheless subjected to such language deprivation. And it's not just the shock of Jim's limited speech. What strikes me is how much insight he provides into the experiences that are required to learn language skills. Psychologists and linguists often explain how complicated it is to unpack the inner workings of language. They describe at length how learning a language involves multiple interrelated steps, such as recognizing units of words as they are spoken, figuring out how to vocalize, associating a word with objects or actions, understanding how words are strung together, and realizing how words relate to one another. But until you encounter a 3-year-old boy who can't talk the way most 3-year-olds do, it can be hard to envision what language learning really requires.

In Jim's case, the television was the only tool available to him, and it fell short. Though he learned words, he didn't seem to pick up on grammar. The TV didn't seem to teach him anything about the glue that holds sentences together, the way words relate to one another, and other essential but hard-to-pin-down elements of communication. Why not?

We don't know much about what Jim was watching on television, but we can safely assume that the words coming out of the box had nothing to do with what he was doing or saying, where he was looking, where his parents were looking, how he was sitting or what his little brother might have been teething on at the time. The speech wasn't contingent on anything happening in his life. And there is the rub. Developmental psychologists and cognitive scientists are starting to discover just how much a person requires real, person-to-person contact to learn language. This interaction is something that televisions, DVDs or even interactive computer programs cannot replicate.

~~~

One afternoon I visited with a mother who was using DVDs to help her 19-month-old son learn to talk. The family lives in a modest ranch house in a quiet subdivision outside Washington DC. Blocks and Legos were piled in the corner of a sparsely furnished living room, near a plastic toy kitchen and an "activity table" with colorful buttons to press and rattles to spin. One television was in the basement, where a basket of half-folded laundry was on the floor. On the coffee table sat that week's *Washington Post Book World*, some VHS tapes that the mother said she was reviewing for her work (she is a part-time high school teacher), and a couple of Baby Einstein DVDs.

"I only let him watch one a day," said the mother, who I'll call Holly.[3] "Thirty minutes."

Holly said that she and her friends with babies often talk about the push-and-pull they feel about turning on the television. The guilt is always there, she said. But so is the sense of exhaustion that sets in around 4 or 4:30 pm, when she has run out of activities, when her son seems bored with his blocks and toy kitchen, and when she is acutely aware that there is at least another hour and a half to go before dinnertime and Dad's arrival. I nodded, remembering draining days with my first baby when I couldn't help but watch the clock all afternoon. "That's when it's his DVD time," Holly said.

Holly told me that she started popping in the Baby Einstein DVDs when her son, Nick, was about 3 months old. His pediatrician had noted that he needed more "tummy time," lying on the floor on his belly. The purpose of tummy time was to strengthen his neck muscles so that he could hold his head up and be prepared to crawl. But Nick squirmed, fussed and cried during these attempts. She read on an email listserv that babies usually tolerate tummy time if they watch Baby Einstein videos at the same time. It was worth a try, she thought.

Now that Nick is walking, tummy time is no longer a concern. But language is. Nick has only uttered a few words so far, Holly said, and she has noticed that many of his playmates are farther along. A friend recommended that she try a DVD called *Baby Babble*.

"It's supposed to help them learn language," she said. The DVD—which on that day happened to be upstairs on a small TV in the kitchen—shows simple objects, like a ball against a white background. A voice-over says the word, "ball," with perfect articulation. The signs for the words are taught, too. The action moves at a snail's pace. After twenty minutes, the video shows parents how to do exercises with their mouths that their children might imitate. "Buh-buh-buh," said Holly, demonstrating. "I hadn't been doing anything like that before. Now I do it. And he watches it. He'll mimic the sounds."

Baby Babble was created by two speech pathologists named Mary Chouinard and Cory Poland. "It is marketed to typically normally developing children, but a lot of parents with children with speech difficulties have grabbed it up," Chouinard told me. The DVD isn't the only one that markets itself as a language tool. A video series called *Bee Smart Baby Vocabulary Builder* calls itself an interactive learning DVD. *Baby Wordsworth*, one of the Baby Einstein videos, says it is "a playful introduction to words and sign language."

Could these videos really make a difference? Or was Holly being led astray? To learn more about language development, I visited an infant lab at Temple University that is co-directed by Kathy Hirsh-Pasek, an expert in how babies learn to talk. Her lab uses video images in experiments with babies to detect how and when children start to associate words with their meanings. But she has no desire to create videos that speed up the process. In fact, she shakes her head with resignation whenever she hears about electronic media that claims it can accelerate language skills. She doesn't understand why parents seem to think that they need extra tools when their very presence—their capacity to talk and play with their kids—costs nothing and usually works just fine. As she wrote in her book *Einstein Never Used Flashcards*, which she co-authored with Roberta Golinkoff, "Parents are not charged with being their children's personal Berlitz tutors on a 24/7 basis. Children work out much of language on their own."[4]

Many child-development experts recommend that, if a child is not uttering many words by age 2, it is time to consult with a speech therapist. But before that age, the onset of speech can be quite variable. Some children have virtually no words at all at 16 months old, while others are speaking in short sentences by then. I asked Chouinard about this variability. Does a parent need to buy *Baby Babble* when her child will most likely learn to speak on his own? Won't a child simply pick up language from interacting with people in his environment? Chouinard replied,

> Yes, you're correct. Most of us learn just in our environment. But you would be surprised how many calls we get from parents—and these are not those with speech-delayed kids—asking, what can I do, what is some advice, what can I do to make sure my child talks? I think it's different than thirty years ago. Back then they didn't have My Gyms and play dates. But nowadays parents just eat it up. They want to know what they can do with their kids. We've just created information for parents, given them information about ways that they can help their child.

The idea that a video could offer ideas to parents made sense to me. I could see in the short time I spent with Holly, for example, that she was happy with the *Baby Babble* video, mainly because it had given her fresh ideas for using language with her son. It wasn't the DVD, but Holly's interaction, prompted by the DVD, that was going to make the difference, and that allowed her to feel that she was on the right track.

If used in that capacity, Hirsh-Pasek said, baby videos have merit. In fact, she agreed to be an adviser on a line of baby DVDs called *Eebee's Adventures* founded by Stephen Gass, whose background includes working as director of education for Sesame Place, the *Sesame Street* theme park, and serving as the editorial director for CBS's Interactive Learning Unit. Gass explained that he was calling on Hirsh-Pasek and other experts to make sure his videos reflected the latest science on language and child development, and Hirsh-Pasek said she was impressed with Gass's approach.

The *Eebee* videos look and feel different from the Baby Einstein model. They don't name objects like "ball" while displaying them against a white background. Instead, they feature eebee, a cute, pre-verbal puppet with purple nubs for hair and an orange face with a button nose. In ten-minute scenes, a woman interacts with eebee as a mother might interact with her baby. She watches as ee-bee tries to stack oversized soft blocks and speaks to the puppet in slow, simple, often repetitive sentences about what he is doing.

"You're making a tower? You're making a tower," the woman says. Eebee continues stacking, and the video is silent for a while. "It's getting taller," the woman exclaims. Eebee points upward, say-ing "Uh. Uh. Uh." She nods and answers, "Look how tall the tower is getting."

Gass explained that he hopes his videos encourage parents to communicate actively with their babies and toddlers. "A lot of ex-perts coach parents to just describe what's going on" to help their children learn language, Gass said. "We, as parents, tend to ask ba-bies questions, knowing full well they can't answer them, instead of just describing things as we're doing them." To get a child to talk, he suggested, caregivers would be well off doing a lot of the talking, too.

Only in the last few years have scientists launched detailed studies on how and whether a baby might pick up language skills from video. At Vanderbilt University, for example, psychologists Geor-gene Troseth and Megan Saylor are comparing the impact on a child of a robot-like, antisocial person versus an amiable, interactive person, as well as videotapes of both these types. They want to know whether a person's social demeanor and proximity to the child enhances the likelihood of learning new words. Preliminary data they showed me confirms the importance of genuine social interaction.

Meanwhile, cognitive scientists have been discovering the significance of face-to-face experience for another member of the animal kingdom: songbirds. Songbirds and human beings are among the few animals that cannot produce speech or song without a tutor, a member of their species demonstrating what a song or spoken word sounds like. Bird calls and human babble don't require this kind of learning, but specific songs and words do. This similarity, as well as others, has led neuroscientists to consider whether birds have something to teach us about learning to talk.[5]

White-crowned sparrows, for example, need to hear from other white-crowned sparrows if they want to sing well. If a baby sparrow hears a tape-recording of a song—but does not see a live sparrow singing in front of him—he can eventually learn something, but it pales in comparison to the songs he can learn from a live tutor.[6]

Zebra finches are even more dependent on social interaction. In one study, fledgling zebra finches were unable to learn from a finch in a nearby cage that they could hear but not see.[7] Was simply the sight of the bird what mattered? To find out, scientists fitted the finches with eye patches but allowed other finches in their cages. The babies thus had the chance to experience all the pecking and grooming that goes on between these avian socialites. The result? Even when blindfolded, the babies could learn from their peers. It wasn't that they needed to see other birds; rather, they needed to interact with them.[8]

Birdsong studies have stirred ideas about the limits of learning from disembodied sounds electronically delivered. Developmental psychologists who work with human babies are now homing in on the importance of socialization. For example, consider the concept of "joint attention," a theory that has been widely adopted by child-development experts. The idea is that if, say, a father is looking at an object, his baby will follow his gaze and pay attention to the way he is talking about it. Without joint attention, the theory goes, the infant would have little incentive to learn the name for that object or even understand that a word is associated with it.

As early as age 6 months, when babies are starting to understand what people say, social interaction makes a difference in how they learn words. One study showed that 6-month-old babies could recognize a new word if it was said following their name. ("Sally, look at the butterflies!") But they showed no signs of recognition when it followed someone else's name.[9]

If you're like me, you probably find something warm and reassuring about these theories and experiments. They make intuitive sense. They replicate the way most parents talk to and interact with their kids. They offer a reminder that, if raised in normal loving households, babies learn to speak without much intervention.

But let's consider another language-learning question that today's parents often ask: What about acquiring a second language? For years, research has pointed out the difference between rapidly absorbing a foreign language as a child versus the grueling experience of trying to learn one as an adult. Parents know that, if their children become bilingual, they will have a huge advantage as they grow up in a global economy.

In the first half-year of their life, babies are "citizens of the world," brimming with the potential to learn any language, says Patricia K. Kuhl, a speech and learning professor at the University of Washington.[10] Her research, which has received widespread attention, has excited many parents who want to find ways to help their babies learn multiple languages. In one of her studies, Kuhl found that infants are able to distinguish the phonemes from a multitude of different languages—phonemes that are imperceptible to adults who did not grow up hearing those languages. Most Japanese adults, for example, cannot distinguish between "la" and "ra" and are unable to hear the difference between "lake" and "rake." Similar weaknesses exist in English speakers when hearing words in other languages. But infants have no trouble with such sounds; they can make distinctions that adults can't.

Video producers have taken those isolated results and run with them, building a market for baby-bound foreign-language DVDs. Products include DVDs titled *Fun with Languages, Bilingual Baby, Mi Casa/My House, I Like Animals!/Me Gustan Animales! Brainy Baby Spanish* and *Brainy Baby French*. Some of these videos are similar to those designed to augment native language skills, with simple objects displayed and named, like electronic flashcards. Others, like Baby Einstein's *Language Nursery*, tell nursery rhymes and songs in Japanese, Russian, German and other languages while bright toys, patterns and wildlife scenes play out on the screen.

Not everyone who buys these DVDs loves them, however. Amazon.com customers have written some scathing reviews. They complain that the words don't connect to what is shown at that moment (a criticism of several Baby Einstein videos), the speakers don't sound native (a slam at *Mi Casa/My House*) or the words are uttered without the gender-based articles (simply using the word *ballon*, French for ball, instead of *le ballon* in *Brainy Baby French*). But even should those flaws be corrected, Kuhl's research offers another reason to hold off on rushing to Amazon.com to snap up these DVDs.

~~~

A few years ago, Kuhl and her colleagues were investigating whether American infants as old as 9 months might still detect the phonemes of Mandarin Chinese. Of course, she couldn't exactly ask the babies to tell her what they heard. They were too young to communicate reliably by pointing, let alone nodding or shaking their heads. And they wouldn't have understood what she was asking anyway. So she used a popular method for determining what babies hear—the head-turn procedure. Babies were brought into a sound booth, placed on their caregiver's lap, and conditioned to turn their heads to the right or left whenever they recognized that a new sound had emanated from the speakers. (You might remember this procedure from the experiments on background noise in chapter 4.)

The infants were first treated to twenty-five-minute sessions of Mandarin training. They sat on a blanket with a native Mandarin speaker who read them storybooks, played with puppets, a train, and a stack of rings, and tried to converse with them—all in Mandarin. Another group of infants had the same experience, but in English. After twelve sessions over the course of four weeks, the infants were brought to the lab to see how they performed on the head-turn procedure. The results showed that the training had worked; the babies with exposure to Mandarin could distinguish between two syllables typically indistinguishable to American adults. The babies in the English training sessions couldn't make out the differences.

Had the auditory exposure by itself led to the learning, or had the social nature of the training sessions mattered? Kuhl wanted to find out. She decided to test what would happen if the language training was presented passively via DVD. She and her research team took pains to ensure that the electronic recordings were as close to the real thing as possible. They used the same Mandarin speakers, with the screen showing them pointing to toys and making conversation. They displayed the DVDs on a large plasma screen so that the people on screen were nearly life sized, almost as if they were physically present in the room. "It was so clear, so beautiful," Kuhl said. "My graduate students thought, oh my gosh, maybe they'll actually learn better" via the video than the face-to-face interaction.

She rounded up thirty-two infants and assigned them to two groups who received four weeks of "training" while sitting on blankets and surrounded by toys in front of the plasma screen. One group was exposed to the sound of the DVD only. The other was exposed to the audio-visual version. The children were then tested using the head-turn procedure to detect how many phonemes they had learned.

The results were dismal. In both cases, the children did no better than their counterparts in the previous experiment who had experienced no Mandarin training at all.[11] "The effect was so dramatic and so complete," Kuhl said, calling the finding a "complete surprise." She had figured that the electronic sessions might not perform quite as well as in-person teaching, but she hadn't expected that they would produce no learning effect at all.

Today, Kuhl speaks at conferences around the world, warning people not to get caught up by claims that a young child can learn language from audio or videotape. "You can't guarantee that it shows any learning whatsoever," she explains. (Rochelle Newman at the University of Maryland said she has come up with negative results, too, in unpublished data from an experiment she conducted on twenty-four American 12-month-olds. She was testing whether they could recognize Mandarin words that they had been exposed to via video ten times in two weeks at home.)[12]

These research results pretty much dashed any hopes I had that children could learn a second language by attending to a television set—at least, at these young ages. But it can be hard to shake the idea. Social workers say that they often hear reports from Spanish-speaking families about their children learning to speak English by watching *Sesame Street*. People from other countries tell tales about learning to speak English after watching American TV. (A 2006 story in the *New York Times*, for example, described Chinese entrepreneurs who were translating shows like *Friends* into Mandarin and streaming them over the Internet. The founders said they learned how to translate by watching American sitcoms.)[13] But at what age were these foreign speakers exposed? Had they already achieved fluency in their native language? Were they watching with subtitles appearing in their native language—cues that can

make a big difference in what children understand once they learn
to read?

Or maybe the reasons for the discrepancy go deeper. As the
story of Jim teaches us, learning words is not the same as learning
language. There is mounting evidence that young children do learn
words from what they hear on video or audiotapes (as you'll see in
the next chapter), and a few studies focused on *Sesame Street*, where
Spanish words have been uttered for decades, have shown that cultural awareness can be heightened by exposure to foreign words.
Popular shows for preschoolers are now rife with foreign-language
words, like the use of Spanish in *Dora the Explorer*, multiple foreign languages in *Little Einsteins*, or Mandarin Chinese in *Kai
Lan*, an animated program scheduled to launch in 2007.

What is lacking is evidence that electronic media alone can
teach someone language, how to string verbs and nouns and prepo-
sitions together in a meaningful way, how to communicate ideas
through speech. In 2000, two researchers at the University of Connecticut decided to compare data on speech and language tests
from sixty children ages 3 to 4, factoring in how much television—
including educational television—they had watched. They found
no correlation to any skill related to language development, save
one: the children who watched the most television performed
worse in tests of grammar than the other children in the sample.[14]
Grammar, it seems, is something that children need to hear and
practice in real-time situations, where what you say is contingent
on what someone else says and vice versa. That interaction is what
was missing for Jim, the 3-year-old at the Connecticut speech
clinic. Passive listening just didn't cut it.

A few years after Jacqueline Sachs met Jim, she moved to Spain
for a brief time. She knew no Spanish, but when she arrived, she
half-hoped that she might pick something up by watching local
television. "First I tried to watch a telenovella," she said, thinking
that the narrative and the characters might help her crack the code.

But she couldn't grasp what anyone was saying. Then she tuned in to cooking shows. "I figured at least they would be moving things around and stirring and giving a context to the language," she said, "but it was just impossible." The experience was a reminder to her of what it must have been like for Jim.

Jim is almost 40 now, assuming that he is still around. After he reached the fifth grade, Sachs lost touch with him and his family. But she suspects that he is probably doing fine. She remembers how much he learned even in the first four weeks at the clinic, when the clinician wasn't making any effort to teach him language but was simply sitting with him, communicating face-to-face. "Even in those four weeks, just by interacting with her, by showing and talking about pictures, he started to make really fast progress," Sachs said. A few years later, when his first grade teacher was asked to report on how Jim was doing, Sachs recalled that the teacher said, "He's a well-adjusted, popular child. My only complaint is that he chatters too much with other children."

NOTES

1. Sachs et al., 1981, pp. 33–54.
2. Pinker, 1994, pp. 271–272.
3. Names have been changed to protect the family's privacy.
4. Hirsh-Pasek and Golinkoff, 2003, p. 83.
5. Doupe and Kuhl, 1999, p. 577.
6. Ibid., p. 618.
7. Gopnik, Meltzoff, and Kuhl, 1999, pp. 190–194.
8. Douple and Kuhl, 1999, p. 592.
9. Hirsh-Pasek and Golinkoff, 2003, p. 72.
10. Gopnik, Meltzoff, and Kuhl, 1999, pp. 103–106.
11. Kuhl, Tsao, and Liu, 2003, p. 9100.
12. Newman, phone conversation about unpublished data, August 29, 2006.
13. Howard French, "Chinese Tech Buffs Slake Thirst for U.S. TV Shows," *New York Times,* August 9, 2006.
14. Naigles and Mayeux, 2001, p. 139.

Chapter Eight

Can Electronic Media
Enrich My Child's Vocabulary?

Anyone who has lived with toddlers knows the exasperation at times of trying to figure out what they are saying. No matter how well we think we know their speech, no matter how many times we ask them to say it again, we remain baffled. In our family, one of those words was "penk weeno."

Don't know what penk weeno means? Neither did I on that weekday evening as I coaxed Janelle, age 28 months, to make her way up to bed. "Penk weeno, mommy. Get the penk weeno." She was becoming insistent. I was utterly lost. Then another puzzling sentence followed. "Get a skew line, mommy."

Skew line?

My daughter, I finally realized, was telling me to "Get a rescue line"—a command shouted by Dora the explorer, that spunky heroine in the popular preschool show. Earlier that evening, she had been watching a *Dora* video that had become something of an addiction. For nearly a week she had asked for the same video, in which Dora and her cousin Diego rescue baby animals from mountaintops and waterfalls. I remembered that one of the animals was a penguin, who was introduced on the show in Spanish as pinguino, or, as my daughter would say, penk weeno.

Before that day, I had been experiencing waves of embarrassment about the fact that my toddler was fixated on that particular *Dora*

DVD. She would sometimes resort to incessant whining, begging me or my husband to put in the video—behavior that never failed to coincide with surprise visits from other parents who I later envisioned whispering about us in disapproval. But now I was beaming. Pinguino! My daughter had learned a new word, one that was even new to me.

At the time, this feat seemed to contradict what I and countless other parents had been told about TV. "Limit!" we were told. "Turn it off if you can! Don't let your children be exposed to too much. There are better things they could be doing with their time!" The American Academy of Pediatrics had loosened its ban on screen media after children reach age 2, but pediatricians still hammered on the point of quantity, on the sheer amount that should be consumed (no more than 1 to 2 hours a day) instead of what types of shows a child might be watching.

Yet I had a real-life example of my daughter learning a word from television that I probably never would have taught her. (Make that several words: "rescue line" isn't a typical utterance in our house either.) Couldn't some forms of electronic media actually work better than parents in some cases? I had alreadyy come to understand that videos are not good for teaching the nuances of speech and grammar, for literally learning how to talk. But couldn't a child's vocabulary—her inner dictionary of known words—be enhanced by what was uttered and labeled on screen? After all, videos can do things that even books can't. Videos can make an object move, drawing attention to that object and its action ("the car is speeding!"). Videos can zoom in and out, showing hard-to-see things, like pores on skin or the way a river carves out the earth. And videos come with songs and sound effects, which have been shown to help children recall content.[1] Surely these attributes give videos an edge when it comes to teaching words. I decided to dig into what was known about *Dora the Explorer* to find out.

First, though, I needed to answer a few basic questions: Are vocabulary words really so important in the first place? Does a child's vocabulary growth tell us anything other than the fact that the kid has a lot of big words in his head? Is it honestly helpful for children at age 2 and 3 to learn words that seem so far removed from their real life?

Yes, yes, and yes. Education experts say that a child's level of vocabulary before entering school is a strong predictor of her academic performance years down the road. Learning to read can be hard enough. Learning to read while coming across words that you've never heard before—that's even tougher. The same can be said about handling experiences even more basic than reading. Without a large reservoir of words to draw upon, it's difficult to communicate needs, understand what a teacher is saying, and negotiate the politics of the playground.

The sad truth is that children with the most impoverished vocabularies typically come from the most impoverished families. Research has shown that low-income households are more likely to have children with smaller vocabularies, putting those children at a significant disadvantage before they step foot in school.[2] Consequently, Head Start and other kindergarten-readiness programs make vocabulary enrichment a big part of their mission. But they can only do so much. First, these programs typically start at age 4. By then, children have already experienced two years of rapid language development. Somewhere around their second birthdays, children experience a dramatic vocabulary spurt. They can go from learning barely a word a week to ten new words a day. Steven Pinker, an evolutionary psychologist, put it this way: "If we divide language into somewhat arbitrary stages, like Syllable Babbling, Gibberish Babbling, One-Word Utterances and Two-Word Strings, the next stage would have to be called All Hell Breaks Loose."[3]

That all-hell-breaks-loose moment is thrilling. It screams with potential, with the possibility that a child now has the power to absorb an infinite array of new words and use them to communicate.

And it happens long before a child is enrolled in preschool. That is why what happens within a toddler's home or daycare center—what is taught by parents, siblings, babysitters and, yes, the television—can have a huge impact on the words she learns.

In 1983, two developmental psychologists named Betty Hart and Todd R. Risley took on a monumental project that would shed new light on the home lives of very young children. For years, while working together at the University of Kansas, they had been running intervention programs at daycare centers, trying to make a lasting impact on children's ability to learn. Time after time they were disappointed. They could raise vocabulary levels in preschool, but the increases were always temporary. The trajectory of growth would stall out, and the children's school performance would eventually show up as well below average. They realized that they needed to observe what was happening when the kids were very small; they needed to get into their homes to figure out what was holding the children back. Not only that, but they needed to get into their homes month after month, watching and recording everything said by every person present so they could tally not only what words the children learned but what level of language they heard around them.

They set out to recruit 120 families, planning to observe and tape-record every word uttered by each family member for one hour every month for at least a year. It was a daunting project, the transcription of audiotapes alone taking hundreds of hours. "You're crazy," said one of their colleagues.[4] Hart and Risley admitted later that, yes, they were crazy. But they did it anyway—scaling back only in the number of households they observed. Eventually they had more than two years' worth of observations on forty-two families across a spectrum of economic circumstances in and around Kansas City. With help from graduate students and assistants, they worked every weekday of the year, always willing to reschedule home visits so that they could fit the needs of the forty-two families. If they missed just one week of observations, their tallies of words uttered each month would be forever out of whack—a statistical horror that could derail their project. For three years, Hart said, she and Risley didn't take any time off. "Three years with no vacation—that's a long time," Hart told me. "A long time."

By the end of the observation period, they had produced more than 1,300 transcripts—one for each hour of observation, each twenty pages long. It took another six years to assemble dictionaries of words spoken by the children, their siblings and their parents, crunch all the data, and learn something from it.

The result of their work was eye-opening. They discovered that the amount of talking at home makes a significant difference in children's vocabulary growth and later IQ scores. Middle- and upper-income families simply talked more than lower-income families. What did they talk about that the lower-income families usually didn't? Feelings, plans, present activities, past events—things that did not necessarily have to do with everyday routines (like the usual "Do you want some milk?" or "No jumping on the bed!") but that employed a richer variety of words ("We need to stop at the intersection to let the 18-wheeler go by"). When they published their results, in the book *Meaningful Differences in the Everyday Experience of Young American Children*, educators and child-development experts raved about the research, and politicians pledged to focus efforts on educating new parents about the importance of talking with their babies. In 2001, the White House convened a summit on early childhood that highlighted Hart and Risley's work.

The impact of television was not measured objectively in their project, and the point of Hart and Risley's book is that dialogue with parents is a child's best teacher. But they couldn't help but note that, in many families, the TV was always on. Sometimes, Hart told me, *Sesame Street* would be on during the visits, and researchers would record how children related to it. "We would see kids imitate the words," she said. If *Sesame Street* focused on words that started with, say, the letter O, children would repeat them. A month later, the same words would crop up again. It was impossible to know whether the children learned the words because of *Sesame Street*, or whether the parents had chatted about the subjects at the dinner table, but when a word like "ostrich" showed up later in transcripts, they had a hunch that *Sesame Street* was responsible. "Ostrich is not the kind of thing you talk about every day," Hart said.

Talking to Hart made me imagine a scenario in which a 2-year-old girl is home with a low-income mother who is depressed, exhausted, or distracted by babysitting multiple kids, trying to make ends meet. Whatever the reason, Mom doesn't engage in much conversation, and the little girl is not exposed to new vocabulary. Now imagine the impact of a video or television program like *Sesame Street*. That one hour could open a new world of words to her. The potential impact was exciting to contemplate. Could it put that little girl on a similar footing, vocabulary-wise, with the middle-class kids in her upcoming kindergarten class? Could it give her enough of an advantage to overcome her circumstances and eventually excel in school?

That hope is exactly what is driving the mission of many educational shows and software programs. But the producers of these programs cannot simply throw a bunch of new words into a script and expect them to have an impact. Adults may think that children will simply pick up new words by hearing them on TV, regardless of how or when they are said. But for young children, it's not that easy. As I came to discover, how well a show succeeds at making words "stick" depends almost entirely on how and when the words are said, how much repetition is employed, and whether the words are spoken in a context that a very young child can comprehend.

⁓

Which brings us to *Dora the Explorer*, a show created by a team of producers at Nickelodeon. Daniel Anderson of the University of

Massachusetts was one of the show's consultants. He had spent decades doing research on how children perceive television at very young ages, and he argued that a strong chronological narrative—an uncomplicated story with a direct path from beginning to end—would be most effective. It might, he thought, even be able to teach vocabulary. "I thought that by really developing a more continuous story line, we could do better," Anderson said. "And I thought that the idea of a journey was the way to do it."

Chris Gifford, *Dora's* executive producer who was involved in its production from the beginning, remembers Anderson drumming that advice into his head—as well as tips about making shifts in time and space very easy to follow. But Gifford's primary goal, he said, was "a good story told well." An actor by training who once eked out a living doing one-man puppet shows (and who also played Danny in *The Great Space Coaster* back in the 1980s), Gifford was intent on capturing and holding preschoolers' attention. Using everything he knew about how preschoolers become engaged in a story, he and the writers and illustrators at Nickelodeon came up with the vision of Dora, a radiant, animated Latina with huge brown eyes and chunky brunette bangs who faces challenges and embarks on one adventure after another, climbing over sand castles, taking submarine rides, swinging through jungles, and scaling mountains. To make the stories as comprehensible as possible, he made sure that the beginning of each episode featured "The Map," a scroll that uses simple icons of mountains and rivers to show exactly where Dora will end up. He tested each episode with audiences of nearly 100 children over several months, making a dozen or more rewrites.

In 2000, *Dora* hit the airwaves and became a big hit. In 2006 it was one of the top-rated preschool shows in the country. The image of Dora is so popular that it has been licensed to appear on everything from girls' bedroom slippers to a Good Humor ice cream pop. Evidently those "good stories told well" are having an impact. But just because a show is popular does not mean it is making a dent in what children learn. Nickelodeon says that studies conducted within the company show that viewers from ages 2 to 5 have made many academic gains, but I wanted evidence from outside sources, people without a vested interest in seeing the program succeed.

Enter Deborah L. Linebarger, a child-development scientist and professor of communications at the University of Pennsylvania, whose studies have discovered some positive links between programs with strong story lines and language development in children between 1 and 3 years old. A few years ago, Linebarger came across a mother of a 15-month-old boy who was chagrined to admit that her son's first word was "backpack"—a word shouted by Dora and her friends as a signal to open Dora's backpack and find tools to help them climb a cliff or cross a chasm. Linebarger found the comment intriguing. Could this mean that children younger than 2 years old might be capable of learning from television in a meaningful way? If a show was designed with what she called "specific language-promoting characteristics," could it help toddlers learn language?

She and Dale Walker, a child psychologist at the University of Kansas, resolved to study infants and toddlers over a period of two years to glean what they might be learning from TV. Fifty-one children were recruited from child care centers in and near Kansas City, Kansas, most of whose parents were college educated with incomes in the middle to upper levels. Every three months, the researchers asked the parents to record how much time their children spent watching television and videos in the past week, as well as the names of the programs watched. Parents also recorded new words that their children uttered, while experts observed the kids to assess how their language skills were developing from age 6 months to 30 months.[5]

Linebarger said that, when she and Walker first analyzed the data, they compared children's skills based on their exposure to two different categories of programming—educational or entertainment oriented. But crunched in that way, the data provided no hints of what might be having the most impact; the educational content was not proving significantly better than the purely entertaining stuff. So they broke it down even further, looking at specific programs and grouping those with very similar formats. *Blue's Clues* and *Dora the Explorer*, for example, were lumped together as shows with simple narratives that try to elicit responses from viewers.

After putting those groups together and including data from children who had watched the programs multiple times, they discovered some interesting—and surprising—correlations. Children who watched *Blue's Clues* and *Dora the Explorer* were able to identify significantly more vocabulary words at 30 months than their counterparts who didn't watch those particular programs. Two shows with storybook formats—*Arthur* and *Clifford*—were also linked to more vocabulary growth in children who watched versus those who didn't.

Expressive language—the ability to produce and utter words, not just understand them—was also studied. Those four programs again came up as being associated with positive growth. The results attested to what Linebarger had observed in past studies: as long as children view the programs repeatedly, it seems they can learn from them.

But here was the unexpected part: some children's programs did not do as well—even with repeated viewings. They appeared to have a negative correlation with language growth. For example, children who watched *Teletubbies* were found to have learned fewer new words than children who didn't watch those programs. *Barney* was associated with gains in expressive language but was linked to negative outcomes in identifying new words. Most surprisingly, *Sesame Street*—the gold standard of educational television—was associated with less growth in expressive language. Children who had watched *Sesame Street* uttered fewer words at 30 months than those who didn't watch the show.

The data were troubling. Numerous studies have shown that *Sesame Street* is beneficial to children age 2 and up. But here was evidence showing a negative link between frequent viewings of the program and a 1- or 2-year-old's ability to learn words. Could *Sesame Street* be doing harm? Linebarger issues many cautions before jumping to that conclusion. First, the study's sample was small and not representative of society. Second, no causal relationships can be determined from the way the research was done. In other words, there is no way to know whether viewing *Sesame Street* and the other shows caused the lessening of expressive language development. All that is known is that there is a relationship between the two. One possibility, for example, is that the parents of children with delayed language skills were actively promoting *Sesame Street*.

There is another compelling factor to consider as well. Remember the story of *Sesame Street*'s recent redesign, in which the producers decided to stop chopping up the story lines and interrupting them with songs and skits? Rosemarie Truglio, a vice president at Sesame Workshop, was one of those pushing for that format change so that the show could take advantage of the power of a narrative in holding children's attention. "Kids are interested in a story," she said. "They want to know how the story is resolved. They want to start looking for the ending." The redesign of *Sesame Street* debuted in February 2002. The data Linebarger was using came from the years 1999 to 2001; it was based entirely on the old *Sesame Street*.

Linebarger suspected that stronger, simpler narratives—and the potential disruption in shows without such structure—could influence how much vocabulary children learn. She decided to look at the data in a different way. Her new approach included a comparison of videotapes with on-air shows. Videotapes, including those that feature *Sesame Street* characters and *Barney*, are usually more thematic, with less jumping in and out of stories or lessons. She hypothesized that these videos would, indeed, help toddlers learn, because they more likely adhered to a story-telling strategy.

Bingo. The children who had watched *Sesame Street* videos used more expressive language than those who didn't. *Barney* also won a reprieve. These were programs that toddlers seemed to want to watch over and over, and Linebarger thinks the easy, linear story lines were probably the reason. "They stay so glued to it because they don't lose the narrative," Linebarger said. And when they can follow the narrative, they are more likely to learn new words. The study confirmed what I had felt instinctively as I watched my daughter watch *Dora*; an on-screen story could, indeed, help her learn new words. It just needed to be designed well enough so that she could follow it.

How do researchers test a preschooler's vocabulary? In some cases, they sit down with the child, pull out a card showing four images, like pictures of vehicles or farm animals, and start asking questions. "Can you point to the goat?" they'll ask, or, "Which one is the jet plane?" (This method is the one used by the oft-cited Peabody Picture Vocabulary Test.) In other cases, parents are asked to report their children's vocabulary level by reading through a list of words and checking off the ones their kids know or can say. Still other tests rely on experts who observe children in a short play period and note the words they express.

These same kinds of tests are used in academic research on the impact of video programs. But simply to test a group of children who watch a video is not enough; researchers must also isolate any external factors that might cause children to pick up those words. One way to do so is to take a group of children and assign them, at random, to two groups. One group watches a particular show repeatedly over a period of time; the other is not exposed to the show at all. Before the children are sent off to watch, researchers test their vocabulary levels. When the study ends, they test them again and compare the results.

Dorothy and Jerome Singer of Yale University did this study using *Barney*. They found that 3- to 4½-year-old children learned
words that appeared on *Barney*, even without intervention from
teachers, whereas children going through their regular daycare routine did not.[6] In another study using *Dora*, Linebarger found that
English-speaking children at age 3 and 4 were able to learn Spanish words from the show.[7] Anecdotes pop up elsewhere as well.
Nancy Kanter, a senior vice president at the Disney channel who
was behind the launch of *Little Einsteins*, told me about an amusing email she received from one parent whose toddler son had just
watched the *Little Einsteins*'s episode that introduced the word
"allegro" along with fast-paced music. Soon afterward, while both
were in the car stuck in traffic, the little boy called out from his car
seat, "allegro! allegro!"

One of the largest studies to assess vocabulary growth and educational programming was published in 2001 and was called the Early
Window Project. The husband-and-wife team of John Wright and
Aletha Huston and their colleagues at the University of Texas
tracked more than 230 children over three years. Using in-home interviews and phone surveys, they collected monthly data on which
shows the children watched and how long they watched them.
Each year, they used tests like the Peabody assessment to determine
how many new words the children had learned. They also tested the
kids on pre-math, pre-reading skills and other indicators that show
a readiness for kindergarten. They found that the children who
watched educational shows like *Mister Rogers* or *Sesame Street* performed significantly better than kids who watched children's cartoons or adult shows, like sitcoms.[8]

I know what you're thinking: These children were probably going to be more advanced at language anyway. They probably came
from the most-educated households, where parents read to them
regularly, right? Not necessarily. I called Huston to talk to her
about the study. (Sadly, John Wright died in a car accident the

same year the study was released.) She acknowledged that people often assume that any positive influence of television can be explained away by a child's home life. So she and Wright had taken into account as many of those variables as they could. First, they chose to study only families with relatively low incomes, including only households in the Kansas City area with annual incomes of less than $25,000 in 1990, when the study started. They also took into account ethnicity and parents' education level. Their analysis showed that those socioeconomic factors were not driving the children's achievement.

There is another reason the Early Window Project is so compelling; it included 2-year-olds. Besides Linebarger's work, very few people have investigated whether words can be learned from video in children younger than 3. But Wright and Huston's study not only started with 2-year-olds, it showed that the biggest gains from educational television happened in the year between age 2 and 3. "We found that, with the really young kids, if they were exposed to *Sesame Street* early on, they were doing better than those who weren't," Huston said. "This is a period of very rapid language growth. The first three years are when they get the basics of language in place." Moreover, she said, the children at the income levels she was studying "really are in need." They are not yet enrolled in preschool programs, so they are either at home or in daycare programs, which for this demographic are of typically low quality.

What was it about these educational shows that worked? Many years ago, a speech pathologist at the University of Kansas named Mabel Rice put the shows under a microscope, so to speak. She already knew that very young children learn best from adults who speak slowly, with lots of repetition and enunciation. Some call this "child-directed language." She decided to compare six shows: *Mister Rogers*, *The Electric Company*, *Fat Albert*, *Road Runner*, *Bugs Bunny* and the adult sitcom *Gilligan's Island*. She counted the frequency of utterances that could be classified as child directed in a sample from

an episode and took note of whether characters on screen pointed
to objects as they talked about them or made other references that
would make the word's meaning clear. She found, not surprisingly,
that *Gilligan's Island* used sophisticated language, spoken quickly.
Often the words used had no reference to objects on the screen. The
cartoon shows used few words in the first place. But with programs
designed to be educational—specifically *Mister Rogers*, *The Electric
Company* and, to a lesser extent, *Fat Albert*—the language included
many features that would make the utterances understandable to a
young child. *Mister Rogers*, in particular, was full of moments when
objects and actions were explicitly labeled. It was, in the words of
Rice, "well-suited to children's competencies."[9]

❧

So, if even 2-year-olds show evidence of learning words from TV,
how much younger can we go? What is the youngest age at which
a child can start picking up words from the screen?

Anecdotes from research provide hints: a 10½-month-old baby
was seen pointing to Big Bird when asked where Big Bird was, a
13½-month-old pointed to *Black Beauty*, repeating "baba, baba"
(obviously hearing the letter b in the horse's name), a 15-month-
old said "backpack" after watching *Dora*.[10] I talked to the mother
of a 12-month-old who noticed that her daughter started saying
"hoo hoo" after repeatedly watching a baby video that included the
sounds of an owl. Parents with infants and toddlers at home all
have their own stories.

Experts in speech development look at anecdotes like this with a
critical eye. Okay, so a baby points to Big Bird on screen or says
"baba" when seeing *Black Beauty*. That simply tells us that the baby
can mimic the "b" sound in "Black Beauty" or that he knows that
the words "Big Bird" go with the yellow fluffy guy. So a 15-month-
old says "backpack." Does that mean he knows what a backpack is?
Is he referring only to Dora's blue, two-dimensional cartoon back-

pack or to all bags that you wear strapped to your back? A 1-year-old might be able to mimic the sounds she has heard, but does she know that these are the sounds an owl makes?

The point of their questions is that learning vocabulary words involves more steps than people realize. A child needs to be able to hear distinctions in sounds and realize that they are individual units that mean something (i.e., words), recognizing that the words go with specific objects, actions or properties. They need to know what word goes with which object, which they can demonstrate either by gazing, pointing or saying so. Then they need to recognize that a word like "apple" refers not only to that specific apple in front of them, but to apples of all kinds. And at an even higher level, to really understand what the word means, they need to be able to categorize it—to understand that the apple is a fruit. Getting all of this straight is a challenge for young minds. Before my daughters turned 2, they called all men "Daddy" if they had a 5 o'clock shadow and were over five feet tall.

In 2003, Rochelle Newman at the University of Maryland tested whether 12-month-old children could learn words from videotapes. She identified seventy-eight infants and randomly assembled them into three groups. She asked the parents of the first group to play a videotape for their babies ten times over two weeks. Another group was asked to watch the tape five times in one week, and the final group was not exposed to the tape at all. The goal was not to see if the children would attend to the screen (which showed colorful shots clipped from some baby videos) but rather to see if they would retain the audio—the words that were said in a voice-over reading of a fairy tale. To make sure that the words were not words infants would already know, the readers of the fairy tales substituted difficult words for easy ones. For example, the "ugly" duckling was "hideous" instead.

When Newman tested the infants in her lab at the end of the viewing period, she used the head-turn procedure. As the children were sitting on their mothers' laps in the sound booth, she played audiotapes of different words. Some of the words were directly from the fairy tales, like "hideous." Some were foils. She wanted to see if the babies turned their heads more often to hear the fairy tale words instead of the foils. If so, then they were, indeed, retaining the sounds of those words and were able to differentiate them from other words.

The results showed exactly that. It was the first study, Newman said, to show that long-term learning can happen with video. "At 12 months," Newman wrote, "infants are capable of acquiring some aspects of their native language from speech overheard in their environment."[11] However, she cautions that this evidence merely shows that 1-year-olds can distinguish between a word they heard on video versus one they didn't. It is not, by any means, full-fledged vocabulary acquisition.

To show that children can actually attach meaning to words, researchers use a different type of procedure called a "split screen paradigm." A baby sits in a room on Mom's lap and faces a large screen. First the baby is "taught" a new word. To do this, the screen shows an object or action that a narrator labels with a never-before-heard word. A common one is "blicking," which often accompanies some silly action, like a person performing one-armed jumping jacks. The narrator labels the action over and over. "She's blicking! See her blicking!" The screen then splits, and two video clips appear side by side. One clip is a repeat of the "blicking"; the other is entirely different. The narrator now asks a question: "Which one is blicking?"[12]

Babies aren't expected to point to an answer (though, depending on their age, many do), but they usually shift their gaze, looking at one clip or the other. Researchers make video recordings of the baby's eye movements and, reviewing them later, take careful notes about which direction the child looked. If a baby consistently looks at the "blicking" clip, researchers accept this as evidence that he or she is not only assigning that word to that image, she is able to pick out that action when faced with a competing image.

What is the youngest age at which children show evidence of achieving this task successfully? Phyllis Koenig, a cognitive scientist at the University of Pennsylvania Medical Center, has seen some hints in children as young as 15 months old. In her dissertation research on how children learn language, she found that, at this age, children who repeatedly heard a noun assigned to an object during video training looked significantly more often at that on-screen object when tested.[13] "They were engaged, and they made consistent answers," Koenig told me, adding that the video was very simple, with no background distractions or piped-in music. Letitia Naigles at the University of Connecticut has shown that verbs—considered harder to learn than nouns—can be taught at 21 months after four minutes of video training that is similarly unadorned.[14]

Laboratory experiments like these are designed to get at basic questions about how and when children acquire language. They are not designed to compare videos to other methods of teaching children. And, of course, they test video clips in an atmosphere that is nothing like home, where children are probably watching videos with much more flash amid all sorts of other distractions. So, let's look at a study that assessed whether toddlers can learn words from a video that children younger than 2 really watch.

The video is *Teletubbies*, one of the first shows to draw the ire of critics who don't want infants and toddlers watching TV. In 2003, two researchers in Connecticut decided to test the best method for teaching toddlers new words. They located forty-eight children, ages 15 to 24 months, and divided them into groups to test a variety of conditions.

In the first condition, the child interacted with an adult who pointed to and labeled objects—a re-creation of the favored "joint attention" method in which baby and adult are attending to the same thing. The adult would pull out an object that a toddler typically does not yet have a name for, like a plant sprayer, and label it with a nonsense word, like "keeg" or "sas." In the second condition, the child would try to watch the adult but would also be distracted by someone else nearby, shaking a toy. The third condition showed a video version of the same "joint attention" adult who was labeling objects. They called this the "adult on TV" experiment. The fourth showed a short clip from *Teletubbies*.

The *Teletubbies* clip was very similar to the program as it looks on PBS. It showed the roly-poly creatures with screens in their tummies, scurrying over psychedelic green hills. But it needed to be doctored. The researchers—Marina Krcmar, now at Wake Forest University, and Bernard Grela at the University of Connecticut— knew that, if they were going to test a toddler's ability to learn a new word, the word had to truly be new, not one they might have heard before, on the show or anywhere else. So they dubbed over a section that included an adult voice-over and changed the language so that the voice-over now said, "Oh, here is a keeg," whenever a periscope appeared on the screen. (For reasons opaque to most adults who watch the show, this periscope is a perennial part of the *Teletubbies* landscape.)

After experiencing one of the four word-learning conditions, the children were tested to see if they had learned the new words. Experimenters set five objects on a table in front of the toddlers and asked them to pick up the "sas" or the "keeg" or whatever object had been previously labeled. For the *Teletubbies* condition, the periscope was fashioned out of papier-mâché and PVC pipe to look identical to the one on screen.

After the data were tabulated, Krcmar and Grela started to see some interesting patterns. The "joint attention" condition was, not surprisingly, the most helpful. More than two-thirds of the time, the children could match the object correctly with its name after they had been taught by an adult sitting in front of them. In contrast, poor results appeared with the condition in which the child was distracted and the one that featured *Teletubbies*. The children in those groups were only able to make correct matches about 40 percent of the time. (Hold tight for the results for the "adult on television" condition.)

The researchers decided to go deeper. Did the children's age play a role? After all, there is a big difference between what a 15-month-old and a 24-month-old understands. And what about a child's vocabulary level going into the study? Some kids are more verbal, showing an understanding of words earlier than their peers. Some of the children in their study, in fact, may have already hit the "all-hell-breaks-loose" vocabulary spurt, whereas others may not have arrived there yet.

Krcmar and Grela had collected a vocabulary checklist from the toddlers' parents, so they were able to sort the children by age and vocabulary level. When they looked at the data through these lenses, they found that the younger children fared as they had expected: they could learn from a joint-attention session with a grownup, but they couldn't gain anything after watching *Teletubbies*. The same could be said for the children with the smaller vocabularies.[15] Krcmar has a theory as to why. "In the program, there is so much going on," she told me. "So many colors, so much to capture their attention, and that may end up backfiring. It's too much." A parent talking to a child, on the other hand, speaks more slowly, holds up objects, and uses "motherese," she said. But something interesting happened with the older children and the ones with more advanced vocabularies. They showed evidence of actually learning from *Teletubbies*. After 22 months, they seemed to be able to get it—in spite of all the color and movement. They correctly matched the periscope with its nonsense label.

Now let's turn to the results from the "adult on television" condition, in which the children were exposed to an adult pointing out objects and labeling them as if he was sitting right there. My hunch was that this situation could be a good one for learning. I had learned from other studies that a child seeing an adult on the screen, facing them like a social partner, talking to them in slow, simple sentences and labeling objects while showing them on screen can be powerful. And that turned out to be the case here, too. The data showed that children could learn from the video when it was designed in that fashion. Even the younger, smaller-vocabulary children showed some signs of learning in those cases.

Given all the research I had read about vocabulary growth and screen media, Krcmar and Grela's study was an eye-opener for me. It spotlighted two critical factors in using media to expose children to new vocabulary words. First, the media design must emulate the way language is used. The closer the product comes to simulating the way a good nursery school teacher or attentive parent talks to a young child, the better. Linear, straightforward story lines will help. Language should be simple. New words should be repeated often and used explicitly as teaching moments, with their meaning described or displayed on screen.

But more importantly, think about the needs of your child. Not every 2-year-old is at the same stage. Not all children learn in the same way. Is your toddler not yet showing signs of the vocabulary spurt? Or has she already started picking up words faster than you can note them? If language skills are slow in coming, take the time to provide lots of one-on-one conversation, giving her the foundation she needs. If she is already picking up words at full steam, the right show could introduce her to even more.

NOTES

1. Calvert, 2006, pp. 10–13.

2. Some of the most compelling research on this topic is by Betty Hart and Todd R. Risley, authors of the book *Meaningful Differences in the Everyday Experience of Young American Children* (Baltimore: Paul H. Brookes Publishing Company, 1995). See pp. 9–11 for the results from a 1968 study,

which compared the vocabularies of professors' children with children from a very poor area of Kansas City.

3. Pinker, 1994, p. 269.

4. Hart and Risley, 1995, p. 23.

5. Linebarger and Walker, 2005, pp. 624–645.

6. Singer and Singer, 1998, p. 336.

7. Fisch, 2004, p. 44.

8. Wright et al., 2001, pp. 1356–1357.

9. Rice, 1984, p. 461.

10. Linebarger and Walker, 2005, p. 626.

11. Rochelle S. Newman, "Learning the Sound Patterns of Novel Words from Passive Exposure," article written for an academic journal but not submitted, 2006, pp. 7–12.

12. Kathy Hirsh-Pasek's lab at Temple University is one of several laboratories that use the "split screen paradigm," which I saw in action during a visit there in the summer of 2006. In fact, Hirsh-Pasek and Roberta Michnick Golinkoff, a psychologist at the University of Delaware, are credited with having developed this technique for investigating what babies are learning about language.

13. Koenig, 1996, pp. 63–64.

14. Telephone interview with Letitia Naigles on July 25, 2006.

15. Grela, Krcmar, and Lin, 2004.

Chapter Nine

Could This Program Teach My Child to Be a Good Person?

Tune in to *The Wonder Pets*, a popular show on Nick Jr., and after watching an amusing story about a guinea pig, duck and turtle rescuing an animal in trouble, you will hear everyone say "Thanks!" four or five times within the space of a few minutes. The characters on dozens of other children's shows are just as polite, if not more so. Cartoon characters, puppets, talking animals, children and grown-ups engage each other with smiles and bright greetings. "Please" and "thank you" are uttered repeatedly. Aside from Oscar the Grouch, it's tough to find a rude, ungrateful character on preschool TV, and even he grudgingly minds his Ps and Qs by the end of most episodes.

Preschool programs aren't the only electronic media to ooze with social graces. Fun on the Farm, a *Barney* software product, chirps with politeness. "Welcome, welcome!" Barney says repeatedly. "Click on a frog and put it on the lily pad, please," says another character. "Goodbye, thanks for helping!" Barney exclaims when a child elects to exit.

I was thinking about all of this on-screen etiquette and wondering just how much of it was really sinking in, when I came across an interesting remark in a book by Betty Hart and Todd Risley, language researchers who recorded hundreds of thousands of utterances between dozens of parents and their toddlers over a two-year period. "Most of the children we observed," they noted, "said 'Thank you' more often than their parents."[1]

The comment made me smile. We parents aren't always the ideal role models we think we are. But it also made me wonder if interactions with parents and teachers are the only route through which a child learns to be "good"? Could what is shown on screen have any significant impact on the way children behave around their peers and elders? Indeed, what I really wanted to know was what psychologists, educators and parents have been pondering for ages: How exactly do children learn—or fail to learn—how to be not only polite but also kind-hearted, generous, patient and fair? The answers could fill a book, and already do, many times over. Volumes for parents and teachers are full of theories and strategies related to discipline, character education and moral development. And books abound with advice on how to get parents and babies to bond emotionally, ensuring that the child has a strong, positive foundation for interacting with other people.

But let's zero in on a few generally agreed-upon points related to very young children. Many parents teach their children to say "please" and "thank you" as soon as a child can talk or express himself using sign language—as early as 9 or 10 months old. Does this mean that a 10-month-old understands how to be polite? Not yet. But with repetition and bribery ("if you want the cupcake, you have to say the magic word"), children start to realize that these words make good things happen. Not until they reach 4 or 5 years old will they understand that the use of these words is a way of showing respect.

Getting a child to share—the holy grail of the play date—takes a lot more effort. I remember the initial horror of watching my little angels grab a toy from another child while shrieking "mine!" Toddlers, the experts say, are just not wired to share. They are possessive and territorial. While it helps to offer gentle suggestions and provide exposure to other children, what kids really need is time—time to mature into 3- and 4-year-olds who see the benefits of sharing with their friends.[2] Teaching children not to be aggressive can be an uphill battle, too. Pushing siblings, hitting playmates, biting Mom—it all comes with being a toddler, and the problems can vary depending on a child's temperament.

In other words, it is the nature of very young children to be self-absorbed and egocentric. The world, as they have learned about it so far, revolves around them. Their ability to feel real empathy may be a few years away. Admonitions like, "how would it feel if I pushed you?" can only go so far. Nancy Eisenberg, a psychologist at Arizona State University, has conducted research for decades on the moral reasoning of children of different ages. She delineates five stages of "pro-social behavior," adapted from the theories of the Lawrence Kohlberg, a Harvard psychologist famous for his theories of moral education. Level one is the stage at which an individual is concerned with his or her own interests rather than moral considerations. This is where toddlers sit, and most preschoolers as well.[3] In one interesting experiment, researchers tested whether children aged 16 months to 33 months old would try to comfort a peer in distress—or at least go get help from the daycare provider. They did so only 22 percent of the time.[4]

How do these cute but oblivious egoists turn into children who are "pro-social"—caring, tolerant, collaborative and willing to give? And what leads some children to become kinder or more accepting than others? Temperament plays a role (a shy or withdrawn child, for example, may be less likely to help or talk with a classmate), and I was surprised to learn that researchers think genes may be implicated too, to a small extent.[5] The child's environment, however, is considered the most critical. Experts say that a child tends to be more pro-social if he is raised by supportive and warm parents who behave in pro-social ways themselves and who expose their children to other pro-social models.[6]

It's that last part—the exposure to other models—that made we wonder about the impact of the media. It wasn't that I wanted television or computer software to replace my role as a moral instructor for my children; I would never give up those tender discussions with my daughters about why we share (or why their Mom got so frustrated one day she needed her own time-out). But my kids do watch some television each day, and after they hit the age of $2\frac{1}{2}$, they started to identify with the characters they saw on the screen. It seemed as if these characters were their role models, too. Could they become parenting partners, effectively modeling good behavior when I was otherwise occupied with sorting outgrown clothes or answering email?

I started to seek out academic studies on how—or if—television programs can have a pro-social influence on toddlers and preschoolers. Unfortunately, I didn't come away with armloads of reading, and what I did find was spotty and often confusing. Social scientists lament the amount of research completed on the extent to which children at these very young ages learn socialization from the screen, and studies that include computer or videogames are practically nonexistent. But insights did burst forth in a few places, and I started to understand more deeply the power of a TV show when watched by parents and their children together.

One eye-opening lesson came from research on make-believe play. This kind of play can make a difference in helping children act pro-socially. After all, children's environments include their invisible fantasy worlds, too—the place where kids direct the conversations of their action figures and where two preschoolers can turn themselves into doctors and the family room into a hospital. That make-believe world is where children can privately practice how to be a good person. The research on pretend play led me to think longer and harder about how TV and computer time affects playtime. Sometimes a child's pretend worlds are stifled by new media, and sometimes they are stimulated by them. I had already learned that the presence of an "always-on" television could detract from the quality of children's play. I had heard social workers moan about preschoolers predisposed to fighting, who had apparently learned their moves from watching *Power Rangers*. But I had also seen the way my girls and other children used TV shows as springboards for some of their nonaggressive play, even at very young ages. Once, when Gillian was 26 months old, she saw an episode of *Dora the Explorer* that featured a big red chicken asleep in the middle of Dora's path. Later that morning, hours after the TV had been turned off, Gillian amused herself by pushing a big exercise ball around the house. She came upon our dog, Bay, who was blocking the way to the kitchen, but instead of barreling against this animal (who was twice as big as she was), she stopped and called out: "Wake up, wed chicken!" Bay lumbered out of the way. (This incident was much preferred, I might add, to the time I caught her climbing into the kitchen trash can; she was pretending to be Oscar the Grouch.)

Screen time's impact on social skills, it seemed to me, could be both good and bad, depending on what, and how much, my kids were watching. I was eager to call some experts on children's play and get their take. But first I needed to better understand the few studies that have probed whether pro-social TV shows have an impact on very young children. Experts pointed me to *Mister Rogers*, *Sesame Street*, *Barney* and *Dragon Tales*—four shows that have solid independent research behind them showing positive effects. I had already spent a fair amount of time with the first three, and, truth be told, I was getting a bit tired of the purple dinosaur. It was time to visit Dragon Land.

⁓

In 1999, Langbourne W. Rust, an independent researcher who designs experiments to evaluate children's media, took on a project for Sesame Workshop. The workshop had just created a new show called *Dragon Tales*, which tells the story of two children, aged 4 and 6, who enter Dragon Land to talk with dragon friends about challenges they face. The show's mission is to help children become resilient, self-controlled, and positive thinkers—to show them the wisdom of the old saw "if at first you don't succeed, try and try again." The creators, Rust told me, thought that, if they could help instill a can-do spirit, children from disadvantaged backgrounds might be better able to rise above their circumstances.

But were they achieving this goal? Rust and his research team were commissioned to find out.[7] He considered various ways to test the children's responses to the show. Bringing kids into a laboratory and then recording their play five minutes later struck him as too artificial. "We had to do it in the field," Rust told me, "and we had to do it over a protracted period of time." He decided to conduct a five-week experiment in preschools in the New York City metropolitan area. He got permission to run the experiment in a dozen schools on 340 children who were 4 and 5 years old.

First, Rust randomly assigned the children to one of two groups. Half of the children were exposed to *Dragon Tales*, and the other half to *Between the Lions*, a show for 4- to 7-year-olds designed to promote reading more than pro-social behavior. Before and after the study, each child was evaluated by parents, teachers and trained observers, who answered questions like, "How frequently does the child choose to do a task that is challenging for him?" or "How often does he or she share?" The children's behavior during those five weeks was recorded, too. Trained observers, who were kept in the dark about the hypotheses being tested, tracked exactly what the children did during their free play period. Each observer held a personal digital assistant, like a Palm, and made notes about behavior as it was witnessed. (Johnny just shared with his friend. Check. Juanita is sticking with the puzzle even though it is difficult for her. Check.)

In yet another series of tests, the observers sat on little plastic chairs at knee-high tables, put out a basket of wooden blocks, and set up three to form a bridge. They invited the children, in one-on-one interviews, to take a look. They then asked each child to finish what had been started, allowing the kids to use their imaginations and persistence to build whatever they pleased. As the children worked, the observers jotted notes on their handheld computers indicating how many blocks were used and exactly what the child said during and after construction.

It was a complex study. Rust was relieved when all the data were collected and the computer started to churn out the analysis. But he was anxious, too. What would the results show? He remembers the exact words his assistant uttered when she brought him the first batch of graphs and numbers: "I am so depressed."

"I said, 'Oh my god, there's nothing there?' She said, 'No, it's the reverse. The idea that kids can show so much change after watching a show for only 5 weeks is really scary. That means that what they are watching on a continuous basis has got to be just overwhelming to them in its power.'"

The children who watched *Dragon Tales* regularly over those five weeks showed statistically significant gains in starting or organizing play with other children, choosing to do tasks that are challenging, asking other children to play, sharing with others, and accepting another choice when the first is not available. In the block-building task, they performed significantly better than the children who watched *Between the Lions*. They talked about what they were building, they described it as a unified whole—something they had purposefully constructed—and they typically used twenty or more blocks to do it. On measures of free play, strangely enough, both groups showed a decline in cooperative behavior after the five weeks. Rust believes this result probably occurred because the teachers were encouraging the children to do independent work. But the *Dragon Tales* kids were the ones who got most involved in construction projects.[8]

To Rust, the research showed that well-designed television programs can change behavior without relying on flashy screen tricks, short, commercial-length segments, or other techniques that seemingly favor instant gratification. "This was an extremely brave thing for Sesame Workshop to try, to make plots and goal-oriented behavior central to reaching out to 3-, 4- and 5-year-olds," Rust said. "And lo and behold it seems to make a big difference."

His findings were fascinating to me—partly because they existed at all. When we first talked, I told Rust about how little I had uncovered in my search for recent studies on whether very young children can learn good behavior from watching TV. In fact, as I told him, I had come to learn that the words "pro-social programming" could send off alarm bells among advocates for high-quality children's TV. Broadcasters, required by law to put out at least three hours of educational programming a week, are notorious for claiming that a program has a "pro-social" message and should therefore count as an educational program for kids. Often, in fact, the only cooperative or kind behavior comes at the program's end, when the conflict is over and the characters hug. In a recent case, Univision is expected to be fined $24 million by the Federal Communications Commission for trying to pass off a soap opera featuring the identity-swapping of 11-year-old twins as "educational."[9] Before the three-hour rule was established, the claims were bolder still. In those days, TV stations claimed that the *Flintstones* was educational because it taught children history, the *Jetsons* taught children about technology of the future, and *Yogi Bear* taught children "ethical values such as not to do something stupid or you will have trouble."[10]

Even should a video creator design a program with a specific social lesson in mind, experts have doubted that it could be fairly evaluated. Who is to say what led Johnny to behave? Was it the TV program he just watched, the fact that he is getting older, or the pancakes he had for breakfast? Linda Simensky at PBS told me that she chose programs that taught both pro-social and academic lessons, partly because shows that only tried to teach pro-social behavior "just weren't as test-able." Evaluating a child's social skills is a lot more complicated than getting a kid to point to a picture that matches a new word.

Rust said that his research shows that, although evaluations might be more complicated, they are possible. He pointed out that, by comparing two randomly assigned groups of children who were relatively similar except for the TV programs they had been exposed to, you can start to isolate behavior that likely stems from what they have seen. And by relying not only on reports from parents or teachers but from detailed records taken by detached observers, you can collect data on specific actions and behaviors.

"If you want to measure good children, yeah, sure, that's hard to measure," Rust told me. "I wouldn't get close to that. But we can talk about task persistence or goal setting or collaboration or a whole range of emotional states that children find themselves in. There is a whole lot that we can look at and measure and validate and make sure we are measuring what we want to measure."

⁓

Yet, so far, it's slim pickings. Few studies include such measurements on children as young as 3, 4, and 5 years old. In the 1990s, two researchers at the Annenberg Center at the University of Pennsylvania started to seek out every academic study ever done that featured data on how children acted after watching pro-social content. In 2001, the researchers—Marie-Louise Mares and Emory Woodard—published a chart showing the bottom-line results of 108 studies. Only ten of them included children 4 years old and younger; of those, only four included 3-year-olds. Studies of toddlers were absent completely.

The data from those few studies of 3- and 4-year-olds sent mixed messages. In one, for example, a group of children was exposed to a *Sesame Street* segment that showed a conflict and its resolution—a common motif in preschool programming. Another group saw the segment with no conflict, just happy, warm moments of pro-social interaction. And a third group—the control group—saw a segment that contained no social lesson at all. When the children were later observed playing a marble game, Mares and Woodard wrote, "the conflict-resolution strategy seemed to backfire. Children who saw the conflict tended to cooperate less than the control group."[11]

As Mares and Woodard looked at the array of studies, they came to realize that the "be nice, be good" messages at the end of some children's programs were not getting through to young viewers. The resolution was drowned out by the usually more-engaging scenes of conflict that drove the plot. In a study published in 2006, Mares found that even older children fail miserably when asked about the moral lessons of movies. She showed *The Sword and the Stone*, a Disney movie, to children around 7 years old and a day later asked them questions about what they had seen. The moral of the movie, which is about Arthur, Merlin, and the value of intellect over physical strength, was obvious to adults. But not one child could cite that moral lesson during the question period. About half of the kids responded with a general moral principle not related to the movie, like "You have to be nice to people." One child, Mares wrote, "remembered that Merlin had told his magical teapot to serve guests first and said the moral was to serve guests first." That answer was the closest anyone got.[12]

How do we square these findings with the bright spot from the *Dragon Tales* research? For one, *Dragon Tales* includes no scenes of aggression, and characters spend most of their time overcoming the problem instead of rehashing it. Mares also suggests that the answer may lie in the particular structure and plot line of a show. Remember, preschoolers need linear narrative. They need repetition. They need a pace that allows them to digest what they've seen. With these pieces in place, a developmentally appropriate social lesson can be learned, she believes. Yet, even then, she added, it would be foolhardy to assume that preschoolers are extracting abstract lessons from a show or movie, particularly if it contains conflict. "Little kids don't get motive, and they don't get consequences," Mares told me. "What they focus on is the action."

Which brings us to the action-packed adventures of superheroes. There are very few studies that try to get at how movies and TV shows about superheroes affect preschool children, but let's zoom in on a classic study from the 1970s that is cited repeatedly in debates about "good" and "bad" television for young children. The study, conducted by Aletha Huston and Lynette Friedrich, was conducted at a preschool at Pennsylvania State University, where ninety-seven children were assigned to one of three groups. One group watched *Mister Rogers*, another group watched *Batman* or *Superman*, and a third group, the control group, watched videos about nature, circuses, or going to the post office, selected to be "neutral" videos. Every day for four weeks, 3-, 4- and 5-year-olds were exposed to thirty minutes of their assigned shows. Before and after the study began, researchers observed the way children acted during their free playtime and while attempting to complete a mildly frustrating puzzle. They recorded persistence and self-control, pushes and shoves, patient waiting, please and thank-yous, toys being grabbed, and toys being shared. After the four weeks of viewing were over, the observers continued to watch the children for two more weeks.

By the end, those in the *Mister Rogers* group had gained ground in being patient, persistent, and able to follow rules. The control groups showed varying degrees of good and bad behavior. The children who had watched *Batman* and *Superman* showed less self-control and were more inclined to break the rules, regardless of their family background, and the relatively aggressive children became even more aggressive with each other.[13] The results from this study and others like it were profound enough to make this type of experiment among the last of its kind. Now persuaded by the impact of violent media, researchers weigh the potential for harm very carefully before exposing very young children to programs that show aggression.[14]

L. Rowell Huesmann, a psychologist at the University of Michigan, has found that the younger the child, the more influential violent media can be. He has documented how, in their early years, children start to acquire "scripts" about how to behave in particular situations. These scripts are usually a string of behaviors, repeated in certain social encounters. A positive script might read, If a friend comes to the door, open it, smile and say hello. A negative one might go, If a boy says something you don't like, yell back and smack him. Toddlers and preschoolers may be too young to understand the motives and reasons behind these scripts, but they learn them, nevertheless, storing them away and retrieving and performing them almost automatically as they get older. In fact, the younger the child, "the more malleable," Huesmann said, adding that children 2, 3 and 4 years old are at the prime age for learning scripts from what they observe in others—on screen or off.

Many parents I have interviewed know this truth intuitively, and they make a point of banning violent cartoons or talk shows that devolve into shouting matches. They see how much their kids love to mimic and imitate at very young ages, regardless of whether they understand what they are seeing or hearing. Before kids can walk, they want to hold the keys and talk on the cell phone. If they see their brothers slam the door in a rage, they want to do it, too. According to a survey from the Kaiser Family Foundation, about 80 percent of parents with children ages 2 to 6 say they have seen their child imitate something from TV.[15] At older ages, the urge to imitate starts to fall away, and reason can take hold. But if a child younger than age 4 sees a favorite TV character kick and punch, real kicks and punches are likely to follow.

Thankfully, not all superheroes kick and punch. Consider *The Wonder Pets*, a show that first aired on Nick Jr. when my younger daughter, Gillian, had just turned 2. Her sister, almost 4, took to it immediately, and I couldn't help being drawn to the show's amusing quirks and the photo-realistic animation. The show's characters, whose job is to rescue animals in trouble, often sing their lines instead of speaking them, and catchy tunes abound. It took less than fifteen minutes of exposure for the whole family, my husband and toddler included, to spend the rest of the morning singing the show's theme song. I doubted seriously whether Gillian was learning any real lessons from what she was seeing, especially given her age, but the music seemed to be getting through. When a few episodes became available on our "on demand" cable channel, we sometimes chose them for our daughters in the morning while we read the newspaper.

The first evidence of imitation came one morning six months later, after watching a *Wonder Pets* episode about a baby pigeon. We turned off the TV and sat down for breakfast. Gillian grabbed a couple of apple slices and proceeded to parade them around her cereal bowl. In this 2-year-old's mind, they had turned into little figures in an invisible drama. One of the apple slices halted its steps and turned to face the other. "Thanks, Mister Pigeon!" it called out to its apple-slice companion. Aha, I said to myself. She may not know why she is saying "thank you," but by this age she seems to be capable of re-enacting it.

I started to wonder if *The Wonder Pets* might one day measure up to the pro-social achievements of *Sesame Street*, *Mister Rogers*, *Barney* or *Dragon Tales*. To adults, at least, its lesson about teamwork is clear. One of the characters, Ling Ling the Duck, always proclaims that she can do the rescuing all by herself, but invariably it becomes clear that the job will only get done if all the animals work together. The message always comes with a singable little ditty— "What's gonna work? Teamwork!"

Later that morning, I contacted Josh Selig, the creator behind *The Wonder Pets*. Had he done any research on whether *The Wonder Pets* was leading children to work together? I was hoping that maybe, in

some not-yet-reported scientifically controlled trial, the show was
the subject of research. The answer was no, but Selig sent me a few
anecdotes from parents about how the show had seemed to help
their kids. Positive reviews of the show also turn up on iTunes,
where the show is available for downloading into a video iPod. One
anonymous iTunes reviewer wrote: "I find that the main theme of
teamwork has helped my young child work out problems with her
friends, such as sharing. 'What's gonna work? TEAMWORK!'"

It's impossible to know whether children watching *The Wonder
Pets* learn teamwork as a result of the show alone, or whether they
are responding to parents who co-view with their children and actively promote its theme. In interviews, parents sometimes told me
how they would half-watch shows with their children, putting away
dishes while adding commentary about the on-screen action when
the time felt right. ("Did you see how they shared?" "That was a
nice thing to do for a friend, wasn't it?") Emory Woodard, the researcher who studied pro-social programming with Louise Mares,
remembered a moment when he was watching *Caillou*, a program
on PBS, with his son. One of the characters on the show—a toddler
named Rosie—was behaving badly, throwing food or having a tantrum. "You see anti-social behaviors, behaviors you may not want
your child to emulate, but I think a child can still walk away with
lessons because it might offer valuable opportunities to talk through
what is portrayed," Woodard said. In the middle of that *Caillou*
episode, Woodard said, "I talked to my son about it, and he recognized that Rosie wasn't behaving in the right way. Now if I hadn't
talked about it, maybe it would have washed over him and he
wouldn't get it." But with Dad there, "it provided an opportunity for
a conversation."

Dorothy and Jerome Singer, the Yale psychologists who have
done years of research on *Barney*, stress that the best way to ensure
that a child learns good behavior from a television program is for
teachers or caregivers to follow up with related activities and con-

versations. In their study of preschoolers watching *Barney*, children nearly doubled their awareness of manners when their teachers followed up on the show's themes with dialogue or activities.[16] In the real world, it is not always possible to watch what your children watch and provide a running commentary. But with toddlers and preschoolers, you at least have more opportunities to put in your two cents, compared to when they become older and no longer need a caregiver hovering nearby. The combination of compelling on-screen entertainment and your trusted word may go a long way.

~~~

While studies are sparse on whether media has a significant prosocial impact, far more research shows the positive effect of pretend play. I wanted to understand why pretend play made such a difference and how those lessons might be incorporated into a parent's considerations of screen time. One of the leaders in this research is Laura E. Berk, a distinguished professor of psychology at Illinois State University, who wrote the 2001 book *Awakening Children's Minds: How Parents and Teachers Can Make a Difference.* She has watched countless numbers of toddlers and preschoolers over three decades, listening to their private dialogues as they play solo and witnessing their interactions with other children as they enter into dramatic make-believe worlds. With every observation, she has taken careful notes on everything the children said and did.

Her work has been guided by the theories of Lev Vygotsky, a pioneering developmental psychologist who focused on the importance of socialization and culture on children's development, including pretend or fantasy play. This play, which is most apparent between the ages of 2 and 6, allows a child to practice social rules and challenge himself to act, as Vygotsky put it, "as though he were a head taller than himself." Many researchers today believe that pretend play is crucial for a child's cognitive, social and emotional development. Vygotsky theorized that this form of play is what leads to growth in a child's ability to self-regulate. A child who can self-regulate is a child who can inhibit impulses, who can delay gratification, who can think before acting out. As toddlers and preschoolers learn to control their emotions, to wait their turn, to let playmates touch their train sets, they are learning to self-regulate. Only with that foundation of self-regulation, the theory goes, can a child move to higher planes of cognitive and socioemotional growth.

Berk has great respect for Vygotsky's theory. When we talked, she called it "remarkable and creative." But is it really true? Have any experiments been done to show that children who engage in a lot of pretend play really are better at self-regulating than children who don't? Berk and Cynthia Elias, then a postdoctoral researcher at Illinois State, reviewed literature on the subject. Studies had shown that, the more often children engage in pretend play, the more socially mature and popular they are, possibly because their playtime has given them the chance to role-play and think about others' feelings.[17] But they found that the impact on self-regulation had never been adequately tested. It was time to do so.

The first phase of their research took shape in the fall of 1999 at two preschools in Normal, Illinois. Trained observers, equipped with clipboards and stopwatches, recorded the actions of fifty-three children of middle-income families during their playtime and clean-up time over several weeks. They conducted observations a semester later so that they could record how the children's "clean-up" behaviors matured over time. As most parents know, clean-up time—when we are urging, cajoling and begging kids to put away their toys—is when a child's level of social responsibility and self-control are definitely being challenged. The idea was to code precisely what each child did when he or she played in the large block area or "housekeeping" area (where children could dress up in hats and boots or pretend to make dinner) and then compare that play to the same child's behavior when it was time to clean up. If Vygotsky's theory was right, the children who engaged in the higher levels of pretend play would be the ones able to take on more socially responsible roles and put their toys away when asked.[18]

The results were encouraging. The children who engaged in the most frequent and longest socio-dramatic play episodes were most likely to be the ones who had learned to handle clean-up time, sometimes even going so far as to help their classmates. They also found that children with impulse-control problems who practiced pretend play had the biggest gains.[19] "The children who are the least well-regulated seem to benefit the most," Berk said.

When I first learned of this research, I wondered if the only real lesson was one I and many parents already stress in our households—that time must be preserved in children's routines for playing pretend, which means careful limits on how much they watch TV. But then I heard about the second half of Berk's research, which offered some insights into how that playtime might be affected by what children see in their everyday lives, on screen and off.

Berk, you see, was well aware of a limitation in her initial research: she had only observed children from the middle class. She wanted to know if pretend play could make an impact with at-risk children. So she and Sara Kay Harris, a graduate student, devised a second experiment. This time they went to a Head Start center, where the only enrollees are children from low-income families. They went through the same drill, with observers taking careful notes over several autumn days, watching the children's behavior while they played and cleaned up, then returning in the spring to observe the clean-up routine again. Berk soon realized that these children were engaged in less socio-dramatic play overall, a troubling finding that has been replicated in other studies of at-risk children, but she still expected that the theory would bear out. She figured that the children who engaged in the most pretend play would be the children with the social maturity to put away toys without major cajoling from their teachers.

Instead, she and Harris found evidence to the contrary. Socio-dramatic play was slightly, though not significantly, linked to poor clean-up performance. The more pretend play, the worse the clean-up behavior. The results were disappointing, but Berk had an inkling why they had turned out this way. Although observers hadn't been specifically instructed to write down the themes of children's make-believe episodes, they started to note that the pretend play was more violent than in middle-class preschools. The children, they said, were enacting fights, killings, robberies and imprisonments. Where they might have learned these story lines is impossible to know, since the study did not delve into the home environments or television viewing patterns of these children. Berk hypothesizes, however, that television played some role, since prior research has shown that children from poor families are more likely to be exposed to lots of television—including viewing at primetime and night-time hours when adult shows like *Law and Order* or *CSI* are on. What's more, she said, "children bring media themes into their play. We see that very easily." Considering the growing literature on how preschoolers learn from what they see on TV, together with her recent research on how the content of pretend play can influence a child's sense of social responsibility, she is prepared to take a leap of faith: "Violent programming creates self-regulation difficulties in children," she said.

The flip side is to ask whether pro-social programming can lead children to engage in more pretend play that, in turn, might improve their ability to self-regulate. We will have to wait for more research to know for sure, but we have a hint from Huston's data on *Mister Rogers' Neighborhood*, which showed a positive influence. The research on *Barney* is worth highlighting, too, since it is one of the only studies to include children as young as 2 from low-income families. Researchers observed toddlers in a daycare center for two weeks who engaged in periods of free play immediately after viewing *Barney*. These 2-year-olds showed significantly more signs of playing make-believe than did their peers who did not see the show, and their play was not of the violent type. The *Barney* group also showed more evidence of being persistent and cooperative.[20]

Did their pretend play have any connection to their level of co-operation, or were they simply better behaved because they were coming off the toddler high of watching *Barney?* The study was not designed to answer that question, but it shows how all of these issues are bound together, entwined to produce what parents and teachers simply know as "good behavior." The Singers are con-vinced that media can be a positive force for pretend play. Over the past few years, they have created their own videos, called *Circle of Make-Believe*, that are part of a training program for children and parents, designed to stimulate more imaginative, pro-social play. When preschool centers at eight sites around the country tested the program, researchers found it to have a significant positive im-pact.[21] Here, it seems, is a mix that works: children benefit when they are given the right kind of screen time along with the oppor-tunity to escape into the right kinds of imaginative play.

Taken together, the studies of Berk and of *Barney* remind me of the risks of over-parenting and under-parenting in the media age. The over-parenting comes in the form of worrying too much about academic skills at the expense of social ones, not giving children enough time to simply play pretend without having to be "taught." The under-parenting comes when a television set is always on, dis-rupting and deferring a child's natural play or, worse, serving as a catalyst for aggressive behavior. Somewhere in between is the happy medium—"just-enough parenting"—where kids use some media and an abundance of playtime to practice self-regulation, cooperation, responsibility, and negotiation skills. Learning to say "please" and "thank you" is an added bonus.

NOTES

1. Hart and Risley, 1995, p. 105.
2. Spock and Rothenberg, 1992, pp. 408–409; and Eisenberg, Murkoff, and Hathaway, 1996, pp. 267–269.
3. Siegler, DeLoache, and Eisenberg, 2003, p. 541.

4. Ibid., p. 549.

5. Ibid., p. 550.

6. Ibid., p. 553.

7. Sesame Workshop paid for the evaluation but played no role in designing or reviewing the study before it came out, Rust told me. Research on *Dragon Tales* was made public through a link to the full report, available for some time on the PBS Web site. (I received the report directly from Rust after finding the Web link broken.) Private research is typically proprietary, but *Dragon Tales* was produced with public funds, so the results are available to anyone who wants to read them. The funding for the show came from the Corporation for Public Broadcasting through the U.S. Department of Education. It was designed for the Ready to Learn programming block on PBS.

8. Rust, 2001, pp. 45–47.

9. Stephen Labaton, "Record Fine Expected for Univision," *New York Times,* February 24, 2007, p. A6.

10. Kunkel, 1998, p. 44–45. Also see, Edmund L. Andrews, "Broadcasters, to Satisfy Law, Define Cartoons as Education," *New York Times,* September 30, 1992.

11. Mares and Woodard, 2001, p. 192.

12. Mares, 2006, p. 227.

13. Huston Stein and Friedrich, 1975, pp. 78–84.

14. From a telephone interview with Huston, September 13, 2006.

15. Rideout and Hamel, 2006, p. 21. As I noted later in this chapter, that imitation can take the form of pro-social behavior, too. In Rideout and Hamel's survey, 66 percent of parents said their children imitated pro-social behaviors they saw on screen, while 23 percent admitted their children imitated aggressive behavior they saw on screen.

16. Singer and Singer, 1998, p. 337.

17. Siegler, DeLoache, and Eisenberg, 2003, p. 260.

18. Berk, Mann, and Ogan, 2006, p. 78.

19. Elias and Berk, 2002, pp. 14–15.

20. Singer and Singer, 1998, pp. 356–357.

21. Singer and Singer, 2005, p. 162.

Chapter Ten

Is Interactive Media
Worthwhile — or at Least
Better Than TV?

I t's November, the cusp of the holiday shopping season. I'm being urged to buy VMIGO, a toy that plugs into the TV and offers what the judges at the *Toy Wishes* magazine call a "completely immersive virtual pet experience." I'm also hearing about the T.M.X. Elmo, the latest incarnation of the Tickle Me Elmo electronic toy that throws himself into fits of giggles when touched. Then there's the Digi Makeover, a "cool new gadget" that requires a digital camera and a TV, and Disney's Magical Talking Salon that features a light-up mirror embedded with voice-recognition software so that "girls can practically become a mermaid themselves."[1]

These marketing messages and many more are peppering the morning news shows, the daily newspaper, monthly magazines and my email inbox. The toys all boast of some sort of electronic component that rings or sings, responds to my child's voice, brings books "to life," records digital messages, employs a child-friendly joystick, or comes with a touch screen or digital display. Whatever the feature, there is some chip-driven device within their plastic casing that has positioned them at the head of the class, carrying the buzzword of the decade: they are undeniably, bet-your-money, wouldn't-have-it-any-other-way interactive.

Before now, this marketing maelstrom had little to do with products for babies. Granted, there have been plenty of baby toys that feature, say, buttons that emit a few musical notes when pressed. But screen-based interactive products, like computer software, educational videogames and plug-and-play controllers that work with TVs, were only being designed for older children, at least those out of diapers. The year 2006, however, marked the arrival of two interactive video products specifically tailored to children as young as 9 months old. One is the V.Smile Baby Infant Development System by V Tech; the other is the Little Leaps Grow-with-Me Learning System by LeapFrog. Both packages contain two parts—a video and a toy-like wireless controller, essentially an oversized remote control. The controller comes with bright block-sized buttons that can send commands to the video player, changing the action on screen.

I got a personal demonstration of Little Leaps a few months before it went on the market. Interactivity was the selling point. Surely, the marketers argued, this is better for a child than passively watching *Baby Mozart* videos that they have no control over. They turned on a segment called "Naked Baby Blues." A song began to play, and the screen showed a smiling, diapered baby about to get dressed. Then the action paused. "Push a button to find baby's pants," a narrator called out. With one press of the round red button on the remote control, the screen responded, showing a pair of plaid pants, accompanied by the spoken word "pants" and another little tune, then lapsing into video of the baby now crawling in those same plaid trousers. Cherie Stewart, a spokeswoman for LeapFrog, said that researchers had taken care to construct the prompts to get parents and their babies involved. "The primary goal was interactivity and cause and effect and really developing that," she told me.

Both Little Leaps and the V.Smile Baby certainly appeared more interactive than plain old DVDs. Moreover, they were toys that usually required prompting and guidance from a caregiver. No electronic babysitting here. But did the babies using these "learning systems" fully realize that they were in control of what was on screen? Did they comprehend that, whenever their chubby hands pressed the buttons, they caused something to happen several feet away? Were these systems really teaching cause and effect?

One critic who wanted to find out for sure was Warren Buckleitner, the editor of the *Children's Technology Review*, a monthly magazine that reviews videogames and educational software for children. He usually asks children to test the products, and he decided to do the same with these two "learning systems," capturing the experiences on video so that he could carefully review them later. I watched a few of the videos. One of them took place in the home of a 28-month-old girl. Her mother sat on the rug with her, showing her the buttons on the toylike remote control. The television screen was several feet away in an open TV cabinet. The girl pushed on the buttons for a minute or two, climbed on Mom for a bit, and then got distracted by the family dog who wandered by. "What happens if you press the yellow button?" asked the mother, who went ahead and pressed it herself when her daughter didn't respond. New images appeared on the TV screen, but her little girl didn't notice. She had barely looked at the TV screen at all.

The other children he observed were similarly disinterested. "These are a state-of-the-art bad idea," Buckleitner told me. "I've pretty much dedicated my last twenty years to trying to understand interactive media and kids, and my standard line is, if you've got an under $2^{1}/_2$-year-old, get a cat." His observations reminded me of the accumulating evidence related to television viewing and what children under age 2 can understand. We've learned that babies do not comprehend images the way adults do, that they are still trying to work out the connections between symbols and objects, between pictures and the real thing. And we've learned that babies and toddlers are not yet ready to absorb much more than the here-and-now, not typically comprehending sequential narratives until after age 2. Understanding the nuances of cause and effect is another developmental milestone, and some experts believe that children have a limited understanding of cause and effect when it isn't close and immediate.[2]

Consider an experiment conducted years ago with infants lying on their backs. Researchers tied string around the babies' ankles and connected it to a mobile hanging above them. Babies as young as 2 months old learned that, if they kicked their legs, the mobile would move. It was a thrilling discovery. The babies would kick excitedly and deliberately as soon as they figured it out.[3] The term experts use for this learning process is contingency, where feedback is contingent upon a child's action. It might seem that contingency is exactly what babies are learning when they press a button and see something happen on screen. But the connection between what they do and what happens next is not likely to be as obvious to them as it is to me and you. They have pressed a button on a chunky plastic thing, and they have witnessed movement on a flat but always changing surface ten feet away. It is hard to tell whether the babies who play these games realize that they caused the effect.

Carolyn Rovee-Collier, a psychologist at Rutgers University, designed the experiment involving the mobile. I asked her whether children as young as 9 months old would notice that they were controlling an interactive game on a TV screen. She didn't rule out the possibility, and she stressed that babies learn more than we give them credit for. But then she offered a telling story about one of her research experiments. She had been testing 6-month-old children. She wanted to see if the babies could learn that, by flipping a lever on a train table, they were responsible for moving the train that chugged by. She discovered that they could. But first she had to fix her equipment, for the kids weren't even looking at the train. They were fixated on the clicking noises made by the lever. "We had to make it quiet so they would actually care about the train," she said.

A few preschools and child care centers now have computers equipped with touch screens that allow children to press the screen and get an immediate response, thus avoiding large distances that separate their movement from the action on screen. They also don't come with any distractions like clicking noises or family dogs. But perhaps those distractions are learning moments in and of themselves. Simply discovering that a lever makes a click is a pretty exciting thing for a little kid to figure out. "I think babies have plenty of ways to learn cause and effect," Rovee-Collier said, suggesting that parents experiment with the doorbell. "That's cheaper," she said.

～♥

If interactive screen media is an expensive and relatively ineffective tool for babies and toddlers, what about children a little bit older? Could 2-year-olds learn from educational computer games or electronic books? Some educational software products are marketed as appropriate for very young kids. For example, the packaging for a CD-ROM software called JumpStart Preschool Advance says it is for "Ages 1½–4." But the natural laws of child development have a way of putting the brakes on just how much a child can do without a lot of help. At age 2, and often at age 3, children have not yet developed the fine-motor skills to operate a mouse. They may know all about cause and effect by that age, but they are still challenged when what they are doing with their hands is causing something to happen in a different physical place. "Usually I'm looking at the object I'm acting on," said Glenda Revelle, vice president of creative development and digital media at Sesame Workshop. "But to use a computer you have to separate that."

Game designers have started to employ a few tricks to make things easier for little hands. One common feature allows children to "click-attach" instead of "click-and-drag" whenever they want to move an object on the screen. One click causes the object to stick to the cursor, going wherever the cursor goes. A second click drops the object. In interactive TV products (videogames that operate via the TV remote control), Sesame Workshop has tailored its offerings to suit 2- and 3-year-olds, allowing them to advance the action on screen with a simple press of a button instead of pressing multiple buttons to scroll or move right and left. In making cartridges for the V.Smile system, which uses a joystick with buttons that plugs into the TV, Sesame Workshop again tried to keep the motor skills of the youngest users in mind. Designers made a point of not using the joystick at all, asking children instead to push the buttons to play.

My daughter Janelle got her introduction to using a computer mouse when she was about 2 years old. We were at the house of a playmate who, at just over 3 years old, could ably insert a CD-ROM into her computer, which was in her bedroom, and click through the menu options like a pro. Janelle, by contrast, was fumbling to keep the cursor from sliding off the screen. I have no doubt that more practice would have helped, but it seemed her time would be better spent with crayons. If children best develop their motor skills from hands-on experience with real objects, I thought, it was probably best to steer away from software programs altogether.

One point, however, encouraged me to keep an open mind. Assume that a child has acquired enough motor skills to operate a mouse. Could interactive software then have something to offer? After age 2, children have been shown to learn from television programs when they are well designed. Can't the same be said of interactive software? And wouldn't it be better for children to genuinely interact with what is on screen instead of watching it pass them by? Most parents allow their children to have some TV or video time each day. Would it be better for those kids to be playing with educational software on a computer or using a handheld interactive game?

Arguments along these lines have been voiced at multiple forums on young children and media over the past few years. Tech-savvy educators hail the ability of computer-based tools to provide children with contingent feedback and positive reinforcement, while being careful not to claim that electronic interactivity is better than real-life interaction. "This isn't an either-or situation," said Mark Bailey, a professor of early childhood education at Pacific University. "It's not that you either play with toys or use technology. It's that technology is one more avenue to exploring the world." Besides, sometimes parents need to be on the phone, balancing the checkbook or helping an older sibling with homework. These new tools, advocates say, could be the next best thing to Mom or Dad. Unlike TV, they argue, interactive screen-based media actively engage children in learning, giving them a feeling of control and motivating them to strive for new levels of competency.

Is there evidence that any of these ideas are true? Educational psychologists and media researchers have only recently started to test these assumptions in large-scale studies. Nothing like the massive longitudinal studies on *Sesame Street* exist for interactive media. And yet new software and online games are appearing every day. Buckleitner's magazine, for example, has been putting out a list of the top 100—yes, that's 100—preschool software programs for several years. It was hard enough for me to figure out the effectiveness of these products, but when I looked into the fast-moving marketplace, I felt like I was an impatient child tugging on some increasingly tangled shoelaces. Only by focusing on some science-based studies of preschool children would I have any hope of unraveling some answers. And, just as with television, I came to learn that the benefits or drawbacks of an interactive media program depend on three important factors: content, context and the individual child.

~⁓

Dora the Explorer, as you surely know by now, is one of those preschool television shows that tries very hard to elicit responses from

children who are watching. Dora is usually pictured looking out-
ward toward the audience, and throughout every show, she pauses
for a few seconds when asking questions to give children a chance
to shout out an answer. But let's face facts. She is not really talking
to anyone in particular. She is a TV character who keeps saying her
lines whether children respond or not. The show might be billed as
interactive, but among researchers, the way to describe it is participatory. *Dora* merely invites participation; no contingent back-and-
forth dialogue is possible.

However, somewhere on a computer server at Georgetown University, there are two other versions of *Dora*, and one of them meets
the definition of interactive. Researchers at Georgetown University
have tinkered with video from the show to create a computerized
version that pauses and won't respond until a viewer clicks on
something that appears on screen. For example, when Dora's backpack opens and objects spill out, children are asked to click on the
appropriate object to solve the problem. The other version of *Dora*
is a stripped-down form of the TV show, with no pauses or cues to
answer questions. It is the opposite of interactive; it requires nothing more than observation.

These re-engineered *Dora*s were created at the direction of Sandra
L. Calvert, a psychology professor at Georgetown, who has heard
more than her share of claims about the benefits of interactivity. She
is the head of the Children's Digital Media Center, which has received multiple grants from the National Science Foundation to
study the impact of new media. Her studies are interdisciplinary but
rooted in scientific method, comparing children's use of media under
tightly controlled conditions. Many of them are trying to isolate various elements of interactivity. Does the child's ability to control what
is on screen make a difference? How responsive does a program have
to be? In short, her role is to tease out exactly what about online
software or videogames might help children at various ages. She was
just what I needed for those knotted shoelaces—an untangler.

"With the new media, all we hear about is how interactivity is going to improve learning," Calvert told me when she described the *Dora* experiment. "But I didn't think we had a good enough sense of what interactivity was or how it worked." At the same time, she said, she strongly resisted the idea that TV was just a passive activity. She is persuaded by the researchers (those you met in chapter 3) who have documented how much children are engaged when they watch TV designed for them. Kids work hard, for example, at following a televised narrative. "One thing that video does is tell a good story," she said. When children are clicking around on a computer screen, whatever narrative may have existed is suddenly interrupted.

So which is better for preschoolers—TV or computers? To find out, Calvert and her Georgetown colleagues loaded the *Dora* videos onto laptops and visited daycare centers around Washington DC, where they had found 131 4-year-olds to participate in their study. The children were randomly assigned to one of the videos, either the interactive, participatory or simple observation versions. A video camera recorded how much attention children paid and exactly how they responded. Directly afterward, researchers asked the children questions about what they had seen.

The results showed that the *Dora* television show could hold its own. The children who watched the participatory version of *Dora*, the one they see on Nick Jr., were able to answer more questions about the content than kids who saw the stripped-down version. The children who used the interactive *Dora* did well, too, but they came in second place compared to those who watched the participatory program. What mattered, Calvert said, was whether the children were engaged with what was on screen—and that was clearly happening with both the interactive *Dora* and the televised version. In both cases, kids were seen calling out to the screen and imitating Dora's movements.[4] "The more children participate with Dora, the better they understand the content," Calvert said. "So, put simply, both the participation and interaction conditions help children get the program messages."

This doesn't mean, of course, that every television show is as good as—or better than—every videogame. There might be something particular about *Dora* that prompts participation, and not every interactive computer program is designed like the one at Georgetown. Complicating the picture, too, are DVDs and CD-ROMs based on printed books, as well as Web sites like OneMoreStory.com that offers a library of beautifully illustrated children's books in which pages can be turned, one after the other, on the computer screen.

The Georgetown study did, however, challenge the prevailing wisdom. Interactive programming is not always an improvement over straight video. Design matters. What kind of design works best for preschoolers? That was my next question.

～つ

When my older daughter was 4, I ordered JumpStart Advanced, the preschool edition. The label on the box called it the "#1 Educational Software." I naively wondered if that meant it got a top rating from educators, but when I found the fine print, I learned that it was number one in dollar sales over the past decade. Still, I knew that the JumpStart line of products had received some high marks from Buckleitner's *Children's Technology Review*, and the activities in this package looked enchanting. One CD was called the Language Club, where kids could be exposed to words in French, Japanese, Spanish and English. Another CD was dedicated to creative work, allowing kids to play with graphics or make their own storybook. Janelle, who sees me using the computer every day, was pestering me to put in the software the minute she opened the package.

At my desk, with Janelle on my lap, we popped in the Language Club CD. She leaned forward, eager to take in the colorful animations and music. She chose the English-language section first—

"that's where we live," she said, pointing to the U.S. flag—and I indulged her. She chose the puppets game, as I helped guide the mouse to the right spot to click it open. A doll-like puppet, unclothed, appeared on a stage. The object of the game was to dress the puppet by clicking on various clothing items, which triggered the software to say the words in whatever language was being taught. Once the puppet was dressed, the software promised, it would perform a dance.

The clothing choices were a hat, shirt, pants and shoes. "I want to pick a dress," she told me.

"That's not an option, kiddo. Pick one of the four on the screen," I told her.

My husband came in, peered over our shoulders, playfully snagged the mouse and chose a black top hat. "No!" Janelle hollered. "I don't want her to wear a hat." The hat came off.

We moved on to the shirt selection. The voice-over on the software said "shirts and dresses." Janelle got excited. "They do have dresses!" But there was no dress on screen. She chose a long-sleeved white shirt instead. Within a few minutes she had chosen two other items, dressing the puppet in red shorts and purple high heels.

"Now I want to see it dance," Janelle told me. But the software had something else in mind. "You're doing great," it said. "You only need one more type of clothing to complete the outfit." Reluctantly, Janelle put the hat back on the puppet's head. And with that, it launched into a little dance that labeled its arms, legs and head, although when it said the word "arms," the hands were moving instead. Meanwhile, lunchtime was upon us. We shut down the software and headed into the kitchen to make a peanut butter and jelly sandwich.

A few minutes into lunch, Janelle asked when she could play the computer game again. Evidently those little frustrations hadn't bothered her at all. I, on the other hand, felt vaguely distressed. I remembered a phrase that had been drilled into my head by Kathy

Hirsh-Pasek, the author of *Einstein Never Used Flashcards*. A good toy, she said, is 90 percent kid and 10 percent toy. But a lot of electronic products for children, she said, are the opposite—10 percent kid and 90 percent toy. They don't prompt children to use their own imaginations or explore what their little brains might be intrigued about.

To be fair, my daughter had not used the software exactly as it was intended. After all, this was a teaching game, not a toy per se. And the idea was to learn foreign-language words, not play dress-up in English. Subsequent interactions with the software were a little less frustrating. But her initial experience highlighted what even advocates acknowledge as the inherent limitations of many software programs for young kids. They are usually programmed to guide children down particular paths, not set them loose. If children want to veer off and explore something programmers didn't intend or never imagined, they will find themselves stuck.

Warren Buckleitner, who was once a preschool teacher, wrote his doctoral dissertation on how the style of an interactive media program affects young children's engagement. He studied how thirty-eight children, ages 3 to 5½, responded to a simple matching game he created for the computer. In the game, children were asked to match cookies to one of three little critters at the bottom of the screen. A cookie sprinkled with stars, for example, was supposed to go to the critter covered in stars. As soon as children made the right match, the critter gobbled the cookie, emitting a low burp with every tenth swallow.

As the kids were playing the game, Buckleitner silently sat just behind them in the room, recording everything they said and using a mirror to observe their facial expressions. One 4-year-old boy, he noted, seemed more concerned about the critters' eating patterns than whether he was getting the right answers. "That one didn't get to eat, that one didn't get to eat," the boy repeated. Another boy, age 4½, was most driven by the sound effects, keeping track of belching and nonbelching critters and exclaiming, "I want him to burp!" One girl, almost 4, wanted to feed every critter equally. "You already ate," she would say.[5] These observations were secondary to the thrust of his research, but they struck him as important reminders of how different children can be, even when they are nearly the same age. Their personalities, their needs and their interests will dictate how they interact with a software program.

The primary point of Buckleitner's research was to uncover whether preschool children could benefit from interactive programs that gave them a feeling of control. He set up the game to provide one of two types of feedback. One mode emitted lots of praise and gave children instructions at every turn. On the software menu, it was called "smother." The other mode was relatively silent, giving off a few dings and beeps to indicate right answers but rarely offering instructions. Buckleitner found that, when kids were given a chance to go forward on their own without waiting for instructions or sitting through multiple seconds of praise, they were more active and engaged, focusing on the task at hand instead of looking around. They spent the same amount of time with the program as the other group but completed three times the number of tasks.[6] The findings seemed to validate his hypothesis: the more children could control the interactive experience, the more they responded to it.

A few months before talking to Buckleitner, I visited Kathy Hirsh-Pasek at her child-development laboratory on the Ambler campus of Temple University. Ambler is a little town north of Philadelphia, with a quaint train station and patches of quiet countryside. From the outside, the Ambler lab looks quaint and quiet, too. It occupies a refurbished old house with white clapboard siding and creaky stairs. But inside, the silence is broken by the sounds of children climbing on colorful bean bags and playing with toy cars. On the day I visited, mothers with their toddlers and preschoolers were arriving every thirty minutes.

One of the subjects that day was a 5-year-old boy in a black T-shirt and shorts. He and his mother were ushered into a nearby room and given an electronic book made by Fisher-Price. Called the PowerTouch Learning System, it is similar to the LeapPad talking book made by LeapFrog. A specialized paper book is inserted into the toy's plastic frame, and an accompanying computer cartridge is plugged into the top. When a child presses an image on the page, the toy "talks," giving voice to the words on the page, sounding out letters and labeling pictures. Books like this are typically marketed to children age 3 and up, although Fisher-Price and other companies also offer simplified versions to be used with babies as young as 6 months old.[7]

In a room nearby, I sat down with Julia Parish, a doctoral student at Temple who is co-authoring the study with Molly Collins of the Erikson Institute in Chicago. "We're curious if kids get anything out of these ebooks," Parish said. Did they allow for the same kind of rich interactions and conversations possible when Mom and Dad read regular books to their kids? Were parents inclined to ask as many questions about characters or depictions of events when the book was electronic? She recruited eighty children, 3- and 5-year-olds, to come to the lab. One group was given a couple of regular storybooks, like those about the Berenstain Bears. Another group was given an electronic book that featured the same stories. The child and parents were instructed to use the books for as long as they wanted and to "do whatever you do with books." Two minutes after the families got settled, a video camera recorded some of their interactions.

Parish was about to tell me about preliminary results when the lab coordinator appeared. "The mother is saying she can't get it to work," she told Parish, who left temporarily to offer assistance. There's one big limitation right there, I thought to myself. In interviews with families who use interactive DVDs, computer software and ebooks, I had often heard complaints about the amount of troubleshooting required. "The usefulness of it all is lost on me when I am constantly asked to fix the game," said a mother of three in State College, Pennsylvania.

The results Parish revealed that day showed that the ebooks had a negative impact on parent-child interaction. For example, instead of following the story, children would play with the device. Parents would respond with, "Don't press that button! Wait to turn the page! No, no, we're supposed to be reading!" As Parish put it, "behavioral directives were through the roof." The final results, tallied later that year, confirmed the problem. Parents in the traditional book group engaged in significantly more talk about the books' content than the parents in the ebook group. In the ebook group, conversations about content seemed to be replaced with conversations about button-pressing.

There is another way to look at data like this, however. Consider Buckleitner's point about control. Maybe the strength of electronic books—whether in a child's lap or on a computer screen—is that they allow children to engage with a book on their own terms. A hovering parent doesn't exactly help test that theory. But work by Allison Caplovitz, an educational technology consultant who did her doctoral work at the University of Texas at Austin, provides some insights. Like Parish, Caplovitz studied the impact of the PowerTouch ebook, but she studied how they are used at home. When she compared the use of ebooks among 138 4½-year-olds, she found that, on the whole, the ebooks were no better than traditional books at helping children with emergent literacy skills. But they weren't worse, either.[8]

More interesting to me was what she found when Mom or Dad weren't reading with their children. "When parents are reading a book, parents are in charge," Caplovitz told me. "They guide the whole interaction." With ebooks, she found that children wanted to take over. "When the parents are there, and the child has the interactive book on his or her lap, parents are pushed to the side," she said. "They may jump in and try to ask their children questions, but a lot of time children feel so in control, they say, 'No, I'm doing it. This is my thing.'" In Caplovitz's study, children with ebooks frequently used them alone, whereas children with the regular books were rarely reading alone. That "alone" time made a difference in some small ways. For example, the more time children spent using the ebooks alone, the better they could match an uttered word to the word in print.[9]

I took this result to be another lesson in the power of context. Learning, as many educational experts will attest, is more likely to happen when children feel motivated and empowered. Calvert and her colleagues at Georgetown have found evidence of this, too. They tested how $4^{1}/_{2}$-year-old children used an interactive *Blue's Clues* storybook. When adults controlled all or part of the action—guiding the mouse, for example—children's attention declined significantly.[10] Calvert put it this way: "The question is, how is the parent involved? Are you following the child's lead? Or are you dictating control?"

~⁓⁓

Imagine a new building under construction. The elevator and stairs have yet to be added. Walls are still to be framed out, windows need to be installed, the façade awaits painting. For workers to get these jobs done, they need scaffolding—temporary bridges that offer support. When work in one place is done, the scaffolds are moved to the next level of hard-to-reach spaces.

Educators have adopted that image of scaffolding as a critical strategy in helping children learn. Think of children as moving from one level of understanding to a higher one. A very young child, for example, might learn to sing the alphabet song, belting it out in that adorable toddler voice, even though he doesn't really know the letters or what they mean. (I know one 2-year-old who would gleefully sing ". . . H, I, J, K, Elmo Pee . . . . ") After a while, the child might start to recognize what the letters look like. Then he learns to print them, followed by the ability to match the letters to the sounds they represent. To get from one level to another, he is aided by parents and teachers who provide scaffolding for the next step, taking into account exactly where he stands developmentally and presenting him with the cognitive framework to get to the next level. "Yea, you spotted the A!" a parent might say. "Now, I bet you can draw an A. Want to try?"

Scaffolding draws on the theories of Vygotsky, the child-development guru of the twentieth century. Vygotsky believed that children learn best when they are in their "zone of proximal development," where children have nearly mastered one skill and are within stretching distance of something slightly more advanced. To enable that stretching, to allow children to climb to a new place, scaffolds can make all the difference. Caring adults are often building scaffolds without even realizing it, and in a perfect world, parents would be the primary source of strong, customized scaffolds to bridge their children's growth. But some parents are better at this than others—for reasons both within and outside their control. Parents who work long hours may not have the time or energy to engage on a daily basis in such rich interactions with their kids. Parents under stress, worrying about money or other children, may not be paying enough attention to see what "zone" a child is in and whether he or she is ready to stretch.

The studies on interactive media that I had found so far emphasized the problems associated with parents taking too much control. But given this emphasis on scaffolding, I was curious about the flip side, too. Can interactive software provide some guidance to a preschooler who isn't getting much of it in person? What can it offer when parents aren't around?

PBSKids.org is one place where these questions are being asked. Sara DeWitt, director of PBS Kids and Parents Interactive, said that when the Web site was revamped in 2006, designers made a big point of providing navigational arrows and symbolic icons to empower the preschool population to take the reins. The idea was to create a Web site that preliterate children could use without always having to ask, "What does that say?" "We decided we wouldn't design any more Web sites for parents," DeWitt said. "We would allow the children to navigate themselves."

Given that a Web site or piece of software is designed to put children in control, designers say, the next step is to create games that can almost sense a child's zone of proximal development and adapt to take it into account. Now, if you're like me, you're probably saying, yeah, right. How can a piece of software possibly tune into the specific needs of a preschooler? How can an electronic game simulate the actions of an attentive parent? DeWitt encouraged me to look at PBS's *Curious George* games to see for myself. I tried out "411," a telephone game. The man in the yellow hat asked me to "dial this number—476—and click the green button." The idea behind the game, the site told me, is to help children practice number recognition. Every time I entered the correct numbers, I got to see a ten-second video clip from the show. After recognizing the correct numbers multiple times in a row, the man in the yellow hat asked me to find 2854. Now I was being asked to recognize four digits in a row, instead of three.

I moved on to the Web site for *Peep and the Big Wide World*. The man who designed the *Curious George* games did the same for *Peep*. His name is Bill Shribman, executive producer of kids' projects for WGBH in Boston. One of the *Peep* games, Paint Splat, is intended to teach children about mixing colors. On the screen, a little red bird holds up a card with a big orange dot. The object of the game is to help another bird named Quack create that same color using a combination of paint from three tubes—red, yellow and blue. After I went through a few rounds giving correct answers, the red bird pulled out a card with a dot that was not just orange but yellowy-orange. Now I was going to have to figure out how much paint from the red and yellow tubes Quack needed.

In short, both games kicked up the difficulty level after realizing that I knew my stuff. (Though, as a 35-year-old playing a game for preschoolers, I'm embarrassed to admit that the switch from secondary to tertiary colors threw me for a loop at first.) I caught up with Shribman to ask about the games' adaptability, which in the industry is known as "self-leveling." One of the reasons his team created the games this way, he said, is because designers don't know the exact age or developmental stage of the children playing. "We don't want children to have to say 'easy' or 'hard,'" he said. "They may not know. How can they calibrate that? Or they might find that it's too babyish to say 'easy.'"

Instead, the games calibrate for the player by paying close attention to what the child is doing. Think of a child on the monkey bars at the playground. A typical kid may simply gravitate to what he has done before. But as a parent you want her to try something new, climbing a bit higher or hanging a bit longer. "When I am making games," Shribman said, "I'm thinking of good parenting." His approach is built on the advice of James Paul Gee, a reading professor at the University of Wisconsin at Madison who has written about the positive impact of videogames. For games to be able to teach, Gee says, they must be "pleasantly frustrating." They need to offer challenges that "feel hard but doable."[11]

~⌒

No large studies have been done to find out if this pleasantly frustrating electronic scaffolding is doing any good for very young kids. Only recently have researchers acquired grants from the Department of Education to test the online games that are packaged with educational TV shows. It will be several years before we see any data. But I could see how my daughters might enjoy some of these games. So one rainy, cold Sunday, I showed Janelle, then 4, the *Peep* Web site.

It had been two weeks since we had tried JumpStart, and Janelle had been aching to get back to the computer. She figured out Paint Splat quickly, with little instruction from me. But after a few minutes of hitting the right color combinations, she wanted to keep clicking on the tubes of paint to see what kinds of colors she could create. The game didn't allow such experimentation. "I have an idea," I told her. I closed the Web browser and opened the old Paint program that comes with the Microsoft operating system. For the next half-hour, Janelle was scribbling, sketching and coloring. My help was required, especially to get her mouse clicks to work correctly, but she was in control. We saved each of her paintings and printed a purple one that featured a tall pink oval. She titled it, "The Magic Tower."

I later learned about KidPix, an inexpensive graphics program designed for children ages 4 and up. Santa gave it to Janelle for Christmas. A month later, my husband and I decided to put a computer on our kitchen desk, where we also keep art supplies that the girls can dig into whenever they want. The software has become a huge hit. Even Gillian, not yet 3, has become more adept at using the mouse by virtue of watching and "coloring" with her older sister. Sometimes they collaborate together on a project, exclaiming excitedly when they're finished, "Mommy, come see this!"

It is true that, for less than the cost of KidPix, my husband and I had already stocked up on magic markers, construction paper, glue sticks and kids' scissors. To my relief, the girls remain just as interested in those hands-on tools. Some days, they are just itching to create something on screen, but on others, the markers are all they need.

Meanwhile, I have resolved to adhere to some general guidelines about computer use with our kids. My first resolution is not even to touch the Web sites that are laden with advertisements. Some game sites have only one goal: to capture a child's attention for as long as possible while flashing ads for Reese's Peanut Butter Cups and Cap'N Crunch. Furthermore, I plan to pick software that allows them to go where their imagination takes them. I will select games that sense their abilities and challenge them to go further. And I will avoid programs that contain what are called "inconsiderate hotspots"—clickable icons that set off bells and whistles but do little to propel the child to a new level of understanding.[12] (Software reviews often highlight these problems. To find the reviews, go to the Web sites listed in appendix II.) More than anything, I promise to hand my kids the mouse and let them steer.

Finally, being on the computer at that moment must jibe with my attempts to provide them with a healthy, fulfilling day. At the age that preschoolers can begin playing independently on computers, they are also old enough to occupy themselves for decent stretches of time with pretend play, coloring books or playing in the sandbox. And I want those things for my kids. But different days and different circumstances call for different decisions. Some families live in apartments without easy access to sandboxes or safe playgrounds. Many children don't have siblings to stimulate and sustain their pretend play. Our family is fortunate to have both of those outlets. Still, when playtime devolves into fuss time, or when I need a surefire way to keep my daughters out of my hair while I finish a phone call, I may opt for screen time. If my choice is between a high-quality participatory TV program or a dead-end computer game, I may turn on the TV. If the options are a TV show or a chance to play with KidPix, the software may win. And if the weather cooperates, and I have the leisure of watching them from the back porch as they jump in the leaf piles in our unfenced yard? No doubts there. I vote for the outdoor frolic.

NOTES

1. Excerpted from "Toy Wishes Holiday 2006 All Stars," a list of the "brightest, most innovative toys in over 20 different categories," according

to the editorial board of *Toy Wishes: The Ultimate Guide to Family Entertainment*, a magazine that comes out twice a year.

2. Siegler, DeLoache, and Eisenberg, 2003, p. 197.

3. I read about Rovee-Collier's classic mobile experiment in a paper she wrote, "Shifting the Focus from What to Why," *Infant Behavior and Development* 19 (1996): 391.

4. Calvert et al., 2007, pp. 11–15.

5. Buckleitner, 2004, pp. 69–73.

6. Ibid., p. 83.

7. As several reviewers on Amazon.com noted about the ebook for children as young as 6 months old, it seems a little much to expect a baby at that age to control her fingers enough to deliberately point and press. And low-tech pictures may be engaging enough without the technology. The mother of a 15-month-old wrote, "My daughter just wanted to hold the book on her lap and look at it. Maybe it's just not the toy for her."

8. Caplovitz, 2005, p. 66.

9. Ibid., p. 86.

10. Calvert, Strong, and Gallagher, 2005, p. 584.

11. Gee, 2005, p. 10.

12. The term "inconsiderate hotspots" comes from Linda Labbo, a language and literacy professor at the University of Georgia.

Chapter Eleven

Will Screen Time
Make My Children Fat?

When I started interviewing families about how they used media in their households, I expected to find two types of parents. One type, I figured, is just going with the flow, not thinking much about media and its impact. In my mind, I called them the "whatevers." The other type, I figured, is as neurotic as I am. They are the "worriers."

I suspect the whatevers are out there, but it was the worriers I kept encountering, across all income levels and ethnicities. One of the concerns I heard repeatedly was how screen time might adversely affect children's quality of life, leading them to a couch-potato existence and an ever-widening girth.

One mother in Washington DC, for example, told me of the angst she felt when her daughter, then between 2 and 3 years old, was under the care of a nanny who also had responsibility for a playmate at a friend's house. Every few days, when her daughter was at her playmate's house, the kids would watch a few *Elmo* videos. This made her nervous. She didn't like the thought of the children sitting in front of a TV screen instead of moving around. "Why engage in something passive?" she asked. "Why set her up for that?"

The father of a 9-month-old girl in DC had similar worries. "I watched a lot of TV as a kid," he told me, and he planned to be more careful with his daughter's consumption. Her exposure so far had been limited to an occasional look at *OyBaby*, a DVD that features Hebrew songs for children. This stay-at-home dad, who is caring for his baby while finishing a graduate degree, was already making plans to limit her screen time and increase her activity levels as she got older. "I don't want her to be one of those kids stuck inside playing videogames on a sunny day," he said.

Obesity among children has become an epidemic, with almost 19 percent of American kids aged 6 to 11 now qualifying as obese, according to the Centers for Disease Control. That percentage is more than three times the incidence in the 1960s, when obesity affected 4 percent of children that age.[1] As scientists try to trace the source of this surge, the list of possibilities keeps growing. Do we blame fast food restaurants? High-fructose corn syrup? Processed foods made with trans-fats? Oversized portions? Uncontrolled snacking? Fruit juices? Poor sleep habits? Less breast-feeding? Fewer bike rides and walks to school? Too much TV viewing after school? Videogames that last for hours?

The quantity and quality of calories ingested by today's children are obviously culprits, but screen media is also a prime suspect. Conventional wisdom tells us that watching TV is so sedentary and so addictive that it must be replacing the time children would otherwise be running around outside. Meanwhile, a rise in media designed for the very young has coincided with a rise in overweight toddlers and preschoolers. This decade started with about 10 percent of children aged 2 to 5 being overweight. In four years, the number rose to nearly 14 percent. (Young Hispanic boys are a subject of particular concern, with nearly a quarter of them now overweight.)[2] Meanwhile, a recent NIH study showed that children who are overweight at age 2 are more likely to be overweight throughout childhood.[3] Given this statistic, parents of babies and toddlers have good cause to be worried about television and computers sucking their children into a vortex of inactivity.

But is that really what is happening? To my surprise, I discovered that many researchers who study obesity and screen time are putting less and less faith in that hypothesis. Television use is associated with obesity. Few people question that fact.[4] Research has shown that heavy television use and heavy kids go hand in hand, even when you control for demographics like income. But talk about whether, or how, television causes obesity, and things get more complicated. If it does have an impact, scientists say, it probably has less to do with displacing physical exercise than we might assume.

Take, for example, a study published in the journal *Pediatrics* in April 2006, in which researchers examined data on nearly 3,000 randomly selected children around the United States. The children's parents or caregivers had been asked to fill out what is called a "time diary," a log providing hour-by-hour details on their children's activities the previous day, including every moment they watched television. Poring over the entries, the authors of the study—led by Elizabeth Vandewater of the University of Texas—sorted every activity into categories. Entries like walking, playing in the backyard or going to the playground were labeled "active play." Then they analyzed the data to find out whether it could be said that, the more children watched television, the less they engaged in active play. With one exception concerning 9- to 12-year-olds on the weekend, the answer was no. "Our findings do not support the notion that active playtime is negatively related to television viewing," the authors wrote.[5]

This result surprised me, but on reflection, it makes some sense. Just because the TV is off doesn't mean a kid is suddenly doing something active. Maybe he is coloring, reading, sitting in a car or sleeping. Conversely, kids who watch TV do not necessarily neglect going to the playground at other times during the day. "In the absence of data, most people believe that kids are sedentary, but there are actually lots of studies that discount that," said Dale Kunkel, a communication professor at the University of Arizona who has been conducting research on television and children for decades.

"For example, some studies compare the activity levels of heavy TV users and light TV users and they find that kids are getting the same amount of exercise. . . . This means that kids are resilient. TV is not driving their lives."

But that doesn't mean that TV is off the hook. Kunkel and other experts believe that something else about television may be having an impact. The past few years have seen a flurry of studies in some promising new directions that examine not only how much time children sit in front of a screen but what they are watching and where they are watching it. Content and context are the words that have emerged over and over again in recent research on media. They are also at the heart of how we parents should think about media's influence over our children's fitness and health.

~⌒

In April 2005, I saw a food pyramid unlike anything put out by the U.S. Department of Agriculture. Presented at a meeting of the Society for Research in Child Development, it was created by Cynthia Scheibe, executive director of a media literacy program called Project Look Sharp at Ithaca College, and it was based on the portrayals of nutrition that children see on commercials during and between children's television shows. "I wanted to know, based on what is on television, what that food pyramid might look like," Scheibe said.

The official pyramid, as you know, is supposed to help Americans remember how to healthfully apportion their diet. It has a wide base of grains, another wide section for fruits and vegetables, a thinner middle section showing meat and dairy, and a tiny triangle at the top representing fats and sugars. The pyramid Scheibe presented didn't look anything like that. In fact, it didn't look like a pyramid at all. It was shaped like a top-heavy hourglass instead, with a huge, precariously placed block at the top representing fats and sugars, a tiny midsection for dairy, fruits and vegetables, and a large block at the bottom representing grains. "Those are refined, not whole, grains," she said, referring to the white bread and pasta variety. "And the vegetables are only there," she said, pointing to the middle section, "because of ketchup." "We can tell kids all we want about eating fruits and vegetables," she said, "but that's not what they are seeing."

Continuing with her presentation, Scheibe showed a photograph of a bowl of apples, oranges and bananas. "This is fruit," she said. She clicked to the next slide, which showed a box of Froot Loops cereal and a package of Fruit Gushers chewy snacks. "This," she said, "is fruit on television." In experiments, Scheibe said, she would put photographs like these in front of children and ask which ones have fruit in them. Sometimes they wouldn't even mention the real fruit. "They'd say Froot Loops."

Junk food commercials on television are nothing new.[6] Most of us are so accustomed to advertisements that we simply wave them away, putting little faith in their messages. But think about the years of training that have led us to such easy dismissal. We may not realize how few of those critical thinking skills have yet to be developed in the minds of very young children.

In the 1970s, when pediatricians and dentists became concerned about the number of dental cavities they were seeing in young children, developmental psychologists started to conduct a number of studies on how children understand commercials. Perhaps, the thinking went, television advertisements for candy, soda pop and sugared cereals were leading children to spend their allowances on sugar-filled treats and to nag their parents to buy them.

Experiments soon uncovered the susceptibility of children, how easily swayed they are by the joyous, bright shots of children and cartoon characters enjoying "part of a balanced breakfast." Kids under the age of 8, researchers concluded, do not understand what they are watching. They can name the products, yes, and they may even be able to label what they are seeing as "commercials," but they do not understand the motivations behind the commercials. They don't realize that they are viewing something purposefully designed to persuade them to buy that product.

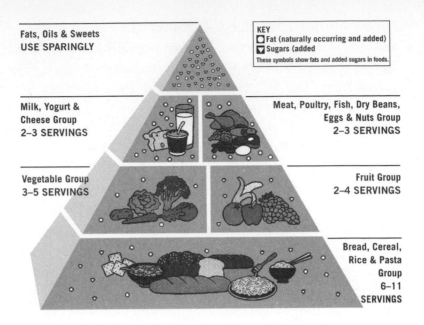

"They say, the purpose is 'to tell me about things I need to get,'" explained Dale Kunkel of Arizona, who has led the American Psychology Association's task force on advertising and children. "There is no cognitive filter. They accept everything that is included in an advertisement as fair, balanced and truthful information." Parents can, and do, try to counter the messages, Kunkel said, "but when you see ads for Twinkies and sugared cereals all the time, it leads children to think that it's acceptable to eat these on a regular basis."

By 1978, the research was strong enough for the Federal Trade Commission to call advertising to children "unfair and deceptive." But a few years later, Congress barred the commission from restricting advertising to children, citing a violation of the country's tenets of free speech. In other countries, stricter measures have stuck. Australia, parts of Belgium, Norway, Greece, the Canadian province of Quebec, and Sweden have since instituted some form of ban on television advertising before, after and during children's

The Food "Pyramid" on Children's TV Commercials

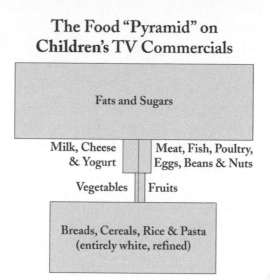

If the traditional food pyramid, left, were redrawn to reflect the foods that children see in television commercials, it might look something like this, right. (Reprinted with permission by Cynthia Scheibe, Ithaca College)

programming.[7] The United Kingdom's regulatory agency recently barred the broadcast of commercials for high-fat and sugary foods during children's programs, on approach that the American Academy of Pediatrics has urged the U.S. Congress to take as well.[8]

Some people have argued that kids today are less naive, that because they are surrounded by advertising and media, they have a much better handle on how they are being manipulated than a generation ago. Children, however, start recognizing brand logos as early as age 3, according to peer-reviewed research.[9] I'd argue that brand recognition starts even earlier than that. My girls have been pointing excitedly to McDonald's golden arches since before they could talk. Could there be any validity to the notion that today's children, exposed to the ways of marketing at such early ages, are better able to sort through the onslaught?

Mark Blades, a psychologist at the University of Sheffield in the United Kingdom, set me straight. For several years, he and his colleagues have been putting children through a series of experiments designed to illuminate how much they understand about the persuasive intent behind advertising. An early experiment, for example, involved television spots for products children had never seen before, like Chappies bubble gum from South Africa. When asked what the advertisements were for, 6-year-olds said that they didn't know; perhaps they were a source of information ("to show you what's new"), or they were supposed to give people a break ("to get time to go to the toilet"). Not one 6-year-old gave any evidence of understanding the advertisement's purpose, whereas about a third of 10-year-olds did (saying, for example, that the commercial was "to convince people to buy things").[10] Since then, Blades has led or been involved with fifteen studies, which have included nearly 1,000 children across a broad demographic spectrum, showing that not until 7 or 8 years old do children show signs of understanding the purpose of advertising.

Advertisers counter that children may know more than they can say. Maybe we are underestimating our kids, they say. Or perhaps parents should simply get better at teaching their children to be more skeptical. Blades, Kunkel and other psychologists shake their heads, arguing that children's minds can only move so far so fast. There are innate hurdles of cognitive functioning to overcome first.

To demonstrate one of these cognitive hurdles, developmental psychologists use a story-telling and interview technique. In one-on-one sessions with elementary- and preschool-aged children, researchers start by telling a story about a little boy who wanted his parents to buy him a bird. No, says the boy's mother, the bird will be too noisy. No, says his father, the bird will be too messy. The researchers then turn to the children and ask, what should the boy say to change his parents' minds? To answer this question well, a child must recognize that his parents have minds in the first place, that they think about different things than what the child himself might be thinking about. This concept, which is known in psychology as having a "theory of the mind," is considered well beyond the ability of toddlers and only in the beginning stages of development for preschoolers. And even if a preschooler is getting there, the child then needs to take another mental leap to mull over some negotiating positions.

"You've got to be working out what is in your parent's mind already, and trying to find a counter argument to your parent's beliefs," Blades said. "The child is saying, Hmmm, my mom's got this in her mind. What should I tell my mom to persuade her?" The child might think, can I convince Mom that this type of bird is quiet? Should I tell Dad that I will clean up the bird's messes? For young children, he said, "it's very hard to do."

Blades and his doctoral students recently used this technique with forty children, ages 6 to 8, and then asked them about their favorite advertisements, questioning whether they understood the purpose of the ad. The children who could come up with ways for the boy to persuade his parents to buy the bird were the same children who understood the intent of advertising. And only the children nearing the end of their seventh year could do it.[11]

Understanding advertising on Web sites may be even more difficult for young kids. There are hints, so far, that young children cannot distinguish between advertisements and content on Web sites, let alone be able to understand the intent behind the ads. In one of Blades's studies, for example, only 12 percent of 6-year-olds could answer the question, "Where is the advertisement?" when shown a Web site with a banner ad.[12] "We were quite shocked at how bad the children are" at simply recognizing Internet advertising, Blades said. Another set of experiments conducted by Mary McIlrath, a marketing researcher in Chicago, showed that even older children—ages 9 to 12—do not judge banner advertising, "advergames," or pop-up animations as anything more than pictures or services designed to inform and entertain.[13]

This type of research has led people to seriously consider whether the fattening of American children has something to do with commercials that feed children unhealthy messages about what to eat. Scrutiny has also focused on the licensing of movie and TV characters that appear on packages of high-fat or high-sugar foods. Even the Federal Trade Commission has become involved, hosting a workshop on the issue in 2005 that resulted in the publication of several recommendations for change, several of which came from the food and media industries. Representatives from those companies, as well as the industry's self-regulation organization called the Children's Advertising Review Unit, are intent on showing that they can regulate themselves and make responsible choices without government intervention.

In 2006, the Institutes of Medicine released a 516-page report titled "Food Marketing to Children and Youth," written by a committee of experts in media and health as well as a few people who work on marketing campaigns for children's products. The report reviewed the findings of 123 published and peer-reviewed journal articles that touch in some way on the consumption of TV, the influence of advertising, and children's obesity. It concluded that "food and beverage marketing influences the preferences and purchase requests of children, influences consumption at least in the short term, is a likely contributor to less healthful diets, and may contribute to negative diet-related health outcomes and risks among children and youth." For children age 2 to 5, the report said, there is moderate evidence that TV ads influence what they eat.[14] But the report stopped short of saying there was evidence that television advertising or marketing strategies cause children to become fat. It could only say that "statistically, there is strong evidence that exposure to television advertising is associated with adiposity [fatness] in children."[15]

What else could be causing this connection between television and obesity in children? There was little evidence for the TV-makes-kids-sedentary argument. There wasn't much evidence, either, for other possibilities, like the theory that obesity causes TV watching (based on the idea that obese children will watch more TV because they are more ostracized). In other words, it didn't look like there were many alternative explanations. Still, the report did not put full blame at the feet of marketers. Instead, it put the ball in their court, calling on the media and marketing industries to show "leadership" in using their influence to send healthy messages to children. "This is a public health priority," the report said, "of the highest order."[16]

~~~

My oldest daughter was not yet 3 when I got a taste of the power of the Princesses—the Disney Princesses, that is. There they were in the grocery store, gracing the boxes of Kellogg's fruit snacks, which sat on the shelves just at Janelle's eye level. The exclamations started immediately: "I want that, Mommy, I want that!"

Margo G. Wootan remembers a grocery-store moment when her daughter was not yet 2 but still reached excitedly for the Frosted Flakes boxes with the *Sesame Street* characters on them. "She was saying 'Big Bird! Big Bird,'" Wootan told me. "She didn't even know what was in the box."

For Wootan, that experience catalyzed a crusade. In 2003, as the nutrition policy director for the Center for Science in the Public Interest, Wootan wrote a report about food marketing called "Pestering Parents." The center now issues guidelines for what it calls "responsible food marketing," which call for media companies to be careful about with whom they do business. If a company like Disney licenses its characters to food manufacturers, the guidelines say, it should at least make sure that the food is of decent nutritional value. Young children aren't thinking about a balanced diet; they just see characters they love and want to have them—now. "Why would you want a strawberry or grape when you can have a grape-flavored fruit snack shaped like a Disney Princess?" Wootan said. "An apple can't compete."

Sesame Workshop, influenced by mounting research on obesity and the power of marketing, came to a similar conclusion in 2004 when it launched a coalition called Healthy Habits for Life, in which *Sesame Street* characters help to promote physical activity and healthy nutrition for young kids. Participants include the U.S. Department of Health and Human Services, the National Association for the Education of Young Children, and the Ad Council, among others. Big Bird and his friends have had nothing to do with Frosted Flakes since.

The strength with which their children identify with commercialized characters has become a hot topic for many parents. What is it about *Dora the Explorer* or *Thomas the Tank Engine* that makes children squirm for anything emblazoned with their faces? Susan Linn, in her acclaimed book *Consuming Kids*, argues that a reliance on commercially generated characters is holding children back from imagining their own world and make-believe figures. But Jackie Marsh, a senior lecturer at the University of Sheffield who studies media literacy and early childhood, suggests that media characters can serve as reflections of identity as well as transitional objects for children, soothing them the way a teddy bear might, always there and always theirs.[17]

Wherever you sit in this debate, the power of commercialized characters on children is clearly strong. It has even become the subject of new psychological research. Sesame Workshop, for example, tested what would happen if children saw Elmo associated with different foods. In a pilot study, researchers showed preschoolers a picture of broccoli and a picture of a partially unwrapped Hershey's chocolate bar. The pictures sat side by side. When asked which one they wanted to eat, 22 percent of children voted for broccoli, and 78 percent preferred chocolate. Then researchers took out pictures that included Elmo and another character. With Elmo affixed to the picture of broccoli and an unknown character (from a TV show that never aired) on the chocolate, the desire for chocolate dropped and the preference for broccoli shot up to 50 percent. When Elmo was affixed to the chocolate, the chocolate became even more desirable, selected by 89 percent of kids.[18]

A larger second study, not yet published, tested real foods with children. Researchers set two little cups in front of the kids, each containing small pieces of broccoli or chocolate. When a cardboard cut-out of a *Sesame Street* character stood nearby to promote the food, children tried more of it. The changes in food preferences were not as striking as with the pilot experiment, said Jennifer Kotler, Sesame Workshop's director of education and research. (Even with the Elmo effect, it's hard for broccoli to compete with real chocolate sitting inches away.) But significant findings remain. "Popeye has been credited with changing the spinach industry," Kotler said. "If we can use our characters in more socially responsible ways, it could help." Sesame Workshop now has licensing deals with companies like Sunkist and Del Monte to encourage children to eat more fruits and vegetables.

Disney recently announced a change of heart, too. For years, the Disney cable channel has been commercial-free—with the important exception of promotions for Disney movies and some spots about physical activity sponsored by fast food companies. But in the fall of 2006, it announced another step: it will serve healthier meals in its theme parks and cut back on its licensing of characters to companies that make high-fat, high-sugar foods. In 2006, 40 percent of Disney's licensing portfolio included inappropriate sweets and high-fat snacks. By 2010, under its new guidelines, the company plans to bring that percentage down to 15 percent (allowing for occasional foods, like birthday cakes and ice cream). Mickey Mouse and company have already started to appear on fruits and vegetables. "The time was right to associate Disney characters with healthier foods," said Disney spokesman Jonathan Friedland.

Disney Princess fruit snacks won't disappear immediately; we have to wait for Disney's contract with Kellogg to run out. But Wootan and other health advocates praised the move, and other companies have since announced strategies for promoting healthier foods to kids. The news brought me some relief. The power struggles in the grocery store will still be there, and it remains to be seen whether these licensing deals will spur the agriculture industry to raise the prices of fruits and vegetables, but if my daughters will be nagging me about frozen corn instead of fruit snacks, I'll take it.

~⌒

In May 2006, the Henry J. Kaiser Family Foundation came out with a statistic that sent jaws dropping: a third of children aged 0 to 6 have a TV in their bedroom. The percentages for babies and toddlers were smaller, but still surprising. Among infants up to age 1, the number is 19 percent. For children 2 to 3 years old, it is 29 percent. A small part of these figures can be explained by children sharing a room with their parents. Another chunk includes children who share a room with a sibling. But a majority of the children with a TV in their room have their own room.[19]

These statistics mystify the worriers. Parents with concerns about television's impact on their kids wonder why any parent would give a young child a TV set and place it in a room that is supposed to be a sanctuary of sleep. Victoria Rideout and Elizabeth Hamel, the authors of the Kaiser Foundation report, wondered too. They found that, in more than half the cases, TVs were put in bedrooms so that parents could watch the TV; grown-ups wanted to free up the family television to watch adult-oriented programs, and the solution was to give the children their own television sets.

What these parents might not know, however, is that scientists are starting to uncover links between televisions in children's bedrooms and the prevalence of obesity. Barbara A. Dennison, a pediatrician and obesity expert who oversees five prevention programs at the New York State Department of Health, published a study in 2002 that included more than 1,400 low-income families with children ages 1 to 4. The data showed a significant correlation between a child's body mass index and the existence of a television in the child's bedroom. The heavier the child, the more likely that he or she had a bedroom TV set. And in this particular sample, the proportion of bedroom TV watchers was high: 40 percent of children had a TV in their rooms.

Those children, on average, also watched 4.6 hours more TV per week than their counterparts without TVs in their bedrooms.[20] Dennison said that she believes a family's dynamics—particularly the habits of the parents—play a large role in how and in what contexts children watch TV. "One of the real problems that people tend not to talk about is that to reduce TV viewing in children, you have to reduce TV viewing in parents," Dennison said. But that isn't easy. "People get angry," she said, at the idea that they have to change their lifestyle.

What about simply asking parents to take the TV out of their child's bedroom? That's not easy either. A few years ago, a team of researchers, including Amy Jordan of the Annenberg Public Policy Center, conducted a series of focused interviews with families in three cities—Chicago, Philadelphia, and Richmond, Virginia. One of their intentions was to generate ideas for getting parents to remove TV sets from their children's rooms. But they encountered huge resistance. "No TV in my kids' rooms? That would be punishing me," said one parent. "They would always be bickering."[21] Jordan has come to realize that the cultural barriers to changing TV habits are daunting. "We're talking about changing a system," she said.

The results have led Jordan and her colleagues to shift expectations. The families they interviewed had children over the age of 6, and two-thirds of the sample had TVs in the bedroom.[22] Maybe the most effective strategy, they realized, would be to reach out to younger families—those with babies and toddlers—who haven't set up a TV in their child's room just yet. "It's a lot easier to not put the TV in than to take it out," said James C. Hersey of Research Triangle Institute (RTI) International, a co-author of the study.

The bedroom conundrum drove home to me how much the location of the TV can make a difference in how it is used. In our house, we have two televisions. One is in our living room, hiding behind cabinet doors when it isn't being used. The other, with a much larger screen, is in the basement, where my husband and I retreat for movie nights, episodes of *CSI*, *House*, and other surround-sound indulgences. Neither set is within viewing range of the dining room table—a fact that irked me during the days of the World Cup, when soccer games would inevitably coincide with meal time.

But in many households, the TV is part of the dining experience—whether on purpose or because of constrained living quarters. About 53 percent of children under 6 eat at least one meal or snack while watching TV or videos, according to recent data from the Kaiser Foundation.[23] "I'll turn on the TV in the morning and [my son] will watch cartoons," a mother in Irvine, California, said during a Kaiser focus group. "My kids will have breakfast, and then we take my daughter to school. I'll turn the TV on for him when we get home. . . . We'll usually watch TV when we're eating lunch. . . . He thinks that you only eat in front of the TV."[24]

Could eating while under the influence of TV be partly responsible for the association between television and obesity? Jordan, Dennison, and others think the notion is worth investigating. Very few research studies have probed this question, and in those few, results are mixed. A study at Pennsylvania State University published in 2006, for example, showed that, while watching a twenty-two-minute cartoon, children ate less food than their nonviewing counterparts. The children who ate more, however, were also the children who made a habit of eating while watching TV at home. Nutritionists say they need to learn more about how home environments affect eating habits in general. Until more research is done, it is going to be hard to pin down exactly what is going on when kids view and chew.[25]

~⁓

A television set cannot make a child fat. But research on what children watch (like commercials for unhealthy food) and where they watch (whether in bedrooms or at the dinner table) is enough to keep me relatively vigilant about how TV is used with our kids. Like many parents I have interviewed, I try to avoid commercials by using video-on-demand services and DVDs instead of television shows. Cable channels that do not accept advertising—like PBS, the Disney channel and Noggin—help, too, though I'm probably not alone in cringing when my children squeal with excitement when the PBS sponsorship spot includes the sign for Chuck E. Cheese's. I hope that the growing number of children's shows encouraging viewers to get up and dance, like *The Wiggles* and *The Doodlebops*, counter other weight-inducing influences.

Another way to lessen the burden of worry about TV and obesity is to think about screen media within the context of your family's lifestyle and food choices. What counts in the end is how many calories your children eat and how many they burn off. If your family eats nutritious foods and has a relatively healthy lifestyle—engaging in physical activity, getting involved in the community, and gathering for TV-free family meals—you may find that you and your kids don't have time to watch more than a moderate amount of TV in the first place. "Media seems to be one piece of the puzzle, not the whole thing," said Hersey of RTI International. "It's easy to look for the simple answer, but what it boils down to is active parents and supportive communities."

NOTES

1. Results are from the National Health and Nutrition Examination Survey. Most recent data is for 2003–2004.

2. Ogden et al., 2006, pp. 1551–1552.

3. "Overweight in Early Childhood Increases Chances for Obesity at Age 12," NIH News, September 5, 2006, accessed November 30, 2006, from www.nih.gov/news/pr/sep2006/nichd-05.htm.

4. See chapter 5 of the Institute of Medicine's 2006 report, *Food Marketing to Children and Youth: Threat or Opportunity?* for a thorough review of peer-reviewed studies that show a relationship between fatness (called adiposity) and television.

5. Vandewater, Bickham, and Lee, 2006, p. e189.

6. In fact, the raw number of food commercials aimed at children has actually decreased since 1977, according to data from Pauline M. Ippolito from the Bureau of Economics within the Federal Trade Commission. (See slide 7 of her 2005 presentation to the FTC, "TV Advertising to Children, 1977 v. 2004.") She did not present data on the number of licensing deals between media companies and the food industry (the mechanism through which the Disney Princesses appear on Kellogg's fruit snacks), but it's not unreasonable to assume that they, meanwhile, have increased in number.

7. Each ban is slightly different, of course. (Greece, for example, bans toy advertising on TV before 10 pm.) For a history of the regulations on advertising to children, see McGinnis, Gootman, and Kraak, 2006, pp. 30–33. The information on Greece, Australia and Belgium comes from p. 239 of a 2001 article by Oates, Blades, and Gunter.

8. Policy statement of the AAP Committee on Communications, "Children, Adolescents, and Advertising," *Pediatrics,* December 2006, p. 2566.

9. McGinnis, Gootman, and Kraak, 2006, p. 31.

10. Oates, Blades, and Gunter, 2001, p. 243.

11. Blades, 2006, slides 36–39.

12. Ibid., slide 44.

13. Interview with Mary McIlrath, December 2006.

14. McGinnis, Gootman, and Kraak, 2006, pp. 8–9.

15. Ibid., p. 9.

16. Ibid., p. 15.

17. Marsh, 2005, pp. 38–40.

18. Kotler, 2005, slides 12–14.

19. Rideout and Hamel, 2006, p. 18.

20. Dennison et al., 2004, p. 1032.

21. From a presentation by James C. Hersey at the biennial meeting of the Society for Research in Child Development, Atlanta, 2005.

22. Jordan et al., 2006, p. 1303.

23. Rideout, 2004, p. 38.

24. Ibid., p. 24.

25. Francis and Birch, 2006, p. 598.

Chapter Twelve

How Do Real Families
Make Smart Media Choices?

The guilt, the guilt. A woman I interviewed one morning laid it on thick. We were talking about toddlers watching television. She is a professor specializing in language development at a northeastern university, and I was asking about some videos she had used in her lab. Though she had witnessed very young children learning words from controlled video training, she saw no reason why they should be exposed to the TV. I asked, "but what about parents who just pop a video in for fifteen minutes so they can go take a shower?"

"I raised twins," she told me. "And when I went to take a shower, I didn't put the TV on. The kids just played in the Ultrasaucer. I'm puzzled by the idea that parents need the TV to take a shower. It's like, isn't there Playdoh? Markers? Blocks?"

I felt my neck tighten. This woman's children were only ten years older than mine, but it seemed she had forgotten the difference between an 8-month-old who might tolerate an Ultrasaucer but who would suck a marker dry and an 18-month-old who wouldn't stand to be restrained for a minute and who still, if given the chance, might suck a marker dry. I tried to sound nonchalant and put a joking tone in my voice. "In our house," I said, "giving Playdoh to my 18-month-old would mean that I'd be picking Playdoh out of the rug for the next hour."

"I put plastic over the rug," she told me. "I'd use water-color paints that wash out."

She went on to tell me how she and her husband had created a safe room for the twins to play in. "All the sockets were covered with plugs," she told me. "The floor was covered with plastic. They had pots and pans to bang on. The living room was blocked off. The bathroom was blocked off. But they could still wander to a certain extent."

I swallowed my agitation and let the matter drop. But my head was teeming with comebacks. What if the open layout of your house doesn't allow for blocking off all the other rooms? Besides, wouldn't you want your children to come get you if something happened to one of them? I'll never forget the panic that ensued one morning when I tried to sneak in a shower and an over-exuberant Janelle, just 30 months old, slammed the door on her crawling sister's finger and split it open, forcing an emergency doctor's visit and multiple stitches. Sure, sure, one solution might be to keep the children with you in the bathroom, securing all cabinet doors and toilet seats for safety. But what if your kid was like my second daughter, who at 20 months of age pushed a stool next to the sink, climbed up to the counter, retrieved a bottle of hand lotion, and squirted it all over the mirror, the floor, and the bedroom carpet until I managed, cold and dripping wet from my half-finished shower, to extract it from her chubby little hands?

It's true that, before the days of television, parents raised children and still managed to take showers. And it wasn't that I needed to pop in a video every day. But I couldn't help thinking that maybe something was different back in the old days. Maybe fathers weren't out the door at 6:30 am trying to beat the dreaded morning commute. Maybe mothers didn't worry about washing their hair because they didn't leave the house as often. Maybe parents resorted to playpens and simply ignored the sound of their babies' wailing to get out.

I calmed down by interviewing parents who were, right that very minute, raising young children. A few interviews were with struggling single mothers and poor immigrant families. Most of the interviews were with middle-class parents who had stable homes and the money to pay for babysitters. In a few cases, I did meet parents for whom the TV was either background noise or filled with content inappropriate for young children, or both. Given what the recent research had taught me about what happens when screen time is used poorly, they were doing more harm than they knew. But more often I found parents who were thinking hard about the media they used with and around their kids, who were trying to set realistic limits and make smart choices.[1]

The interviews taught me how much our generation's reliance upon and desire for media shapes what we want for our children. As one mother put it: "I love reading—and I love television." I heard from movie buffs, sports nuts, software designers, Web-news junkies and parents of all stripes who revel in well-written television shows that make them think more deeply about the world. Nearly all of them grew up watching *Sesame Street*; nearly all harbored the belief that TV shows can do good.

I also learned how much parents' decisions are theirs to make. Families are microcosms of peculiar and particular cultures, little worlds unto themselves. Everyone's emotional stresses and financial pressures are different, everyone's family routine is different, everyone's children are different. Stay-at-home parents who can afford to vary their days with Gymboree classes and periodic relief from a babysitter may not need as many video breaks as a stay-at-home parent without those resources. A working mother who comes home to a partner who helps with dinner and bedtime may see TV differently than a mother coming home with a headache and no one to help.

That said, families do want models to follow. Many interviews ended with questions to me, such as: What are other families saying? How do other parents handle TV time? What rules do they institute in their households?

The following is a roundup of rules, guidelines, and ways of thinking that I heard from the families I interviewed. I have chosen stories and tips that synchronized best with what I learned from developmental psychologists on what is most appropriate for young children. And in many cases, whether they realized it or not, the parents described below had chosen to integrate the TV and computer into their lives according to the three principles that I've noted elsewhere in this book: They were thinking about content. They were thinking about context. And they were thinking about the needs of their child.

Families Instituting Time Limits

The American Academy of Pediatrics recommends no screen time before the age of 2 and no more than two hours a day for children over the age of 2. Several parents said they had a hard time with the first half of this recommendation and an easy time with the second. As children get older, as routines get established, and as child care and preschool opportunities expand, it can become easier to fill the days with alternate activities.

"When she didn't come to school, she watched a lot of TV," said a Spanish-speaking mother with a 4-year-old daughter whose household income was low enough to qualify for subsidized preschool in northern Virginia. Now that her daughter has school each day, the mother told me, she has much less time at home in front of the television. Her routine has become more settled. "Now when she comes home, she watches *Dragon Tales*, some other shows on PBS, then plays and draws," her mother said.

A mother in Washington DC told me that her family's rule is "one video a day." Her 3½-year-old son and a 22-month-old daughter are allowed to choose from a limited supply of thirty-minute videotapes and DVDs that the family has collected. "For me, thirty minutes of screen time is what works for our family. My husband and I have talked about it at length."

Another mother, who stays at home most of the time with her 19-month-old son, said she also tries to stick to a limit of thirty minutes a day. They live in a suburban area of northern Virginia. She pops in a Baby Einstein or Baby Babble video in the late afternoon and folds laundry or does paperwork while he watches. "It's that last half-hour before dinner," she said. "That's when you're like, how are we going to fill this time?"

One mother I spoke to had twins who were almost 2 years old. She said she didn't use any TV or videos. They had been relatively easy to care for so far, she told me, a fact she attributed to them having each other to play with. The mother worked part-time, teaching classes in New York City a few mornings a week. Her husband worked long hours, so she had hired a nanny to help five days a week. "I'm lucky because I have our caregiver," she said. "I think if I didn't have that, I would probably put them in front of the TV. I'm fortunate that I can do that."

Families with Rules About When to Turn the TV On

The vast majority of families talked about using television shows, videos and computer games as ways to fill small holes in their days instead of being the default or primary activity. Their media use was considered in the larger context of their daily routine—one that became increasingly full as their children grew up. Think of all the pieces that child-development experts say should be part of a young child's day—time to play independently, time to become immersed in make-believe play with friends, time to sit at the table learning socialization during meals, time to pick up and inspect every stone in the driveway. And that's not including story time, naptime and grocery-cart time.

As a friend in Baltimore, the mother of two boys aged 2 and 4, wrote me in an email message: "We are in the habit of not having the TV on, and so our afternoons go by quite nicely, playing in the yard, having play dates, going to the zoo, the science center and napping." As a part-time working mom, she notes that she is not home with them every day. "I only have 3 days during the week at home with them. If I were home every day, the TV thing would probably change."

A few parents talked about being very purposeful with putting in a video at nearly the same time each day so that their children saw electronic media as being used at a particular time, for a particular purpose, with a beginning and an end. A mother on the Upper West Side of New York City with twin 3$\frac{1}{2}$-year-old boys told me that she uses videos only in the late afternoon, when it is too late to go out and too early to eat dinner. "If we lived in the suburbs and had a backyard," she said, it might be different. "But here, to get dressed, down the elevator and to the park—it's not realistic to do that in forty-five minutes."

A close friend of mine in Alexandria, Virginia, instituted a new rule for her children when they were 2 and 4 years old. "No TV when it is light outside," she declared. "It is just easier," she told me. "We don't have to negotiate." After dinner, she turns on the TV and clicks to the children's shows offered by her cable's on-demand service. The videos, she said, calm her kids down and serve as a good transition to bedtime, which still includes books.

A mother of a 4-year-old and 7-year-old in Arlington, Virginia, told me that her rules depend not on the time of the day, but the day of the week. Her kids are allowed only one thirty-minute TV show a day on the weekdays, but more on weekend mornings, usually from 7 am to 10 am. This way, she and her husband can sleep in—at least a little bit—and read the newspaper over coffee. "The AAP would frown at our household," she said. "But oh well."

For parents who work, the timing of television and computer use can make a significant difference in the way they relate to their children. Several mothers and fathers, for example, said that they set aside special "movie nights" to promote family togetherness. But electronic media can divide families, too. I didn't learn this from my interviews, but I will note it here to sound a warning: Elinor Ochs, director of the Center on Everyday Lives of Families in Los Angeles, has been studying how TV, computers and video-games are used among families in the Los Angeles area. Her team of researchers has been following families with video cameras to capture their daily routines. She said she was disturbed to find that many children are so engaged in their shows or videogames in the late afternoon that they do not even notice when their parent walks in the door from work. "Eighty-seven percent of the time," Ochs said, "they did not look up."

Families Controlling What Content Their Children Can Watch

Social workers at a northern Virginia preschool center told me the story of a low-income single mother who worked nights, some-times from 5 pm to 7 am, while her child stayed overnight with a babysitter. When her boy was around 3 years old, he was enrolled in the preschool, giving the mother time to rest during the day. But he was starting to act out. "He would use terrible language," his case worker said. He used the F-word. He kicked and lashed out at his classmates. It was soon discovered that the boy's babysitter watched television around the clock, and the boy seemed to be im-itating a lot of what he saw. "He would walk by a student and say, 'Loser,'" said a supervisor at the preschool. "I said, 'That sounds a lot like Nickelodeon.'"

"The mother figured out that she couldn't do the night shift anymore," the case worker continued. "And she didn't want any more babysitters who watched television." The mother found a day job and was able to put her son to bed at night. "He's not as hyper now," she told me. "He did a whole 180-degree turn."

Several parents said they made a point of avoiding programs with characters that acted aggressively and used adult language. They avoided the nightly news, soap operas, game shows, sitcoms or crime-scene dramas. They relied on children's shows only. But as research tells us, children's shows can vary widely in their appropriateness for young children, and many parents said they struggled to make good choices. Sometimes they discovered that a video was inappropriate only after turning it on.

The mother of a 13-month-old daughter in Hawaii said she recently bought a Scholastic video of children's stories. She saw it for sale in Costco and figured it was worth a try, even though it was labeled for children "3 years and up." When she tried it out at home, the result was a disaster. The stories seemed "surreal and strange," the mother told me, with characters that looked "kind of scary." One scene featured a dog that meowed like a cat, with a veterinarian pulling a cat out of the dog's body. "My daughter freaked out. She got really upset," the mother said. "I was holding her. I said I think it's going to be okay."

The mother in Arlington with two boys aged 4 and 7 said she learned to hold a hard line against any media made for older children. "I was the queen of innocuous," she said. "I may hate *Barney*, but we did *Barney*." She would not let her boys see any Disney movies before the age of 3, she said, and still refuses to let them see anything with shooting scenes. "I still let them watch *Teletubbies*," she said.

Some parents have watched TV with their children closely enough to make critical judgments about whether even "innocuous" programming was worth their children's time. A mother in Austin, Texas, with a 3½-year-old son and a 1-year-old daughter did not like Baby Einstein's *Language Nursery* video. She didn't think her son was getting anything out of it because words were uttered that held little relation to what was shown on the screen. "After that I said I'm watching everything with him," she told me. She said she came to love *Dora the Explorer* because she saw how her son responded to the use of the map. Because the map showed exactly how the story would progress, it enabled him to feel like he knew what was going to happen, and he could pay more attention to the moments of counting or sorting out shapes. "Dora always goes three places," she said. "It's predictable."

For this mother, time limits didn't mean as much as controlling content. The day before we talked (a day that had been so scorching hot in Austin that playgrounds were unbearable), her son had watched about two hours of television. "People say, they shouldn't have more than an hour of TV. I say, 'What are they watching?' You couldn't pay me to put on an hour of *Spongebob Square Pants*." She said she didn't like the way the characters on that show talked to each other.

Families Limiting Exposure to Commercials and Big-Business Marketing

A few parents said they objected to what they saw as the commercialization of childhood and had tailored their children's video, television and software consumption accordingly. To do so, they avoided broadcast television and instead used DVDs and video-digital recorders that allowed them to fast-forward through ads.

The mother in Washington DC with the 3½-year-old girl and a boy of 22 months told me that she avoided any programs tied to licensed merchandise. "I've been afraid of getting into problems with 'I will only wear my Dora T-shirt,' or 'I will only use my Dora fork.'" Her household does include toys from the LeapFrog company, she acknowledged, adding, "they have identified with Baby Tad, though we've tried to avoid that commercialization."

A mother with two boys, age 3 and 5, in Alexandria, Virginia, relayed that her older son has started to play the videogames offered on the NickJr.com Web site; "but I don't love how he can wander from games into ads," she told me. She prefers that he play with purchased software that doesn't feature any advertising.

It was interesting to hear parents' comments about PBS, the U.S. system of publicly funded television stations. Years ago, PBS programs ended with a simple announcement that the programming had been made possible by corporate donations and "viewers like you." Now PBS highlights its corporate donors, including Chuck E. Cheese and McDonald's, with short spots that include their logos. A mother of two girls, aged 4 and 7, in Washington DC said that, as a preschooler, her older daughter pined for what she used to call Mickledonalds, "because my nanny introduced her to McDonald's, and then she was fed the marketing through PBS." "They may not call them commercials," this mother said, "but they are commercials. Period."

On the other hand, several parents said they considered advertising and the licensing of television characters like Dora to be a necessary evil. A mother in New York City said that, because she believed in the value of Sesame Workshop's shows, she made a point of buying products with Elmo and Big Bird emblazoned on them. She said she figured that the nonprofit company needed the revenue generated from selling the rights to use images of *Sesame Street* characters.

Families Being Careful
About Where Screens Are Located

For many immigrant families who have come from third-world countries, having a television is a symbol of the good life, and having a TV in a bedroom is even better. I heard stories of bedroom TVs from social workers at multiple agencies that work with poor immigrant mothers. A Spanish-speaking mother of three children—ages 9, 5 and 1—told me that she tries to shield her baby from the noise of the TV by staying in the living room while her older children watch TV in their shared bedroom. In some cases, social workers explained, the TV is in the bedroom because the bedroom is essentially the living room for poor families who share living quarters. I visited a mother with a 7-month-old baby who, along with her husband, spent the entire evening in the bedroom, starting at 5 or 6 pm, because they shared their apartment with another immigrant family that was granted use of the living room at night. For this mother and her husband, there was nothing to do but watch TV.

Several middle-class parents with their own homes told me that they put the television in places that would discourage their family members from automatically turning it on when they came home. The mother of a 9-month-old in Silver Spring, Maryland, told me in an email, "We only have one TV, and we keep it in the basement. [The baby] is never down there, and my husband and I watch a few shows in the late evening. Consequently, there is no temptation to turn it on upstairs." Another mother said: "We have doors on our TV, so we can close it up."

The mother I spoke with from Austin, Texas, said: "The TV needs to be in public places where I can see it." The family computer, which her 3½-year-old son often uses to play educational software, is also purposefully and publicly placed. "At the point my son learns about chat rooms," she said, "I'm going to be on him like a hawk. I want him to know at that any moment I'll be there with him."

Watching during meals was forbidden among many families I interviewed. "We don't watch with dinner; that's not allowed," said a mother of two in Arlington, Virginia. What about watching videos in the car? Some parents described in-car DVD players as essential for long trips. For children over 30 months old and, therefore, following narratives, the videos staved off whining, at least for a few hours. But a few parents said they made a point of not allowing DVD-watching on shorter trips, like visits to the grocery store or the commute to nursery school. That time, they said, was good for parent-child conversation, though it often occurred over the din of the children's music CDs they opted for instead.

Families Limiting Background TV

Everyone has a story to tell about what they were doing on the morning of September 11, 2001. One of the mothers I interviewed said the events of that day caused her to change her morning viewing habits around her first child, who was 2 at the time.

"I'll never forget," she said. "We were watching the *Today* show, and we watched the plane hit. I was tying her shoelaces. We just didn't expect to see . . . I hope she doesn't remember it."

The mother wanted to keep watching, but she switched to the video player. "My impulse was to go to the TV, but I just couldn't. I declared it an all-*Barney* day," she said. She held off watching anything until her husband, who had been in downtown Washington DC, arrived home. "It was very hard," she said. "But it was pivotal in my thinking that day. I said, 'This is too much. I can't watch TV that is scary to her. I just have to turn it off.'"

Many parents said they decided to change their own viewing patterns a few months after their babies were born, but breaking habits wasn't easy. A mother of 20-month-old twins in New York City said she loved watching morning news shows. At one point in our interview, she told me, "I purposefully don't watch them around the twins." But at another point, without realizing the contradiction, she gave me an example of a morning in which her children played with toys while she watched a morning show in the same room.

A mother in northern Virginia with a 19-month-old son related that, before her boy was born, she and her husband watched a lot of TV. These days, she said, they have cut back, though her husband will not give up watching Sports Center in the morning. Her son, she said as an aside, has started to learn sign language and will make the sign for "ball" whenever he sees one on screen.

A stay-at-home mom in Westchester County, New York, said that, before her twin daughters were born, "we had the TV on all the time." Now, with her daughters nearing age 2, she makes a concerted effort to keep it off. When her parents visited recently, she said, "they were surprised that we didn't have the TV on."

How do these self-reported TV addicts cope with the changes? Several mothers and fathers told me that the TV (or, in many cases,

TiVo) comes on as soon as the children are in bed. Others say they have decided to get their news fix from the Internet instead, where it isn't as easy for their children to see and hear what is on. I'm a news junkie myself and could relate to the newsgathering strategies described by a mother of two in Washington DC: "We do it mostly online, and we subscribe to the *Washington Post*. We try to do it by other means."

Families Integrating Other Forms of Electronic Media into Their Lives

The Internet. Handheld videogame systems. Educational computer software. Electronic books. Interactive TV. These are among the technologies parents told me they use, have bought, or have received as gifts for their children. "It's overwhelming," one mother told me, talking about all the electronic toys and software programs available these days.

The families who seemed at ease with their electronic media choices said they used media as catalysts for interacting with their children or encouraging creative play. A mother in Alexandria, Virginia, with two children under 5 and another on the way, said that she often has her older son sit on her lap while they play games on PBSKids.org or the Disney Web site. "We also use the Internet a lot for explaining things to him," she said. "For example, we had a good conversation about space, so we went to the NASA Web site to show him pictures of different planets and astronauts."

My sister-in-law in Norwalk, Connecticut, reported that my 14-month-old nephew gets a kick out of Hallmark e-cards that she plays for him. "Especially ones with singing animals that dance across the screen," she wrote me in an email message. "I must have played the animated chicks birthday card for him about 35 times this week. It never seems to get old **sigh** except, maybe for his mama!"

Often parents told me about interactive electronic products that were not being used as advertised. A friend whose sons own a

LeapPad—a popular electronic book system—said that pressing the icons and buttons had become a game. "The boys mostly treat the books as a sort of odd synthesizer, mixing up the sounds in random ways," she said. A mother with a 3-year-old who was given a Barbie laptop for Christmas said that her daughter doesn't operate most of the functions. She uses it in pretend play instead.

I heard several comments about software, toys or educational videogames that were never played—either because children weren't interested or technical problems thwarted their use. One mother said of her 4-year-old daughter and an interactive gaming system called the VTech V.Smile TV Learning System: "She got the V-Tech for Christmas last year but has not really liked it." A friend with preschool-aged twins in Bethesda, Maryland, told me that her family has an InteracTV system, which is designed to allow children to play educational games on the TV with the remote control. But it requires a lot of her time to set it up and guide her kids on using it. "The way I look at it," she said, "is if I am going to be that engaged with my kids then why does the TV need to be on at all?"

Families Coping with Multiple Children of Different Ages

Most parents with more than one child will tell you that life changes drastically when the second child arrives. Parents who used to be overly protective of their first baby become understandably less attentive when they have two, three or, Lord help them, four little munchkins to cope with.

A mother in Washington DC said that she had tried to avoid TV and videos altogether with her first child. "That said, once her brother was born and we were getting no sleep, we discovered the joys of early morning DVDs," she said. "Now she asks for TV pretty much every morning and it just makes our lives so much easier, we've given in."

Many parents with more than one child said that they find it difficult to abide by the American Academy of Pediatrics recommendations. When an older child is watching a *Blue's Clues* video, what are they supposed to do with their kids under age 2? When the younger children grow old enough to have opinions about what to watch, life gets trickier still. How do parents grant kids some choices and keep content appropriate to different age groups, while also holding down the total amount of viewing time? Some parents urge their children to negotiate with each other; other parents resort to dictating what is watched. A mother in Washington DC with a 3½-year-old girl and 22-month-old son said that they have an "even day, odd day" rule in their household, giving each child alternate chances to pick the day's video. Often, she added, her older child "successfully lobbies" the younger one to go with her choices.

When You Are a Single Parent — or Feel Like One

Single parents have a difficult juggling act to maintain, holding together their health and their children's well-being while working enough hours to make a living. Many rely on relatives. One of the mothers I interviewed was in her early twenties, unmarried and living with her parents while raising her 1-year-old daughter. Throughout our interview, the TV was on, as she said it is every day, all day, to keep her company. A social worker visits her monthly to give her parenting tips and ensure that she isn't becoming depressed.

Another view of single parenthood came from a woman on New York City's Upper West Side who had twins not yet 2 years old. She and her husband had recently separated. She said she was trying to maintain limits on the use of videos and TV. "But every once in a while, I come to weakness and I put on the Oprah show in the afternoon," she admitted. "And when [the kids] are cranky and we're all going batty, those are the days that we put on the videos."

Some parents told me that they relied on children's videos to keep them from losing their cool. Take the case of a mother of three in Lincoln, Nebraska, who stays at home and often babysits for other children to help pay the bills. She isn't single, but she often feels like it, given that her husband works so much. She relies on animated children's movies, especially when she is trying to cook dinner. "Yes, I use video as a babysitter, but what are you going to do?" she asked me. "I'm exhausted and my husband is away a lot—four nights a week and, in the winter, every weekend."

I talked to a mom whose husband works on the weekends and who has 3½-year-old twin boys, one of whom has been diagnosed with mild to moderate autism. She said she copes with the bad days by relying on what she considers quality children's TV shows. Illnesses, especially, throw her for a loop. "If I'm sick," she said, "I lie on the couch in a semi-comatose state," holding the remote control. "I try to make it good stuff."

Talking to Caregivers and Babysitters

Many families said they made a point of telling babysitters their views on what kind and how much media was appropriate for their children. A mother who owned several Baby Einstein videos said that she understood the temptation of using them to occupy her children. "Trust me, it would be easy to do it every day," she said. "I had a conversation with the nanny asking her to limit it from 1 hour to 30 minutes."

Another mother said that, when she hired her babysitter, she told her it was okay to tune into children's shows "in emergencies." But she discovered that the babysitter was turning on the TV whenever she felt the need to wash dishes or straighten up. "I had to tell her I didn't care if things didn't get done around the apartment."

One mother told me that she took the lead from her caregiver, whose mode of operation was to involve the children in arts and crafts projects. "Our nanny will not turn the TV on—that's her philosophy," she said.

Making Good Use of TiVo and Other Video-on-Demand Systems

Many parents I interviewed made a big distinction between watching videos and watching TV. To them, watching TV was an idle activity, full of commercials and at risk of lasting far longer than they had planned. Watching videos, on the other hand, was an advertising-free activity that lasted a set amount of time. When the video ended, their children knew it was time to move on.

Many of these families did not have vast libraries of children's DVDs, but they were affluent enough to have a digital video recorder, like TiVo, or a subscription to their cable company's on-demand system. Those with recorders had set the machines to capture their children's favorite programs so that they always had a store of new and age-appropriate shows to watch. A mother in Austin, Texas, told me that she programs her machine to record PBS's afternoon programs. "We don't have to stop what we are doing to watch them," she said. "We can watch them when we want to."

Video players help parents with another aspect of their children's media use: they enable parents to comply with their 2- and 3-year-olds' requests to see the same show over and over—a behavior that child-development experts say is perfectly normal for children this age. One mother told me about an episode of *Little Einsteins* that her son was particularly drawn to. "We had to TiVo it," she said, "because he loves it, and God forbid if that episode ever went off the air. . . ."

Parents praised the way digital video recorders allowed them to capture an adult program and watch it when the children were asleep—rather than missing the show or exposing their children to it. "I TiVo now," said one mom. "It's my way to relax. I really look forward to it when they're in bed."

Our Family's Media Choices

By now, you're probably wondering exactly what screen time looks like at my house. To start, we have a newfound awareness of how much content matters. I used to think that there wasn't much difference to a 2-year-old between a *Winnie the Pooh* video and *Dora the Explorer*. By the time our second child turned 2, however, I came to understand that *Dora the Explorer* was designed with features like simple story lines, repetition, and calls for participation that hold a very young child's attention and provide an opening for learning. *Winnie the Pooh* videos, on the other hand, sometimes frightened my 2-year-olds, and from what I could tell, they didn't make much sense to them, anyway. So exactly what content have we relied on? Staples for my children at age 2 and 3 have been *Dora*, *Blue's Clues*, *Caillou*, *JoJo's Circus*, *The Wonder Pets*, some *Barney*, and *Elmo* videos of all stripes. Now, at age 4, Janelle is enchanted with shows that teach pre-reading skills, like *Pinky Dinky Doo* and the first three-quarters of *Sesame Street* (the last quarter of *Sesame Street* is "Elmo's World," and according to Janelle, it is now "too young" for her).

I also pay a lot of attention to the way in which my girls watch TV. We rely heavily on prerecorded videos—whether DVDs, VHS tapes, or on-demand selections from our cable company—so that our children see TV time as "multimedia story time" with a definite end. When the video is over, my kids have learned, it is time to do something else. (Though I'll admit that they still have moments when they just whine for more.) Before embarking on this video strategy, I would invariably turn on Noggin or Playhouse Disney in the middle of a program, which meant that the kids saw the end of one show, then another show, and then—if I didn't reach for the remote in time—the beginning of yet another show. What was supposed to be a thirty-minute event became an hour that included two chopped-in-half story lines, and my girls would roar in understandable frustration at having a story cut off in the middle.

Exactly how much TV time are my kids exposed to? My girls, now $2\frac{1}{2}$ and $4\frac{1}{2}$ years old, watch about an hour a day. Our routine, at the moment, includes thirty to sixty minutes of TV time in the early morning. Gillian has a habit of waking before 6 am, and though in theory we could simply return her to her bed, we would rather not subject ourselves to the shrieking protests that wake her sister and half the neighborhood. So, before the sun is up, you will probably find our youngest watching a video, while my husband and I make the coffee, feed the pets, let the dog out, retrieve the newspapers, attempt to read them, let the dog in, prepare breakfast, clean up last night's messes, and unload the dishwasher. If there is time before preschool starts, Janelle, too, gets to watch a video of her choosing. If not, we save it for a lull in the afternoon.

On rare days, there is no screen time at all. On bad-weather "climbing the wall" days and special "movie time" Sundays, my girls probably watch about two hours. On sick, feverish days, the sky's the limit. A few years ago, in that can't-catch-a-breath era of nursing a baby and chasing after a toddler, I relied pretty heavily on TV. In those months, an hour of TV time for Janelle could easily become an hour-and-a-half—especially when her baby sister would not settle down and required my full repertoire of pacing, swaying and singing before drifting off for naptime.

I have learned not to feel guilty about those exceptions. Using baby videos to give myself a break in those early days was necessary for my sanity. Given that my children were otherwise getting huge doses of "Mommy time," I came to understand that using videos occasionally was not going to harm my children and, hey, they probably needed a break from me, too. Today, as long as my girls are watching age-appropriate content, as long as I am within earshot to hear how they are responding to it, as long as they get plenty of time in the day to run around and escape into fantasy worlds of their own making, I figure they are going to be just fine. I know not to rely on media as a superior stimulator for their brains or a foreign-language instructor. But I do believe that the world my kids inherit is going to be increasingly rich in audiovisual information, so I see a value in exposing them to media tools that foster new kinds of expression. I have discovered that the right video stories can catalyze good conversations, spark new interests and lead to happy pretend play. They can trigger little "aha" moments for me, too. I can't say that our household is as perpetually nurturing as that of *Caillou*'s (in the show, both parents work, yet they always have an abundance of time for their kids and never lose their cool), but from watching I have gleaned some hints about the emotions coursing through a 4-year-old's mind during a tantrum. And I will forever thank *The Wonder Pets* for giving my husband a model for clever bedtime stories, an unending series that we call The Adventures of Super J and Super G.

Digging into the science of screen time and child development has given me a new appreciation for how my children learn. Now I'm hooked. I eagerly await upcoming research that may shed even more light on how young kids respond to media of all kinds. But in the meantime, instead of worrying about how screen time affects my children, I can take delight in watching them watch.

NOTES

1. I took several routes to find parents to interview, including sending notes to listservs, emailing friends to give me their thoughts, asking friends to forward my email requests to their friends, and meeting people at child-friendly events who then introduced me to other parents with young children. Most interviews were by phone; a few took place at families' homes. I also met with social workers at a preschool with a predominantly Spanish-speaking population, interviewed Spanish-speaking parents in an E.S.L. class (with the teacher's help as a translator), and conducted group interviews with social workers at three agencies in northern Virginia. In a few cases, I was able to accompany case workers on trips to visit low-income families. In all interviews, to elicit honest responses, I told parents up front that I would not use their names in the book.

Epilogue

In 2007, when this book was first published, many child development experts were genuinely puzzled over the idea that babies—even as those as young as three and six months old—had become the target audience for sales of DVDs. Could there really be a market for such things?

Looks that way. My story at the beginning of this book, about my desperate dive for the *Baby Einstein* DVD to calm my colicky firstborn, has some company. Just a few years later, a group of researchers found 218 titles on the market. In 2010, the average family with a six-month-old had four baby DVDs. By the time their children were eighteen months old, that number had grown to more than seven.[1] The average number of minutes that infants and toddlers spend daily with TV and video has increased from forty-seven minutes in 2005 to sixty-one minutes in 2011, according to a recent Common Sense Media survey.[2] Two-thirds of children under the age of two have watched TV.[3]

But just as DVDs for babies are becoming more deeply embedded in the fabric of family's lives, they already represent old news. Touchscreen technology has arrived, with tablet computers like the iPad becoming the platform for interactive screen-based games that babies can play while sitting on Daddy's lap. One company is even selling a $389 interactive tablet—the Vinci—designed for children from six to forty-eight months. New games for babies show up in the iTunes App Store every day. Six-month-olds in homes across America are now served up brightly colored graphics of touch-to-listen barnyards, with mooing cows that sound eerily lifelike.

Older tots—toddlers and preschoolers—are the beneficiaries of the touchscreen revolution too. ABC preschool apps are now a dime a dozen (actually, it's more like 99 cents apiece). And even two-and three-year-olds are thought to be part of the audience for motion-sensing gaming systems like the Nintendo Wii and Microsoft Kinect—products that require parents to clear their living rooms, lest a child engaged in virtual snowboarding find herself leaping off a cliff and into the coffee table.

Keeping up with all this technology is not easy. Keeping up with the way it changes child-rearing adds another layer of complexity. In our house, where our two daughters are now seven and nine, my husband and I alternate between astonishment at the amazing experiences our kids have at their fingertips and chagrin at how routinely they co-opt our iPads and become oblivious to the world around them.

What is the impact of this new phase of screen time for young children? What should we be worried about? When are we allowed to let down our guard? Many of the same scientists you read about in the previous pages are still trying to unearth some answers. In fact, the research on screen time for young children has become deeper—and even more interesting—than ever before. Happily, the latest studies reaffirm the mantra that echoes through this book. The advice still holds: remember the Three Cs. Think about the *content* of what your children see on-screen. Think about the *context*—who is with them, how are they talking about what they see, how much the DVD or online game dominates their day. And think about what makes sense for your individual *child*, whose needs and interests will be unique to him or her alone.

I still run the Three Cs mantra through my head whenever I'm faced with a question about technology and kids. And I keep dig-

ERRATA TO LISA GUERNSEY'S *SCREEN TIME*

A technical issue led to printing errors in the epilogue, which begins on page 253.

On page 255, the first paragraph after the text break is missing; it should read as follows:

"Just as the first edition of this book was appearing in bookstores, a new study emerged that splashed cold water on the claims of 'educational' value that were attached to baby videos. Three researchers at the University of Washington—Frederick Zimmerman, Dimitri Christakis, and Andrew Meltzoff—published an article that showed a link between watching more than an hour of baby videos a day and reduced language development in babies. The data came from a telephone survey of approximately one thousand parents who were asked about what kind of videos or television, if any, their babies and toddlers watched. The survey also asked about the number of words their babies already understood. Parents responded yes or no to an inventory of ninety common words that babies may know, such as 'cup' or 'fast.' When the researchers analyzed the answers, they discovered that 17 percent of parents reported that their babies watched an hour or more of baby videos a day—and that those babies knew significantly fewer words than the other children in the study.⁴"

On page 264, the same error occurred. The first paragraph after the text break should be added as follows:

"All this talk about book-reading compared to video-viewing might lead one to think that we're still back in 2007, when books were books and videos were videos, and it was pretty easy to tell which was which."

On page 268, the first paragraph after the text break should be added as follows:

"The preceding experiments all assume that the content that children see on screen is designed for them. But the sad truth is that too many toddlers and preschoolers are still watching TV shows, viewing DVDs, and playing online games that were not made by people who understand how young kids think. One might also assume, given the arrival of touchscreens and the plethora of online games now made for young kids, that screen time for young children is all about interactivity. But that's not the case either."

And on page 274, the first paragraph after the text break should be added as follows:

"Four years from the first publication of this book, we now have more confirmation of the importance of two of our Three Cs: We know that *content* really matters (sorry, SpongeBob). We know that *context* is even more important and complicated than we may have thought, demanding that parents come up with thoughtful ways to balance screen time with other activities and engage in back-and-forth conversations with their children about what they see on screen."

The complete, corrected epilogue is available at www.lisaguernsey.com.

ging to learn more. Following are a few of the new insights that scientists have unearthed over the past few years. As with the book as a whole, I hope they will trigger insights for you too—or at least fuel some animated dinner table conversations about what is or isn't best for the kids living under your roof.

～〜

As far as children's research goes, the study had many weaknesses. It was based on parents' reports of what their children knew, instead of observations and assessments conducted by trained professionals. And it represented only a snapshot in time. There was no way to know what caused what. Did the videos cause the decrease in vocabulary or was the reduced vocabulary already there, perhaps even leading parents to think they needed videos to help their children learn more words? Was there something about parenting styles that might be contributing to the difference in vocabulary growth? Could it be that those parents were not so good at paying attention to how many words their babies were learning in the first place?

The University of Washington study struck a chord nevertheless,[5] probably because it was among the first to try to determine whether infants and toddlers could learn anything from baby videos. In its wake, more child advocates started vocalizing their concerns about videos that claimed to be good for babies. The Campaign for Commercial-Free Childhood had already filed a complaint with the Federal Trade Commission, protesting the marketing as deceptive. It soon followed with a class-action lawsuit against Baby Einstein and Brainy Baby, two of the most well-known makers of videos for the very young. Within a year of the study, Baby Einstein changed the taglines on its products, eliminating references to making babies smart. And by 2009 the Disney Company, which owned the Baby Einstein brand, had settled the lawsuit by offering refunds to parents who purchased the DVDs between June 2004 and September 2009. (Want to recoup your $15.99? Too late. The refund offer expired in 2010.)[6]

There's nothing like a juicy little controversy involving Disney to capture people's attention. During those years, I was visiting preschools and libraries around the country to talk about the ideas in this book. The Baby Einstein saga came up at nearly every event. I sensed parents were becoming savvier about what to expect from baby videos. But I am not convinced that most parents have stopped buying the baby videos, nor do I sense that they are much more inclined to avoid baby TV-viewing than they were before. The American Academy of Pediatrics still encourages parents to avoid screen time before age two,[7] but a study in 2010 showed how difficult it is for us to abide. The study asked parents of infants and toddlers if they had any rules about TV or videos. Only 8.6 percent specified a "no TV" policy. Parents were also asked to keep diaries, hour by hour, of how they used media in a twenty-four-hour period. Half of the parents who reported a no-TV policy had exposed their child to television the day before. "The American Academy of Pediatrics recommendation is not being followed even by those who adopted it," the researchers wrote.[8]

One aspect of the University of Washington study that got little attention, however, was a finding related to older children. Researchers had grouped the kids into two discrete age categories. They didn't have one category called "two and under." Instead they compared the responses from parents of babies (eight to sixteen months old) to parents of toddlers (seventeen to twenty-four months old). When the researchers crunched the numbers for the toddlers, they found no relationship between baby videos and language development. The baby videos weren't having any effect whatsoever, neither helping nor hurting vocabulary growth. What did this mean? Some researchers hypothesized that by seventeen months children typically undergo a growth spurt in language development and may be in a better position to understand the content on the screen. They may be able to withstand the negative impact—if there is one—of the baby videos.

To me, this study provided another reminder of the need for all of us—parents, researchers, media producers—to be more specific about age groups and the content of the media. Let's get precise about exactly what ages we're talking about, given that so much brain development occurs across the span of a month or two. And let's learn more about whether different types of dialogue and character-to-character interactions make sense to children at these different ages. If media is going to be part of their lives, shouldn't we know a little more about when it can or cannot be useful to them?

Going deep on age differences and delving into exactly what is shown on-screen are among the many contributions made by researchers in the past four years. Social scientists have started to put baby videos and preschool TV under a microscope—examining features of different types of videos and how those features may relate to learning at different ages. For example, one analysis of baby DVDs showed that the majority of the DVDs on the market featured print on-screen[9]: typed text with words like "ball" or "baby." As cognitive scientists and child development experts will tell you, print means very little to babies. They certainly see the vertical lines or humps in a word like "ball," and, depending on their age, they may even memorize the letters. But they do not appear to be cognitively equipped to associate the letters with specific sounds, decode those sounds to form words, and recognize that those words are symbols for actual objects of different sizes and colors. Given what is known about how infants develop language, it may be much more helpful for babies to see a human being on-screen pointing to a ball, naming it, and asking open-ended questions about its color and shape.

This quest to get specific about on-screen *content* has led scientists into new terrain regarding *context* as well: Could science get

About Baby Videos, The Latest Science Says . . .

- Beware of claims that videos can make babies smarter.
- Based on parents' responses to a 2007 survey, researchers found a connection between lower levels of word learning and high levels of baby-video watching among children eight to sixteen months old.
- Videos that include labeling and pointing to objects are likely to make more sense to babies than the appearance of printed text.
- Text on-screen may be helpful to parents but is highly unlikely to be genuinely read by babies.

more precise about how much a child might be able to learn from media with a little assistance from mom and dad? And once we put parents back into the picture, could that defuse concerns about videos having a negative impact? What if a baby might actually be able to learn quite a bit from a video if mom is using that video as a conversation starter, a spark for songs and stories, or even a simple screen-based equivalent to a book?

But I'm getting ahead of myself. Let's first check in with researchers who have looked at whether mom or dad can keep the negatives in check before we think about the potential for learning.

Alan L. Mendelsohn, a pediatrician and professor in the school of medicine at New York University, came to study screen time in a roundabout way. The overarching theme of his work is to examine the connections between a child's healthy development in infancy and the ability to succeed at reading in elementary school. In 2005, he started the Bellevue Project for Early Language, Literacy and Education Success centered at a public hospital in New York City that serves mostly low-income Latino patients. That's where he and his colleagues met with nearly three hundred mothers who agreed, just after delivering their babies, to participate in a study to track their baby's health and development, as well as their parenting skills, for at least three years.

What's interesting is how Mendelsohn asked those mothers about screen time when their infants were six months old. Instead of simply recording tallies of hours of TV watched, or even names of programs, the researchers were also looking for evidence of what they called *verbal media interactions*: Was the TV mostly for watching or just background noise? Did you talk to the child about the program while it was on?

Child development research in the past ten years has zoomed in on the importance of those little moments of connection between parents and their children. Studies show that when parents talk to their offspring—including infants too young to talk back—they are stimulating the child's brain, preparing it for learning and eventually speaking and reading words. And when parents talk to their children about something both of them are looking at—whether it's a dog at their feet or a character on TV—they are prepping their children for even more language development. These are the kinds of processes that Mendelsohn was probing by asking these mothers whether they talked to their six-month-olds about what was on the screen. Could they be counterbalancing the harm by chatting them up?

To see how children fared, research assistants tested the children's language skills at fourteen months. What they found confirmed Mendelsohn's hunch: The babies with mothers who talked to them about TV did better than those who were exposed to TV at six months without any input from mom. The study also found that the verbal media interactions with educational programming were significantly related to better language skills eight months later. Putting six-month-olds in front of a screen is not recommended, the researchers stress, but if that's what parents are going to do any-way, talking about what they see on the telly seemed to serve a pro-tective role.[10]

At the same time that Mendelsohn was conducting these studies in New York, Rachel Barr, a developmental psychologist at Georgetown University, was collecting data from hundreds of par-ents in the Washington, DC, area about whether they watched baby videos with their babies—and if they talked to them while doing so. The results, captured in hour-by-hour diaries by mostly middle-class white moms, showed that parents were in the room with their babies during DVD time for about an hour a day, on av-erage, and that 70 percent of the time the parents were sitting and talking with their infants.[11]

Barr wanted to know more about the impact of the co-viewing on these babies. If parents talked with their infants or toddlers dur-ing a video, did that cause the children to pay attention? Were they more engaged? Barr and her colleagues Ashley Fidler and Eliza-beth Zack, both at Georgetown, visited the homes of one hundred parents with babies of various ages to find out. They arrived with a Baby Mozart DVD and a videocamera to record how parents in-teracted with their children while watching the thirteen-minute show. Some parents were highly involved—pointing to and label-ing people or objects on the screen. Their infants responded by di-recting their attention to the screen, as if trying to process what mom was talking about. By contrast, in cases where parents were less engaged, their children were too.[12]

There's almost a "no-duh" quality to these findings. Babies learn from watching and interacting with their parents. The science seems to be confirming that videos, if used the right way, could be considered in the same realm as books: vehicles for strengthening learning language. Barr and others are now interested in what hap-pens when you apply the lessons of book-reading to video.

"You wouldn't just leave a baby with a book," Barr said. A twelve-month-old might glance at pictures or try to chew on the spine, but he wouldn't be able to access and understand the story without some help. In the same way, she continued, "you wouldn't just leave a baby with a video." Just because a video can enable images to move past a child's face and sounds to reach a child's ears doesn't mean the child is getting it.

Even at older ages—with preschool and elementary school children—books are not the end-all-be-all by themselves. In the field of reading research, scientists have established that adults can make a major impact on young children's learning if they disengage from autopilot, in which they simply read words and turn pages, and instead become guides and partners throughout the book-reading journey, pausing and asking children questions before, during, and after the book is read. This strategy, known as *dialogic reading*, is widely accepted as a way to improve children's later reading skills and comprehension. It includes techniques such as questioning what's going to happen next and prompting children to think about how the story relates to them.

Wouldn't it be interesting to set up an experiment? Get a DVD that is essentially a book on video. Put parents in different groups: One group simply plays the DVD for their young children. Another group uses specific dialogic reading techniques while playing the DVD. Another group is asked to interact with their children in a less intentional way, simply by pausing the on-screen action and talking about it. A fourth group is shown a DVD that features an actress doing the reading, using those same dialogic techniques, posing questions about the story. In which condition would the children be most likely to learn from what they saw?

That experiment is almost exactly what Gabrielle Strouse designed in 2009 as part of her dissertation research at Vanderbilt University, where she and her advisers are trying to determine what

mix of parent involvement and social interaction is necessary to ensure that very young children are helped and not harmed by screen
time. Strouse used Scholastic DVDs that were video versions of
books that most children don't have at home. (For example, they
included *A Weekend with Wendell* by Kevin Henkes and *The Wizard*
by Jack Kent.) She recruited parents of three-year-olds, assigned
them to one of the four groups, and asked them to view the DVDs
three to five times a week. At the end of the experiment, Strouse
brought the children into the Vanderbilt lab and tested whether
they had learned vocabulary words from DVDs, whether their vocabulary in general had improved, and whether they comprehended the stories.

The results, not yet published, showed significant differences
among the groups, Strouse said. Children from the dialogic video
group—the parents who were trained to ask their children
questions—were able to learn words from the DVD at a significantly higher rate than the other groups. Story comprehension
was higher too.

But the parents who were told to simply interact with their
three-year-olds didn't do as well. Strouse surmises that those parents were interacting in some basic ways—making comments
about what was on the screen, for example—but because they
weren't trained, they didn't think to ask questions or employ other
techniques that characterize dialogic reading. A University of Virginia study with younger children ages twelve months and fifteen
months—showed a similar result: When parents were asked to
watch a commercial baby DVD with their children for four weeks
and "interact with their child in whatever way seemed natural to
them," the DVD viewing did not make any difference in their children's ability to learn new words.[13]

Another surprise from Strouse's study is that children in the
fourth group—the one with the DVD that featured an actress on
the screen reading the book—didn't benefit as much as might be

expected. Previous research, much of it highlighted in this book, has shown that by age three, children are certainly capable of learning words from video. In fact, a few studies have shown that video-based word-learning may be possible as early as fifteen and eighteen months under certain conditions in lab settings.[14] But clearly, learning from video at such young ages is not easy. Researchers theorize that the "video deficit" could still be having an impact even among two-and three-year-olds, depending on what sort of learning is expected of them. The video deficit, as you'll recall from chapter 2, is a phenomenon that has been replicated in multiple studies of media and children around the world. It refers to the finding that young children are slower to learn from an on-screen activity (like a vocabulary lesson or hide-and-seek game) than from the exact same activity conducted live in front of them. Evidently, when it comes to book-reading techniques used with videos, it's hard to beat the presence of an adult who knows the child asking questions and prompting responses.

Advances in technology, however, are ensuring that social scientists have yet more scenarios to test before declaring that children will always need a person by their side to get the most benefit from screen time. What would happen if that adult wasn't sitting next to the child, but instead present via a video link, through Skype or Face Time? The story of Georgene Troseth's web-cam study in chapter 6 hints at this possibility, showing that when twenty-four-month-olds are guided by a social partner on the screen they can overcome the video deficit in a hide-and-seek game. A new study by Marina Krcmar of Wake Forest University takes the social-partner concept even further. Krcmar created customized videos for children that featured their own mothers demonstrating specific actions and introducing them to new words. She found that a group of six-to twelve-month-old children did not seem to learn from their own mothers on screen, but an older group—thirteen to twenty months of age—could. They performed significantly better

---

Engage Your Children in Conversations About What You're Both Watching

- Conversing with your children—even when they are infants—is stimulating the child's brain, preparing it for learning and eventually speaking and reading words.
- New studies are pointing to the importance of *verbal media interactions,* which are moments when parents talk with their babies and toddlers about what they both are watching on the screen.
- Just as with books, young children learn the most from videos and TV shows when a parent or teacher uses dialogic reading techniques. These techniques include asking questions about what is shown on the page and prompting children to talk about what might happen next.

---

watching videos of mom than watching videos of strangers, and they could learn from mom on TV almost as well as if mom had been in the room.[15] (The videos—dubbed "Mama TV" by the families in the study—became such a hit with the children that many parents asked to take copies home.)

～❜

Alas. If only it were still so easy. One of the most profound changes since the first edition of this book has been the appearance of touchscreen tablets, such as the iPad and the Nook, which are blurring the boundaries between what were once discrete types of media. Yes, books that are downloaded to these devices can be static, pixilated versions of what we see on printed paper. But now they don't have to be. The graphics can become animated, the stories can be narrated by a disembodied voice, the text can be pressed to repeat itself—and all of this can happen while a child is relaxing on the sofa, instead of uncomfortably situated in front of desktop computer made for adults.

Pat the Bunny, the children's classic, is now one of hundreds of picture books that can be delivered to these tablets. The cottontail is no longer soft and fuzzy—defeating the beauty of the book, if you ask me. As compensation, children now can tuck bunny into bed by pushing their finger across the screen. They can also blow bubbles and pop balloons while lively music plays in the background. Is the book still a book?

Or take another example: *Toy Story*. It's a movie, right? But there's a book-like version available for smartphones and tablets that features text, page-turning, audio, and animated clips that can feel a lot like watching the movie. In fact, is this just an abridged and subtitled form of the movie? Or is this a new kind of book?

How parents answer these questions could change the practice of reading books with young children. For many child development experts, picture books should lead to those magical, quiet, one-on-one moments between an adult and a child. What will happen to those interactions when the picture book becomes a busy box?

In chapter 10, I introduced you to Julia Parish, a doctoral student at Temple University who was studying how preschoolers were affected by electronic console books, such as the Fisher Price Power Touch Learning System. (These systems use paper books that are specially designed to be inserted into an electronic console. The consoles come with a stylus that, when pressed on certain areas of the page, activate an electronic narrator.) One of her experiments asked whether the consoles would cause parents to interact differently with their children compared to reading the same story in a traditional paper book. Preliminary data showed that yes, indeed, the interaction was completely different. Instead of talking about the content of the book, parents were most likely to direct their kids' behaviors: "Don't press that button! Wait to turn the page!" Final results of the study, soon to be published, include data on how well the children comprehended the books in each case. Both types of book-reading led children to correctly identify characters and settings. But among the three-year-olds, only those who read the traditional book with their parents could correctly answer questions about the sequence of events and the plot. They were significantly better at comprehending the story.

There's an interesting side story to Parish's study, however. When she and her colleagues at Temple started to design these experiments, they invited children in the lab to play with the electronic consoles and reading books. The kids were so enamored with the electronic consoles that they showed little interest in the regular books. It was as if they couldn't get enough of being able to press buttons and make things happen.

The dawn of the touchscreen—a device so much easier to use than an electronic console—shows just how compelling that interactivity is. Parents are finding that their toddlers can be well occupied in the backseat of the car if they simply pass back their smartphones. (There's even a name for this phenomenon: the Pass-Back Effect.[16]) YouTube is filled with videos of children as young as nine months old giggling and smiling while touching and sliding their fingers over their parents' iPads. Warren Buckleitner, the editor of the *Children's Technology Review*, has built an online archive of those videos, many of which show parents giddy with excitement over all the touching, swiping, and screen-jiggling that their children can do. As Buckleitner quipped: "Back in the good ol' days, you videotaped your child's first steps. Today it seems it's your child's first app."[17]

Touchscreen devices are probably going to blow a few holes in current theories about what babies, toddlers, and preschoolers are capable of. Until these interfaces arrived, a young child had to move a mouse or push buttons on a remote control to make something happen on the screen. They were required to keep at least three dynamics in mind at one time: the movement of the device in their hands, the changes on the screen, and the way that one affected the other. That's a lot of cognitive juggling for a young brain. But with a touchscreen, action and reaction are about as tightly coupled as possible. Touching a picture of a balloon can make it pop right under a child's fingertip. The physical interface is no longer a barrier to what's possible.[18]

Can young children learn more easily when interactivity is this seamless? Science has not caught up with technology on this question. Published peer-reviewed research of whether toddlers or preschoolers can learn more readily from touchscreens is still to come.

But there are several new studies that get us much closer to real answers than four years ago. One is based on an experiment at Georgetown University that requires children to simply touch a space bar to interact with a screen, and it shows that interactivity holds real promise for three-year-olds—at least for the type of learning tested in the Georgetown lab. Here's how it worked: Researchers created three conditions that revolved around puppets playing hide and seek in a laundry room. (The scenarios were adapted from an online game from Nick Jr. based on *Curious Buddies*, a video program for toddlers.) In the first condition, children would watch the hide-and-seek game on video. In the second, they would play the game themselves by pressing on a space bar on a computer to change the action on screen. And in a third, they would observe a live-action version of the game by watching through a window. Seventy-two children, ages thirty months and thirty-six months, were randomly assigned to one of these three conditions. After they watched, they were brought into the room where the live action had played out—a room designed to mimic the exact scene from the video and computer. Could the children find the puppets in the same hiding places they saw on the screen? For example, if the dog puppet had been hiding behind pants that were hanging on a laundry line, would the children know to run up to the real laundry line and pull back the pants to find the dog? In short, would they be able to learn from the screen and transfer that learning to the real world?

When unleashed to the room to find the puppets themselves, the kids in each condition scampered to and fro, excitedly rifling through the laundry baskets to show researchers that they knew where each puppet was hiding. But not all children could do the task: on average, the children who had watched the game on video had a tough time, while the kids who had played the interactive game or watched the live action performed quite well. Their ability to retrieve the puppets was significantly better than those who had just watched the video. Even the younger children—the thirty-month-olds—had success. "Interactivity may be an important part of the puzzle that has been missing in understanding the video deficit," wrote Alexis Lauricella, a postdoctoral researcher at Northwestern University and lead author of the study.

~~~◟

So let's pause for a reality check. TV time is still a huge part of the lives of young children. A recent Common Sense Media report showed that of all the screen time that young children experience, 74 percent of it comes through the TV set, while less than 13 percent comes through the computer, and an even smaller percentage appears on smartphones or videogame players.

And what are these young children watching on TV? Unfortunately, a large proportion of it includes shows made for older children and adults. This *adult-directed media*, as researchers call it, can be highly challenging for toddlers and preschoolers to follow and therefore it is less likely to help them learn or develop their lan-

---

The Blessings, and Limitations, of Interactive Touchscreens

- With touchscreens, young children no longer have to divide their attention between operating an input device (such as a mouse) and the screen.
- Touchscreens may give us a much more accurate view of what young children are capable of as they use screen media, but scientific studies have yet to provide information on their impact.
- In a study that compared the impact of an interactive computer game, a passive video, and a live-action demonstration, children could learn from the interactive game and the live-action demo at thirty months of age. But they could not learn from the video.
- Reflect on whether computer interactivity is leading you to issue a bunch of directives to your children (such as "press that button" or "don't click there!") instead of authentic conversations about stories and ideas.

---

guage skills. What's more, background television is still ubiquitous, with 79 percent of families of children ages zero to eight reporting that the television is on some, most, or all of the time regardless of whether anyone is watching it.[19] Research continues to show that these always-on TV sets could be having a negative effect on the way children play with toys and interact with their parents.

In 2011, a study on *SpongeBob Squarepants* shined a spotlight on why these facts are so troubling. *SpongeBob* wasn't designed for preschoolers—Nickelodeon says it is aiming for ages six to eleven—but that hasn't stopped it from becoming part of the American media diet for some preschoolers. The show has been known to turn up near the top of cable and broadcast ratings for two-to five-year-old viewers, and studies by marketing firms have shown that SpongeBob is well recognized by preschoolers. Even toddler sippy cups are sold emblazoned with his bright yellow, googly-eyed image.

The study, led by psychologist Angeline Lillard at the University of Virginia, found that *SpongeBob* has a negative impact on four-year-old children's short-term thinking skills.[20]

Lillard randomly assigned sixty four-year-olds to one of three nine-minute activities. One group of children watched a *SpongeBob* episode, another group watched an episode of *Caillou* (that preschool show about a four-year-old boy that I've described before), and a third group was invited to color with crayons. Before the experiment, each group seemed pretty similar. They came from relatively well-off families, and their parents had reported no differences in their behavior or ability to pay attention. There was no significant difference in how much TV they watched at home.

Immediately after watching the shows, the children were asked to perform four tasks that tested their "executive function"—the scientific catchall term for the cognitive work involved in paying attention, focusing on, and following through with activities, and being able to hold back impulses. Good executive functioning has been increasingly connected to a child's ability to do well in school, and scientists have designed some short tests to determine whether children are developing these skills. One, for example, is a "game" called Head-Toes-Knees-Shoulders, which requires a level of mental discipline. When the test administrator directs the children to touch their heads, they are supposed to touch their toes, and vice versa. Children listen and react to a repeated series of directives and are scored on their ability to follow the games' rules. It's all about paying close attention and thinking before you act.

In this test and three others, *SpongeBob* watchers didn't do so well. Compared to the other two groups, the *SpongeBob* audience performed significantly worse on all four tasks. It was as if something had impaired their ability to focus on what they had been asked to do.

Could it have been that *SpongeBob* was just so hysterically funny that it temporarily rewired their brains? "Everyone keeps saying, maybe the children have just been laughing so much while they've seen *SpongeBob* that they can't focus," Lillard said. "Trust me, they weren't laughing. Their facial expressions looked just the same as when they were watching *Caillou*: transfixed and serious."[21]

Another study on adult-directed television found a similar impact, and it deserves even more attention because it used evidence gathered over a period of time, instead of in a short-term snapshot. The study, led by Barr at Georgetown, found connections between exposure to *adult-directed* television at age one and children's cognitive functioning at age four. The data in that study came from home visits conducted with sixty children from middle-income families during a three-year period. Researchers gathered information on how much TV their children watched at age one and age four and what TV programs they saw. They also surveyed parents on how well their children were able to pay attention and persist with tasks. When the children were four, the researchers sat down with the children and administered a series of tests and games to measure their level of executive functioning and cognitive skills.

One of their first findings was that, on average, infants were put in front of adult-directed television an hour a day. They experience almost four times as much adult-directed TV as preschoolers. But most important were their findings on the negative links between adult-directed television and children's thinking skills. The children with poor attention skills—according to parents' reports and as shown in the scores from the tests—were the ones who experienced high levels of adult-directed TV as infants. Poor scores on the tests also coincided with watching a lot of adult-directed TV at age four. When the researchers controlled for a parent's level of education, the results still held. Watching these kinds of shows was significantly associated with poor cognitive performance.

What constitutes adult-directed TV? According to the researchers, *SpongeBob* would fit in that category, as would sitcoms, game shows, pre-teen programming like *That's So Raven*, nature shows for adults and the news, as well as *Power Rangers* or other cartoons that are not designed to be followed by young children.

Shows that were designed for infants, toddlers, and preschool children were in a separate "child-directed TV" category that included PBS preschool programs like *Arthur, Sesame Street*, and *Clifford*; Nickelodeon preschool programs like *Blues Clues* and *Dora the Explorer*; baby-directed videos like *Baby Mozart*; and Disney movies, such as *Finding Nemo*. (That last subgroup—the Disney movies—surprised me, given that many Disney movies include flashbacks and abstract dialogue that are more characteristic of adult-directed programs. It would be interesting to learn if some of these child-directed programs were more associated with cognitive skills than others, a question that would require a much larger sample size to answer.) When researchers examined the data in this category, they found no correlation between children's performance on executive functioning tests and the amount of child-directed television they had watched.

In short, social scientists are finally paying attention to the *content* of what's on screen.

Remember the study that led me to write this book? I was curious—and alarmed—about a 2004 study in *Pediatrics* that showed a connection between poor attention skills at age seven and television viewing at ages one and three. As became clear in my journey through the research, that study had a fatal flaw: it didn't make any distinctions between what kind of television viewing these children were exposed to. This latest study by Barr on executive functioning and adult-directed television was designed to fill that gap. Yes, the sample size is small and much more research is needed to tease out what is causing what, but Barr's study lends support to one theory that explains the negative impact of TV discovered in the 2004 *Pediatrics* report: perhaps the attention problems came from one- and three-year-olds watching television that was not designed for them. Given that the data in the *Pediatrics* study came from the 1980s and 1990s when fewer toddler and preschool-oriented programs were on TV, there is a good chance that those kids were watching adult-directed TV.

It can be tempting to take these results as a license to simply let our the kids watch child-directed TV and be done with it. That's a lot easier than enforcing rules about the quantity of programming, such as how much time a child is allowed to play on a computer or watch videos. (In our house, whenever I declare that computer time is coming to an end, I still get howls of protest.) But experts on child obesity and pediatricians who specialize in sleep problems continue to sound warning bells about the need for young children need to be physically active each day and turn off screens before bedtime to ensure a good night's sleep. Parents need to help children recognize when enough is enough, no matter how well-designed the on-screen content may be.

We can take a cue from Dash, the cartoon character on PBSKids.org. Dash shows site visitors which videos they can watch and which games they can play. But he isn't just a media pusher. When the website first launched streaming videos in 2009, developers were stunned—and more than a little worried—about how many videos their young viewers were gobbling up. They had expected visitors to watch about four million video streams per month, because that was the norm at the website for older children. But in the first month, the number of video streams skyrocketed to 87 million[22]—an astonishing sign of the popularity of the PBS videos and the online "player" that serves them up. It was becoming evident that children at these ages were not terribly good at knowing when to call it quits. So the developers introduced a

> ## More Reasons to Avoid TV
> ## That Isn't Designed for Young Children
>
> - Several studies show a connection between exposure to adult-directed television and reduced "executive functioning," meaning a child's ability to focus, persist in tasks, and follow directions.
> - Adult-directed television shows are any shows that are not designed to be followed by preschoolers and toddlers. They include soap operas, game shows, SpongeBob, and Power Rangers.
> - Studies have not uncovered links to attention problems when children watch programs that are designed for them, such as educational children's television shows.
> - But even when the screen-based shows or games are designed for young children, parents must ensure that their children get enough physical exercise and sleep. Parents will need to closely monitor how much time their children have been on the computer or watching TV.

nudge: after children have watched several video clips, Dash appears on the screen with a friendly reminder: Isn't it time to take a break?

~⌒

What about the third C—the individual child? Certainly the latest science is showing why it is critical for parents to consider their children's age and stage of development. As the word-learning research has shown, for example, learning something from the screen at eighteen months appears to be a lot more difficult than at twenty-four months. But there are still many questions hanging out there about specific subgroups of children and their specific needs. When I visit preschools, I hear from parents who are asking for more help. They want to know whether a child who has trouble falling asleep should watch *The Good Night Show* on PBS Sprout. They wonder whether their two-year-olds who are not yet speaking should be introduced to specific videos or iPad games that the family can play together. They ask about whether children from disadvantaged families may now be exposed to online storytelling and books that they might not get at home. They ask for advice on which movies might be best to calm their asthmatic children when it's time to pull out the nebulizer.

The scientists I've met while writing this book will be working hard to find answers. But in the meantime, those of us with young children should continue to do our jobs: tuning in to what our children need. In the razzle-dazzle of new iPhone apps and touchscreen toys, we cannot forget how much our presence makes a difference. If there is one thing that continues to show up in the research, it is that adults' engagement with children while they watch and interact with e-media leads to far more learning than when the kids are using the technology by themselves. Advances in technology are not pointing to a day in which young children can simply plug in and learn without us. On the contrary, we parents are more necessary than ever.

NOTES

1. Vaala et al., pp. 628–648.
2. Common Sense Media, p. 24. Note that the number of minutes for infants' and toddlers' daily screen time in 2011 is slightly less (53 minutes) on p. 18 of the report where the age range is zero months to twenty-three months, not six months to twenty-three months as was the case in the 2005 survey.
3. Ibid, p. 18.
4. Zimmerman, Christakis, and Meltzoff, pp. 364–368.

5. Many newspapers covered the findings, and I wrote about the results in an op-ed for the *New York Times*, "The Genius of Baby Einstein," on August 16, 2007.

6. Lewin, p. A1.

7. Brown, *Pediatrics* 128.

8. Barr et al., p. 117.

9. Valla et al., p. 643.

10. Mendelsohn et al., pp. 577–593.

11. Barr et al., pp. 107–122.

12. Fidler, Zack, and Barr, pp. 1–21.

13. Deloache, p. 1572.

14. Vandewater et al., p. 4; Koenig, pp. pp. 63–64.

15. Krcmar, pp. 31–53.

16. Chiong and Shuler, p. 7.

17. Buckleitner, "Taxonomy of Touch," pp. 36–37.

18. For more on children's physical development and touchscreens, see Buckleitner,.

19. *Common Sense Media*, p. 35.

20. Lillard and Peterson, pp. 772–774.

21. For more, see "Your Kids' Brains, Spongebob-ed," *Zocalo Public Square*, September 28, 2011.

22. In-person interview and e-mail correspondence with Sara Dewitt, vice-president for PBS Kids Interactive, September 23, 2011 and October 4, 2011. Dewitt said that recent numbers are even higher: In August 2011, the PBS Kids video player served 132 million video streams to online computers and other devices, including iPads.

Appendix I:
Movie Review Web Sites

The following review sites can help parents sort out which children's movies are appropriate for very young children and avoid the ones that contain content that might be upsetting to them.

Parents' Choice
www.parentschoice.org
A well-designed site that spotlights media that is appropriate and engaging for children. Using the product finder you can do a search on, say, home videos for 2-year-olds. Parents' Choice is the guiding hand behind the Kid-Zone on TiVo, a "safe mode" that only displays shows that parents pre-approve for their children.

Family Entertainment Finder from ParentCenter.com
parentcenter.babycenter.com/reviews/
This site makes clear from the outset whether a movie, DVD or show will be appropriate for a child under 4. You'll see "4+" or "3+" next to the symbols at the top of the review. You can also search for various types of media by age groups, like "preschooler (2–4)."

The Movie Mom
movies.yahoo.com/mv/moviemom/
Nell Minow, the "Movie Mom," can also be heard on radio stations around the country every week. To search for her take on whether a movie or DVD will be appropriate for your child, use the main Yahoo search box and then, once the general description of the movie pops up, click on the "Movie Mom" link on the left-hand side of the site.

Parents Television Council
www.parentstv.org/ptc/publications/moviereviews/main.asp

Although it is known primarily for its analyses of violence and sex in television programming, the PTC also offers movie reviews with age guidelines and descriptions of the parts of the movie that might upset very young viewers.

Appendix II:
Web Site Reviews
of Interactive Media

As software, Web sites, and videogames are designed for babies, preschoolers, and toddlers, reviewers are trying to keep up. On the sites below, products for school-aged children predominate, but items for younger children can be found by browsing and conducting keyword searches. (Note: Some sites that cater to parents are not listed here. I chose to include only sites that provide guidance to parents on what might be developmentally appropriate for children under 5.)

Parents' Choice
www.parentschoice.org
This attractive, easy-to-navigate site provides reviews of all kinds of media, including software, videogames and interactive toys. Only products that have received a commendation from the Parent's Choice Foundation are listed. No advertisements.

Children's Technology Review
www.childrenssoftware.com
With a subscription, you can tap into a database of thousands of reviews, a few of which don't hold back in saying which products are not worth the money. But be sure to read the text of the reviews because the numeric ratings alone can be deceptively high. Software is tested by kids as well as adults. The $96 subscription includes a monthly e-magazine. Free sample issues and old top-100 lists are available. Review alerts cost $15/yr.

Little Clickers
www.littleclickers.com
A free subsite of the *Children's Technology Review* that lists educational Web sites for children aged 3 to 12. Organized by topic areas, like "Sites about Dogs," or "When I Grow Up."

Edutaining Kids
www.edutainingkids.com/software.html
For my taste, this site is a little too certain that software for babies and toddlers can be educational. But it does include some critical evaluations of whether software is engaging or just distracting.

Appendix III:
Resources on the Use of
Electronic Media with Children
Who Have Special Needs

A comprehensive look at this topic was beyond the scope of this book, but as I delved into studies about the screen's impact on typically developing children, I came across a few experts and resources that might be useful to parents with children who have physical or developmental disabilities. This list is by no means complete, so consider it merely a starting point.

- The Impact of Technology for Diverse Learners, a set of presentations from the 2005 "Ready to Learn" Summit at PBS. Presenters included Carol Bell, a co-director at the Center for Best Practices in Early Childhood Education at Western Illinois University, and Libby Peet, an educational consultant and an expert in the use of assistive technologies. To read their presentations, go to http://www.pbs.org/readytolearn/resources/2005_summer_institute/summer_institute_tues.html.
- *The Transporters*, a line of DVDs for autistic children designed by Simon Baron-Cohen, director of the Autism Research Centre at Cambridge University, and David Lammy, Culture Minister for the United Kingdom. See the National Autistic Society at www.nas.org.uk for more information.
- How Media Can Contribute to Early Literacy, an academic colloquium hosted by Leiden University in the Netherlands. The colloquium included a few presentations about new research on how media can help children with learning disabilities. See http://athena.leidenuniv.nl/fsw/opleiding/peda/emergent_literacy/ and scroll to lectures by Michael

McKenna of the University of Virginia and Victor van Daal of the University of Stanvanger in Norway.

- Vocabulary Acquisition for Children with Autism: Teacher or Computer Instruction, a brief report by Sandra Calvert and Monique Moore of Georgetown University, showing that autistic children show more attention and more motivation to learn words when using computer software as opposed to in-person instruction. Published in the Journal of Autism and Developmental Disorders 30, no. 4 (August 2000).

- LEARNS Early Childhood Project, an initiative from the University of Maine's Center for Community Inclusion and Disability Studies. Bonnie Blagojevic, a research associate for the project, works on issues related to how technology can assist children with disabilities. See http://www.ccids.umaine.edu/service/learnsearly/index.htm.

- Tech for Tots VHS Set, a video, book and CD package developed by the University Affiliated Project at Childrens Hospital in Los Angeles. Describes the use of assistive technology for children from birth to age 5. Available for purchase from Program Development Associates in Syracuse, New York. See PDAssoc.com for ordering information.

- Technology and Young Children Interest Forum, a branch of the National Association of the Education of Young Children, hosts a Web site and listserv that features child-development experts who are looking into how software and other computer technologies can reduce barriers to learning. See http://www.techandyoungchildren.org/.

- *Journal of Computer Assisted Learning*, a peer-reviewed academic journal of recent research on how computers may help children learn. See http://www.blackwellpublishing.com/journal.asp?ref=0266–4909&site=1.

Acknowledgments

The labor of writing a book has been compared to the labor of having a baby, but I see it more like the labor of caring for a child—tremendously rewarding but also time-demanding, all-consuming, sleep-depriving, and impossible to do well without perpetual assistance and moral support.

I got the idea to write about toddlers and television from watching my children, but I thank Craig Stoltz, health editor of the *Washington Post*, for giving my story its first audience. I am indebted to Mick Gusinde-Duffy, former acquisitions editor at the Zero to Three Press, for encouraging me to write a book on the topic, and to my agent, Jim Levine, for helping to refine my proposal and find me a very happy home with Basic Books. Many thanks to my editors, Jo Ann Miller, whose sharp insights helped me focus the initial chapters, and Amy Scheibe, whose empathy, humor, smarts and good sense became an inspiration.

When I embarked on this research, I had a lot to learn about children, despite having two of my own. A journalism fellowship in child and family policy at the University of Maryland gave me a much-needed grounding in the science of early childhood development; I am thankful for the opportunity to learn from the many talented people who led and participated in that program. I greatly appreciated the insights I gained in talking with social workers, educators and parents at Child and Family Network Centers in

Alexandria, Virginia, especially Blanca Leyva who provided introductions and translations. Many thanks as well to the social workers and staff members of Northern Virginia Family Services, who opened their meetings to me and introduced me to several of the parents they work with. Special thanks to Carol Freeman, Alicia Russo, Delmy Florez and Karina Andrade.

I could not have written this book without the benefit of email, phone and in-person interviews with parents from all over the country whose names will remain anonymous but whose compelling stories and probing questions kept me going. I thank friends and relatives for helping me reach new families and for responding with many of their own insights when I needed a broader view or a gut check. I also thank Nina Ribas and Marina Silva for being so kind, creative and competent in caring for my girls when I closed my office door and went to work.

I bow in gratitude to my friends who read and commented on early drafts, particularly Laura Dove, who never shied from helpful critiques, and Sabrina Detlef, whose clear-eyed, detailed editing helped immensely. Special thanks to my brother, Daniel Guernsey, who as a new father was a valuable test audience. My mother, Betty Guernsey, and my father, Roger Guernsey, have always been incredibly supportive of my undertakings, and this book was no exception. Every day I am filled with thanks and admiration to them for giving me and my brother the wings to fly. I thank my girls, Janelle and Gillian, for being a wellspring of inspiration, motivation and just plain joy. And lastly, with much love, I thank my husband, Rob Krupicka, for never doubting me, even when I felt reason to doubt, and for providing intellectual and emotional support from start to finish.

Bibliography

Acevedo-Polakovich, Ignacio David, Elizabeth Pugzles Lorch, and Richard Milich. "TV or Not TV: Questions and Answers Regarding Television and ADHD." *ADHD Report 13*, no. 6 (2005): 15–25.

Anderson, C., L. Berkowitz, E. Donnerstein, L. Huesmann, J. Johnson, D. Linz, N. Malamuth, and E. Wartella. "The Influence of Media Violence on Youth." *Psychological Science in the Public Interest 4*, no. 3 (2003): 81–110.

Anderson, Daniel R. "Watching Children Watch Television and the Creation of Blue's Clues." In *Nickelodeon Nation*, ed. Heather Hendershot, pp. 241–268. New York: New York University Press, 2004.

Anderson, Daniel R., Jennings Bryant, Alice Wilder, Angela Santomero, Marsha Williams, and Alisha Crawley. "Researching Blue's Clues: Viewing Behavior and Impact." *Media Psychology 2* (2000): 179–194.

Anderson, Daniel R., Hyewon Park Choi, and Elizabeth Pugzles Lorch. "Attentional Inertia Reduces Distractibility During Young Children's TV Viewing." *Child Development 58* (1987): 798–806.

Anderson, Daniel R., and Patricia A. Collins. "The Impact on Children's Education: Television's Influence on Cognitive Development." Working paper #2, Office of Educational Research and Improvement, U.S. Department of Education, April 1988.

Anderson, Daniel R., Katherine V. Fite, Nicole Petrovich, and Joy Hirsch. "Cortical Activation While Watching Video Montage: An fMRI Study." *Media Psychology 8* (2006): 7–24.

Anderson, Daniel R., and Stephen R. Levin. "Young Children's Attention to 'Sesame Street.'" *Child Development 47* (1976): 806–811.

Anderson, Daniel R., and Tiffany A. Pempek. "Television and Very Young Children." *American Behavioral Scientist 48*, no. 5 (2005): 505–522.

Bakalar, Nicholas. "At Risk: Premature Birth Is Linked to Attention Disorder." *New York Times*, June 13, 2006.

Barkley, Russell A. "ADHD and Television Exposure: Correlation as Cause." *The ADHD Report 12*, no. 4 (2004): 1–10.

Barr, Rachel. "Attention and Learning from Media during Infancy and Early Childhood." In *Blackwell Handbook of Child Development and the Media*, ed. Sandra L. Calvert and Barbara J. Wilson. Boston: Blackwell Publishing, in press.

Barr, Rachel, and Harlene Hayne. "Developmental Changes in Imitation from Television during Infancy." *Child Development 70*, no. 5 (1999): 1067–1081.

Barr, Rachel, Catherine Danziger, Marisa Hilliard, Carolyn Andolina and Jenifer Ruskis, "Amount, Content and Context of Infant Media Exposure: A Parental Questionnaire and Diary Analysis," *International Journal of Early Years Education 18*, no. 2 (June 2010): 117.

Berk, Laura E. *Awakening Children's Minds: How Parents and Teachers Can Make a Difference*. New York: Oxford University Press, 2001.

Berk, Laura E., Trisha D. Mann, and Amy T. Ogan. "Make-Believe Play: Wellspring for Development of Self-Regulation." In *Play=Learning*, ed. Dorothy G. Singer, Roberta Michnick Golinkoff, and Kathy Hirsh-Pasek. New York: Oxford University Press, 2006.

Bickham, David S., John C. Wright, and Aletha C. Huston. "Attention, Comprehension and the Educational Influences of Television." In *Handbook of Children and the Media*, ed. Dorothy G. Singer and Jerome L. Singer, pp. 101–120. Thousand Oaks, CA: Sage, 2001.

Blades, Mark. "When Do Children Understand the Reason for Advertisements?" Paper presented at the annual conference of the Psychological Society of Ireland, Galway, November, 9–12, 2006.

Bloom, Paul. *Descartes Baby: How the Science of Child Development Explains What Makes Us Human*. New York: Basic Books, 2004.

Bright, John. "Disney's Fantasy Empire." The Nation, March 6, 1967.

Brown, Ari. "Policy Statement: Media Use by Children Younger than 2 Years," *Pediatrics 128*, no. 5 (November 2011).

Buckleitner, Warren. "The Relationship between Software Interface Instructional Style and the Engagement of Young Children." PhD diss., Michigan State University, 2004. (An abridged version was published in 2006 in Early Education and Development 13, no. 3, pp. 489–505.)

Buckleitner, Warren. "Taxonomy of Touch," *Children's Technology Review*, November 2010.

Burns, John J., and Daniel R. Anderson. "Attentional Inertia and Recognition Memory in Adult Television Viewing." *Communication Research 20*, no. 6 (1993): 777–799.

Calvert, Sandra L. "Production Features as Scaffolds for Children's Learning: Lessons for Instructional Design." Paper presented at Pathway to Literacy Achievement for High Poverty Children: A Ready to Learn Research Agenda, University of Michigan, Summer 2006.

Calvert, Sandra L., Bonnie L. Strong, and Lizann Gallagher. "Control as an Engagement Feature for Young Children's Attention to Learning of Computer Content." *American Behavioral Scientist 48*, no. 5 (2005): 578–589.

Calvert, Sandra L., Bonnie L. Strong, Eliza L. Jacobs, and Emily Conger. "Interaction and Participation for Young Hispanic and Caucasian Girls' and Boys' Learning of Media Content." *Media Psychology 9*, no. 2 (2007): 1–15.

Cantor, Joanne. "Long-Term Memories of Frightening Media Often Include Lingering Trauma Symptoms." Poster presented at the Association for Psychological Science Convention, New York, May 26, 2006.

Cantor, Joanne. "The Media and Children's Fears, Anxieties, and Perceptions of Danger." In *Handbook of Children and the Media*, ed. Dorothy G. Singer and Jerome L. Singer, pp. 207–222. Thousand Oaks, CA: Sage, 2001.

Cantor, Joanne. *Mommy, I'm Scared: How TV and Movies Frighten Children and What We Can Do to Protect Them.* New York: Harcourt Brace, 1998.

Caplovitz, Allison Gilman. "The Effects of Using an Electronic Talking Book on the Emergent Literacy Skills of Preschool Children." PhD diss., University of Texas at Austin, 2005.

Carver, Leslie J., Andrew N. Meltzoff, and Geraldine Dawson. "Event-Related Potential (ERP) Indices of Infants' Recognition of Familiar and Unfamiliar Objects in Two and Three Dimensions." *Developmental Science 9*, no. 1 (2006): 51–62.

Chiong, Cynthia, and Carly Shuler. "Learning: Is There an App for That? Investigations of Young Children's Usage and Learning With Mobile Devices and Apps." New York: Joan Ganz Cooney Center, November 2010.

Choi, Hyewon Park, and Daniel R. Anderson. "A Temporal Analysis of Free Toy Play and Distractability in Young Children." *Journal of Experimental Child Psychology 52*, no. 1 (1991): 41–69.

Christakis, Dimitri A., and Frederick J. Zimmerman. *The Elephant in the Living Room: Make Television Work for Your Kids.* New York: Rodale, 2006.

Christakis, Dimitri, Frederick J. Zimmerman, David L. Giuseppe, and Carolyn A. McCarty. "Early Television Exposure and Subsequent Attentional Problems in Children." *Pediatrics 113*, no. 4 (2004): 708–713.

Committee on Public Education, American Academy of Pediatrics. "Media Education." *Pediatrics 104*, no. 2 (1999): 341–343.

Common Sense Media, *Zero to Eight: Children's Media Use in America*, October 2011, http://www.commonsensemedia.org/

De Jong, Maria T., and Adriana G. Bus. "Quality of Book-Reading Matters for Emergent Readers: An Experiment with the Same Book in Regular or Electronic Format." *Journal of Educational Psychology 94*, no. 1 (2002): 145–155.

DeLoache, Judy S. "Mindful of Symbols." *Scientific American*, August 2005, pp. 73–77.

DeLoache, Judy S., Sophia L. Pierroutsakos, David H. Uttal, Karl S. Rosengren, and Alma Gottlieb. "Grasping the Nature of Pictures." *Psychological Science 9*, no. 3 (1998): 205–210.

DeLoache, Judy S., M. S. Strauss, and J. Maynard. "Picture Perception in Infancy." *Infant Behavior & Development 2* (1979): 77–89.

DeLoache, Judy S., David H. Uttal, and Sophia L. Pierroutsakos. "What's Up? The Development of Orientation Preference for Picture Books." *Journal of Cognition and Development 1* (2000): 81–95.

Deloache, Judy S., et al, "Do Babies Learn From Baby Media?" *Psychological Science*, 2010.

Dennison, Barbara A., Theresa J. Russo, Patrick A. Burdick, and Paul L. Jenkins. "An Intervention to Reduce Television Viewing by Preschool Children." *Archives of Pediatric and Adolescent Medicine 158* (February 2004): 170–176.

Doupe, Allison J., and Patricia K. Kuhl, "Birdsong and Human Speech: Common Themes and Mechanisms." *Annual Review of Neuroscience 22* (March 1999): 567–631.

Eisenberg, Arlene, Heidi E. Murkoff, and Sandee E. Hathaway. *What to Expect in the Toddler Years.* New York: Workman Publishing, 1994.

Elias, Cynthia L., and Laura E. Berk. "Self-Regulation in Young Children: Is There a Role for Sociodramatic Play?" *Early Childhood Research Quarterly 162* (2002): 1–23.

Eliot, Lise. *What's Going on in There?* New York: Bantam Books, 1999.

Erikson, Erik H. *Childhood and Society.* New York: W. W. Norton & Company, 1950.

Evans, Gary W., and Lorraine Maxwell. "Chronic Noise Exposure and Reading Deficits: The Mediating Effects of Language Acquisition." *Environment and Behavior 29*, no. 5 (1997): 638–657.

Evans, M. K., T. A. Pempek, H. L. Kirkorian, A. E. Frankenfield, and D. R. Anderson. "The Impact of Background Television on Complexity of

Play. Poster session presented at the biannual International Conference for Infant Studies, Chicago, May 2004.

Fidler, Ashley E., Elizabeth Zack, and Rachel Barr, "Television Viewing Patterns in 6-to 18-Month-Olds: The Role of Caregiver–Infant Interactional Quality," *Infancy* (2010): 1–21.

Fisch, Shalom M. *Children's Learning from Educational Television: Sesame Street and Beyond.* Mahwah, NJ: Lawrence Erlbaum Associates, 2004.

Fisch, Shalom M., and Rosemarie T. Truglio, eds. *"G" is for Growing: Thirty Years of Research on Children and Sesame Street.* Mahwah, NJ: Lawrence Erlbaum Associates, 2001.

Foulkes, David. *Children's Dreaming and the Development of Consciousness.* Cambridge, MA: Harvard University Press, 1999.

Francis, Lori A., and Leann L. Birch. "Does Eating During Television Viewing Affect Preschool Children's Intake?" *Journal of the American Dietetic Association 106*, no. 4 (2006): 598–600.

Frankenfield, Anne E., John E. Richards, Alexis R. Lauricella, Tiffany A. Pempek, Heather L. Kirkorian, Daniel R. Anderson, and Marie K. Evans. "Looking at and Interacting with Comprehensible and Incomprehensible Teletubbies." Poster at the biennial meeting of the Society of Research in Child Development, Atlanta, 2005.

Garrison, Michelle M., and Dimitri A. Christakis. "A Teacher in the Living Room? Educational Media for Babies, Toddlers and Preschoolers." Report by the Henry J. Kaiser Family Foundation, Menlo Park, California, December 2005.

Gee, James Paul. "Learning by Design: Good Video Games as Learning Machines." *E-Learning 2*, no. 1 (2005): 5–16.

Ginsburg, Kenneth R., and the Committee on Communications and the Committee on Psychosocial Aspects of Child and Family Health. "The Importance of Play in Promoting Healthy Child Development and Maintaining Strong Parent-Child Bonds." Clinical report issued by the American Academy of Pediatrics, October 9, 2006, pp. 1–32.

Gladwell, Malcolm. *The Tipping Point.* New York: Little, Brown & Company, 2000.

Golinkoff, Roberta Michnick, and Kathy Hirsh-Pasek. *How Babies Talk.* New York: Dutton, 1999.

Gopnik, Alison, Andrew N. Meltzoff, and Patricia K. Kuhl. *The Scientist in the Crib: What Early Learning Tells Us About the Mind.* New York: Harper Collins, 1999.

Graham-Rowe, Duncan. "Sounds Alarming." *New Scientist 169*, March 17, 2001, p. 5.

Greenspan, Stanley, with Nancy Breslau Lewis. *Building Healthy Minds: The Six Experiences That Create Intelligence and Emotional Growth in Babies and Young Children.* New York: DeCapo Press, 1999.

Grela, B. G., M. Krcmar, and Y. J. Lin. "Can Television Help Toddlers Acquire New Words?" May 18, 2004. Retrieved from http://www .speechpathology.com/articles/arc_disp.asp?article_id=72&catid=491.

Harris, Sara Kays, and Laura E. Berk. "Relationship of Make-Believe Play to Self-Regulation: A Short-Term Longitudinal Study of Head Start Children." Poster presented at the biennial meeting of the Society for Research in Child Development, Tampa, Florida, 2003.

Harrison, Kristen, and Joanne Cantor. "Tales from the Screen: Enduring Fright Reactions to Scary Media." *Media Psychology 1* (1999): 97–116.

Hart, Betty, and Todd R. Risley. *Meaningful Differences in the Everyday Experience of Young American Children.* Baltimore: Paul H. Brookes, 1995.

Healy, Jane M. "Early Television Exposure and Subsequent Attention Problems in Children." *Pediatrics 113,* no. 4 (2004): 917–918.

———. *Endangered Minds: Why Our Children Don't Think and What We Can Do About It.* New York: Simon & Schuster, 1990.

Hendershot, Heather, ed. *Nickelodeon Nation: The History, Politics and Economics of America's Only TV Channel for Kids.* New York: New York University Press, 2004.

Hersey, James C. "Family Strategies for Limiting Children's Television Viewing and Media Use." Paper presented at the biennial meeting of the Society for Research in Child Development, Atlanta, 2005.

Hertenstein, Matthew J., amd Joseph J. Campos. "The Retention Effects of an Adult's Emotional Displays on Infant Behavior." *Child Development 75,* no. 2 (2004): 595–613.

Hirsh-Pasek, Kathy, and Roberta Michnick Golinkoff, with Diane Eyer. *Einstein Never Used Flashcards.* Emmaus, PA: Rodale Books, 2003.

Hollich, George, Rochelle S. Newman, and Peter W. Jusczyk, "Infants' Use of Synchronized Visual Information to Separate Streams of Speech." *Child Development 76,* no. 3 (2005): 598–613.

Huber, Diane. "Goals Offered for Early Childhood." *The Olympian Online,* January 21, 2007, http://www.theolympian.com/112/story/61634.html.

Huesmann, L. Rowell, Jessica Moise-Titus, Cheryl-Lynn Podolski, and Leonard D. Enron. "Longitudinal Relations between Children's Exposure to TV Violence and Their Aggressive and Violent Behavior in Young Adulthood: 1977–1992." *Developmental Psychology 39,* no. 2 (2003): 201–221.

Huston Stein, Aletha, and Lynette Kohn Friedrich. "The Effects of Television Content on Young Children." In *Minnesota Symposia on Child Psychology,* vol. 9, ed. Anne D. Pick, pp. 78–105. Minneapolis: University of Minnesota Press, 1975.

James, William. *The Principles of Psychology.* New York: H. Holt and Company, 1905. Text of chapter 13 at http://psychclassics.yorku.ca/James/Principles/prin13.htm.

Jones, Gerard. *Killing Monsters: Why Children Need Fantasy, Super Heroes and Make-Believe Violence.* New York: Basic Books, 2002.

Jordan, Amy B. "Learning to Use Books and Television: An Exploratory Study in the Ecological Perspective." *American Behavioral Scientist 48,* no. 5 (2005): 523–538.

_____. "The State of Children's Television: An Examination of Quantity, Quality and Industry Beliefs." *Annenberg Public Policy Report,* University of Pennsylvania, June 1996.

_____. "The Three-Hour Rule and Educational Television for Children." *Popular Communication 2,* no. 2 (2004): 103–118.

Jordan, Amy B., James C. Hersey, Judith A. McDivitt, and Carrie D. Heitzler. "Reducing Children's Television Viewing Time: A Qualitative Study of Parents and Their Children." *Pediatrics 118,* no. 5 (2006): 1303–1310.

Jusczyk, Peter W., and Richard N. Aslin. "Infants' Detection of the Sound Patterns of Words in Fluent Speech." *Cognitive Psychology 29,* no. 1 (1995): 1–23.

Kirkorian, Heather L., Lauren A. Murphy, Tiffany A. Pempek, Daniel R. Anderson, and Marie Evans Schmidt. "The Impact of Background Television on Parent-Child Interaction." Poster session at a meeting of the Society for Research in Child Development, Atlanta, 2005.

Koenig, Phyllis Leslie. "The Effects of Prosody and Syntax on Young Children's Acquisition of Word Meaning." PhD diss., Yale University, 1996.

Kotler, Jennifer. "Healthy Habits for Life Initiative at Sesame Workshop." Presentation at a workshop on marketing, self-regulation and childhood obesity sponsored by the U.S. Federal Trade Commission and Department of Health and Human Services, Washington, DC, July 15, 2005.

Krcmar, Marina. "Can Social Meaningfulness and Repeat Exposure Help Infants and Toddlers Overcome the Video Deficit?" *Media Psychology* 13 (2010): 31–53.

Kuhl, Patricia K. "Early Language Acquisition: Cracking the Speech Code." *Nature Reviews: Neuroscience 5* (2004): 831–843.

Kuhl, Patricia K., Feng-Ming Tsao, and Huei-Mei Liu. "Foreign-Language Experience in Infancy: Effects of Short-Term Exposure and Social Interaction on Phonetic Learning." Proceedings of the National Academy of Sciences 100, no. 15 (July 22, 2003): 9096–9101.

Kunkel, Dale. "Policy Battles over Defining Children's Educational Television," *Annals of the American Academy of Political and Social Science 557* (May 1998): 39–53.

Kunkel, Dale, Brian L. Wilcox, Joanne Cantor, Edward Palmer, Susan Linn, and Peter Dowrick. "Report of the APA Task Force on Advertising and Children, Section: Psychological Issues in the Increasing Commercialization of Childhood." Report by the American Psychological Association, Washington, DC, 2004, http://www.apa.org/releases/childrenads.pdf.

Lewin, Tamar, "No Einstein in Your Crib? Get a Refund," *New York Times,* October 24, 2009.

Lillard, Angeline S., and Jennifer Peterson, "The Immediate Impact of Different Types of Television on Young Children's Executive Functioning," *Pediatrics* 128 (October 2011): 772–774.

Linebarger, Deborah L., and Dale Walker. "Infants' and Toddlers' Television Viewing and Language Outcomes." *American Behavioral Scientist 48,* no. 5 (2005): 624–645.

Linn, Susan. *Consuming Kids: Protecting Our Children from the Onslaught of Marketing & Advertising.* New York: Random House, 2004.

Linton, Michael. "The Mozart Effect." *First Things 91* (March 1999): 10–13.

Mares, Louise Marie, and Emory Woodard. "Prosocial Effects on Children's Social Interactions." In *Handbook of Children and Media,* ed. Dorothy G. Singer and Jerome L. Singer, pp. 183–206. Thousand Oaks, CA: Sage, 2001.

Mares, Marie-Louise. "Repetition Increases Children's Comprehension of Television—Up to a Point." *Communication Monographs 73,* no. 2 (2006): 215–241.

Marsh, Jackie, ed. Popular Culture, *New Media and Digital Literacy in Early Childhood.* New York and London: Routledge/Falmer, 2005.

McGinnis, J. Michael, Jennifer Appleton Gootman, and Vivica I. Kraak, eds. *Food Marketing to Youth: Threat or Opportunity?* Washington DC: National Academies Press, 2006.

Meltzoff, Andrew N. "Born to Learn: What Infants Learn from Watching Us." In *The Role of Early Experience in Infant Development,* ed. N. Fox and J. G. Worhol, pp. 145–164. Skillman, NJ: Pediatric Institute Publications, 1999.

Meltzoff, Andrew N. "Imitation of Televised Models by Infants." *Child Development 59* (1988): 1221–1229.

Mendelsohn, Alan L., Carolyn A. Brockmeyer, Benard P. Dreyer, Arthur H. Fierman, Samantha B. Berkule-Silberman, and Suzy Tomopoulos, "Do Verbal Interactions with Infants During Electronic Media Exposure Mitigate Adverse Impacts on Their Language Development as Toddlers?" *Infant and Child Development 19* (2010): 577–593.

Mifflin, Lawrie. "Pediatricians Suggest Limits on TV Viewing by Children." *New York Times,* August 4, 1999, p. A1.

Morison, Patricia, and Howard Gardner. "Dragons and Dinosaurs: The Child's Capacity to Differentiate Fantasy from Reality." *Child Development 49* (1978): 642–648.

Mumme, Donna L., and Anne Fernald. "The Infant as Onlooker: Learning from Emotional Reactions Observed in a Television Scenario." *Child Development 74,* no. 1 (2003): 221–237.

Naigles, Letitia R, and Lara Mayeux. "Television as Incidental Language Teacher." In *Handbook of Children and Media,* ed. Dorothy G. Singer and Jerome L. Singer, pp. 135–152. Thousand Oaks, CA: Sage, 2001.

National Autistic Society. "Do Children with Autism Spectrum Disorders Have a Special Relationship with Thomas the Tank Engine, and If So, Why?" Research undertaken by Aidan Prior Communications for the National Autistic Society. Executive Summary, February 2002, pp. 1–4.

National Scientific Council on the Developing Child. "Children's Emotional Development Is Built into the Architecture of Their Brains." Working Paper 2, Winter 2004.

National Scientific Council on the Developing Child. "Excessive Stress Disrupts the Architecture of the Developing Brain." Working Paper 3, Summer 2005.

Newman, Rochelle S. "The Cocktail Party Effect in Infants Revisited: Listening to One's Name in Noise." *Developmental Psychology 41,* no. 2 (2005): 352–362.

Newman, Rochelle S., and Peter W. Jusczyk. "The Cocktail Party Effect in Infants." *Perception and Psychophysics 58* (1996): 1145–1156.

Nigg, Joel T. *What Causes ADHD: What Goes Wrong and Why?* New York: Guilford Press, 2006.

Oates, Caroline, Mark Blades, and Barrie Gunter. "Children and Television Advertising: When Do They Understand Persuasive Intent?" *Journal of Consumer Behavior 1,* no. 3 (2001): 238–245.

Ogden, Cynthia L., Margaret D. Carroll, Lester R. Curtin, Margaret A. McDowell, Carolyn J. Tabak, and Katherine M. Flegal. "Prevalence of Overweight and Obesity in the United States, 1999–2004." *Journal of the American Medical Association 295,* no. 13 (April 5, 2006): 1549–1555.

Pempek, T. A., H. L. Kirkorian, A. F. Lund, M. Stevens, J. E. Richards, and D. R. Anderson. "Infant Responses to Sequential and Linguistic Distortions of Teletubbies." Paper presented at the biennial meeting of the Society for Research in Child Development, Boston, March 2007.

Piaget, Jean, and Barbel Inhelder. *The Psychology of the Child.* New York: Basic Books, 1969.

Pierroutsakos, Sophia, and Georgene Troseth. "Video Verite: Infants' Manual Investigation of Objects on Video." Infant Behavior & Development 26 (2003): 183–199.

Pinker, Steven. *The Language Instinct.* New York: William Morrow & Company, 1994.

Purdue News Service. "Less Noise at Home Makes for Better Adjusted Kids." June 1997, news.uns.purdue.edu/html4ever/1997/9706.Wachs.chaos.html.

Rashad, Fatimah F., and George J. Hollich. "What Did You Say, Mommy? Infant Word Learning and Comprehension in Varying Levels of Noise." Poster at a meeting of the Society for Research in Child Development, Atlanta, 2005.

Rice, Mabel L. "The Words of Children's Television." *Journal of Broadcasting 28,* no. 4 (1984): 445–461.

Richards, John E. "Attention." Entry in *The Cambridge Encyclopedia of Child Development,* ed. Brian Hopkins, pp. 282–286. Cambridge, UK, and New York: Cambridge University Press, 2005.

Richards, John E., and Daniel R. Anderson. "Attentional Inertia in Children's Extended Looking at Television." In *Advances in Child Development and Behavior,* vol. 32, ed. Robert V. Kail, pp. 163–212. New York: Academic Press, 2004.

Richards, John E., and Erin D. Turner. "Extended Visual Fixation and Distractibility in Children from Six to Twenty Four Months of Age." *Child Development 72,* no. 4 (2001): 963–972.

Rideout, Victoria. "Parents, Media and Public Policy: A Kaiser Family Foundation Survey." Report by the Kaiser Family Foundation, Fall 2004.

Rideout, Victoria, and Elizabeth Hamel. *The Media Family: Electronic Media in the Lives of Infants, Toddlers, Preschoolers and Their Parents.* Menlo Park, CA: Henry J. Kaiser Family Foundation, May 2006.

Rideout, Victoria, Elizabeth A. Vandewater, and Ellen A. Wartella. "Zero to Six: Electronic Media in the Lives of Infants, Toddlers and Preschoolers." Report by the Kaiser Family Foundation, Fall 2003.

Roberts, Susan, and Susan Howard. "Watching Teletubbies: Television and Its Very Young Audience." In Popular Culture, New Media and Digital Literacy in Early Childhood, ed. Jackie Marsh, pp. 91–107. New York: Routledge/Falmer, 2005.

Rust, Langbourne W. "Summative Evaluation of Dragon Tales Final Report." Report commissioned by the Sesame Workshop, 2001.

Sachs, Jacqueline, Barbara Bard, and Marie L. Johnson. "Language Learning with Restricted Input: Case Studies of Two Hearing Children of Deaf Parents." *Applied Psycholinguistics 2* (1981): 33–54.

Salomon, Gavriel. "Introducing AIME: The Assessment of Children's Mental Involvement with Television." In *New Directions for Child Development: Viewing Children Through Television*, vol. 13, ed. Hope Kelly and Howard Gardner. San Francisco: Jossey-Bass, 1981.

Samuels, Adrienne, and Marjorie Taylor. "Children's Ability to Distinguish Fantasy Events from Real-Life Events." *British Journal of Developmental Psychology 12*, no. 4 (1994): 417–427.

Shonkoff, Jack P., and Deborah A. Phillips, eds. *From Neurons to Neighborhoods: The Science of Early Childhood Development*. Washington DC: National Academy Press, 2000.

Siegler, Robert, Judy DeLoache, and Nancy Eisenberg. *How Children Develop*. New York: Worth Publishers, 2003.

Simensky, Linda. "Programming Children's Television: The PBS Model." In *The Children's Television Community*, ed. J. Alison Bryant. Mahwah, NJ: Lawrence Erlbaum Associates, 2006.

Singer, Dorothy G., Roberta Michnick Golinkoff, and Kathy Hirsh-Pasek. *Play=Learning: How Play Motivates and Enhances Children's Cognitive and Social-Emotional Growth*. New York: Oxford University Press, 2006.

Singer, Dorothy G., and Jerome L. Singer, eds. *Handbook of Children and the Media*. Thousand Oaks, CA: Sage Publications, 2001.

Singer, Dorothy G., and Jerome L. Singer. *Imagination and Play in the Electronic Age*. Cambridge, MA: Harvard University Press, 2005.

Singer, Emily. "Peering into the Brain." *Technology Review 109*, no. 5 (2006): 78–80.

Singer, Jerome L., and Dorothy G. Singer. "Barney & Friends as Entertainment and Education: Evaluating the Quality and Effectiveness of a Television Series for Preschool Children." In *Research Paradigms, Television and Social Behavior,* ed. J. K. Asamen and G. Berry, pp. 305–367. Thousand Oaks, CA: Sage Publications, 1998.

Spock, Benjamin, and Michael B. Rothenberg. *Dr. Spock's Baby and Child Care, 6th ed.* New York: Pocket Books, 1992.

Stevens, Tara, and Miriam Muslow. "There Is No Meaningful Relationship between Television Exposure and Symptoms of Attention-Deficit/Hyperactivity Disorder." *Pediatrics 117,* no. 3 (2006): 665–672.

Traverso, Debra Koontz. "Do You Know What Your Child Is Watching?" Sesame Workshop Web site, http://www.sesameworkshop.org/parents/advice/article.php?contentId=25600&&, February 1999.

Troseth, Georgene L., and Judy S. DeLoache. "The Medium Can Obscure the Message: Young Children's Understanding of Video." *Child Development 69,* no. 4 (1998): 950–965.

Troseth, Georgene L., Megan M. Saylor, and Allison H. Archer. "Young Children's Use of Video as a Source of Socially Relevant Information." *Child Development 77,* no. 3 (2006): 786–799.

Vaala, Sarah E., et al, "Content Analysis of Language-Promoting Teaching Strategies Used in Infant-Directed Media." *Infant and Child Development 19* (November 2010): 628–648.

Vandewater, Elizabeth A., David S. Bickham, and June H. Lee. "Time Well Spent? Relating Television Use to Children's Free-Time Activities." *Pediatrics 117,* no. 2 (2006): e181–e191.

Vandewater, Elizabeth A., David S. Bickham, June H. Lee, Hope M. Cummings, Ellen A. Wartella, and Victoria J. Rideout. "When the Television Is Always On: Heavy Television Exposure and Young Children's Development." *American Behavioral Scientist 48,* no. 5 (2005): 562–577.

Elizabeth Vandewater et al. "A US Study of Transfer of Learning from Video to Books in Toddlers," *Journal of Children and Media* 4 (2010): 4.

Waldman, Michael, Sean Nicholson, and Nodir Adilov. "Does Television Cause Autism?" National Bureau of Economic Research Working Paper #12632, October 2006. Also available at http://www.johnson.cornell.edu/faculty/profiles/waldman/autpaper.html.

Weber, Deborah S., and Dorothy G. Singer. "The Media Habits of Infants and Toddlers: Findings from a Parent Survey." Report by Zero to Three, September 2004.

Wilensky, Joe. "Quiet Zones for Learning." *Human Ecology 29,* no. 1 (2001): 15.

Winn, Marie. *The Plug-In Drug: Television, Computers and Family Life, 25th Anniversary Edition.* New York: Penguin Books, 2002.

Wolock, Ellen, Ann Orr, and Warren Buckleitner. "Child Development 101 for the Developers of Interactive Media." Handout packet for design workshop, updated for Dust or Magic Institute, Flemington, New Jersey, November 2006.

Woolley, Jacqueline D., and Henry M. Wellman. "Young Children's Understanding of Realities, Nonrealities and Appearances." *Child Development 61,* no. 4 (1990): 946–961.

Wright, John C., Aletha C. Huston, Kimberlee C. Murphy, Michelle St. Peters, Marites Pinon, Ronda Scantlin, and Jennifer Kotler. "The Relations of Early Television Viewing to School Readiness and Vocabulary of Children from Low-Income Families: The Early Window Project." *Child Development 72,* no. 5 (2001): 1347–1366.

Yonas, Albert, Carl E. Granrud, Mey H. Chov, and Amelia J. Alexander. "Picture Perception in Infants: Do 9-Month-Olds Attempt to Grasp Objects Depicted in Photographs?" *Infancy 8,* no. 2 (2005): 147–166.

Zimmerman, Frederick, Dimitri Christakis, and Andrew Meltzoff, "Associations Between Media Viewing and Language Development in Children Under Age 2 Years," *Journal of Pediatrics* 151, no. 4 (October 2007): 364–368.

Index

AAP. *See* American Academy of Pediatrics (AAP)
ADHD. *See* attention deficit/hyperactivity disorder (ADHD)
The Adventures of Super Why, 130
advergames, 224
advertising. *See* commercials aimed at children; marketing of children's merchandise
ages of children as factor
  in background TV, 84
  in distinguishing reality from fantasy, 91–92
  for learning from educational television, 103–104, 116, 120
  in selections of media, 246–247
aggression in children
  linked to viewing of superhero shows, 183
  and on-screen violence, 103, 239
Aigner-Clark, Julie, 45, 46
Aladdin movie, 104
always-on television. *See* background television
Amazon.com, 145
American Academy of Pediatrics (AAP), 1–4, 19, 20, 24, 71, 152, 247
American Sign Language. *See* sign language
Anderson, Daniel R., 29–40, 50, 63, 70–72, 96, 124, 156
Applied Linguistics journal, 137

Arthur television program, 159
attention deficit/hyperactivity disorder (ADHD), 8–16
attention disorders, 8, 13–14, 70
  as causing television use, 15
attention to television, 33, 38
  of babies, 36–37
  as background, 73
  differences among individual children, 40–42
  linked to comprehensibility of message, 34, 35
"Attention to Television: A Summary" (Anderson, Collins), 29–30
attentional inertia, 35–36, 37
auditory capabilities of babies, 52–53
autism, 16–19, 248
Autism Research Centre, Cambridge University, 18, 19
autism spectrum disorder, 18
Awakening Children's Minds (Berk), 187

Baby Babble DVD, 138–139
Baby Bach video, 41
Baby Einstein Company, 45, 47, 48
Baby Einstein Language Nursery video, 45, 128, 145, 240
Baby Einstein videos/DVDs, 2, 138, 139
Baby Mozart video, 2, 17, 32, 41, 45, 46, 128
Baby Newton video, 41
Baby Van Gogh video, 41

baby videos, 23
   combined with parent interaction,
      24–25, 253
Baby Wordsworth video, 140
BabyFirst TV, 48
babysitters/caregivers, 235, 248–249
   and always-on TV, 239
background television, 67–84,
      155–156, 247
   demographics, 68–69
   distracts children's playtime, 72, 73–74
   vs. foreground television, 83
   head-turn preference experiment,
      78–80
   limiting, 243–245
   noise of. *See* noise of
      always-on television
   and parent-child interactions, 76–77
   repercussions to child development, 70
Bailey, Mark, 199
Barkley, Russell A., 9–10, 12, 13, 15–16
Barney, 115, 122, 128–129, 250
   on-screen teaching moments, 127, 128
   promotes pretend play, 190
   and social skills, on-screen etiquette,
      173, 177, 186–187
   videos linked to expressive language
      development, 160
   and vocabulary growth, 159, 162
Baron-Cohen, Simon, 19
Barr, Rachel, 60, 62, 63, 96
Batman, 183
bedrooms with televisions, 70, 228–230
Bee Smart Baby Vocabulary Builder
      DVD, 140
behavioral problems, 12–13, 17
Berk, Laura E., 187, 188, 189
The Best of Elmo video, 127
Between the Lions television program,
      29, 178
Bickham, David, 35
Big, Big World television program, 124
Big Bird character from *Sesame Street*, 91,
      164, 225

Bilingual Baby DVD, 145
bilingual language learning. *See*
      second-language acquisition
Bill Nye the Science Guy television
      program, 120
birds, social interaction among, 143
Blades, Mark, 222, 223
Blue's Clues television program, 62, 84,
      247, 250
   academic, social benefits, 115
   cognitive on-screen teaching
      moments, 128
   and flexible thinking scores, 128
   linked to increased vocabulary, 159
   pause technique, 119
   storybook software, 208
books vs. ebooks, 207, 208
BoxOfficeOffenders.com, 88
brain development of babies, children, 4–7
   capacity model for information
      processing, 126
   fear reactions of amygdala, 91, 94
   and long-term learning, 51
   visual, auditory capabilities, 52
brain imaging, 50–51
Brainy Baby Company, 46, 48
Brainy Baby French DVD, 145
Brainy Baby Spanish DVD, 145
Branch Davidian sect, 70
Brazelton, T. Berry, 29
Brody, Michael, 89, 109
*Brown Bear, Brown Bear, What Do
      You See?* (Carle), 53
Buckleitner, Warren, 195, 199, 204
Bugs Bunny television program, 163

Cable News Network. *See* CNN
Caillou television program, 186, 250, 252
Calvert, Sandra L., 200, 201, 208
Campaign for a Commercial-Free
      Childhood, 24, 48
Campbell, Don, 45
Cantor, Joanne, 95–96, 104, 106,
      109, 110

capacity model for information
processing, 126
Caplovitz, Allison, 207, 208
Carle, Eric, 53
Cartoon Network, 103
cause and effect, understanding of,
195, 196
Child Development journal, 33
child-advocacy groups, 24
child-directed language, 163–164
Children and Media Research
Advancement Act (CAMRA),
130, 253
Children's Digital Media Center,
Georgetown University, 200
*Children's Dreaming and the Development of
Consciousness* (Foulkes), 98
Children's Technology Review magazine,
195, 202
Chouinard, Mary, 140, 141
Christakis, Dimitri A., 9, 10–11, 21–22
The Chronicles of Narnia movie, 88
Circle of Make-Believe videos, 191
clean-up time, 188
Clifford television program, 159
CNN, 8, 70, 72, 83
cocktail party effect (babies' coping
abilities), 78, 79–80, 81
cognitive engagement with TV, 34,
35–36, 96
cognitive growth/development
as marketing claim for baby videos, 46
and overcoming susceptibility to
advertising, 222–223
Piaget's theory, 90
pretend play as critical factor, 187–188
related to ages of children, 102, 120
tied to level of chaos in home, 81
cognitive skills
required to make sense of video, 52
for *Sesame Street* viewers, 128
stimulated through videos, 46–47, 48,
49, 64
Cohen, Michael, 110

Collins, Molly, 206
Collins, Patricia A., 29
commercials aimed at children, 224.
See also food marketing; marketing
of children's merchandise
avoided by parental controls, 241–242
avoided by using TiVo, videos, 249
brand recognition, 221–222
labeled deceptive by FTC, 220
and obesity, 223–225
and power of characters, 226–227
and susceptibility to snack food, 219
on Web sites/game sites, 212–213,
223–224
comprehensibility of television/videos,
50, 51
for babies, 39, 40
and dialogue unrelated to action on
screen, 125
guidelines, 124
for preschoolers, 34
of stories, 116
computers, 243
educational games for toddlers, 194,
195, 197
vs. TV/video narratives for
children, 201
conflict and resolution in stories, 182–183
Connecticut, University of, 135
Consuming Kids (Linn), 226
content of media
in multiple-child families, 247
parental control of, 238–239
in plot line, 126
contingency learning process, 196
Cooper, Anderson, 8
cooperation and teamwork, 185–186,
190–191
courtesy. *See* on-screen etiquette;
social skills
CSI televison program, 88, 190, 230
Cul de Sac cartoon (Thompson), 105
Curious Buddies videos, 46, 62
Curious George, 109, 210

Davenport, Andrew, 38
daycare centers, research using, 122, 123, 128–129, 190, 201
DeLoache, Judy S., 53–54, 56–57, 58
Dennison, Barbara A., 229
DeWitt, Sara, 210
digital video recorders. *See* TiVo and video-on-demand systems
Disney Corporation. *See* Walt Disney Company
Disney Princess fruit snacks, 225, 226, 228
distractibility, 37, 73–74, 168
Dora the Explorer, 30, 64, 250
  academic, social benefits, 115
  linked to increased vocabulary, 157, 159, 162
  The Map, 157, 240
  re-engineered to be interactive, 200, 201–202
  and Swiper the fox, 97, 99, 107–108
  uses foreign-language words, 148, 151–152, 162
Dragon Tales television program, 115
  impact on persistence, social skills, 177–181, 190–191
Dragons and Dinosaurs (Morison, Gardner), 91
dreams of babies, very young children, 97–99
dual representation skill of understanding symbols, 56–58
DVDs, 138, 146, 243. *See also* videos

Early Window Project, 162–163
eating while watching TV, 230–231, 243
ebooks for preschoolers, 197, 206–208, 246
Education, U.S. Department of, 29, 130, 211, 253
educational programming, 113–116, 124, 243. *See also* programming for children

age-specific audience required for effectiveness, 119–120
claims pro-social messages, 180
cognitive on-screen teaching moments, 127–128
defined, 116–118, 131
leads to more pretend play, self-regulation, 190
lessons integrated into story lines, 126
and *Sesame Street* reformatting, 122–123
viewers tracked over 10 years, 129
and vocabulary development, 153, 162–164
Eebee's Adventures DVDs, 141
Einstein Never Used Flashcards (Hirsh-Pasek, Golinkoff), 71, 140, 204
Eisenberg, Nancy, 175
The Electric Company television program, 124, 163, 164
The Elephant in the Living Room (Christakis, Zimmerman), 10–11
Elias, Cynthia, 188
Eliot, Lise, 31
Elkind, David, 71
Elmo character of *Sesame Street*, 107, 122, 127, 193
  used for food selection research, 226–227
  used for marketing purposes, 242
Elmo Goes to the Firehouse DVD, 107
Elmo in Grouchland movie, 107
Elmo videos, 17, 64, 250
"Elmo's World" on *Sesame Street*, 121–122, 250
emotional contagion from video viewing, 101
emotions, 18–19, 99–101, 187–188
Endangered Minds: Why Children Don't Think . . . (Healy), 27, 28
environmental stress, 101–102
Erikson, Erik H., 90
Evans, Gary, 81

Evans, Marie, 72
expressive language. *See* speech
　development
Eye Care Facts and Myths (AAO), 21

Fat Albert television program, 163, 164
fear of being left behind, 109
fear of the dark, 106
fear reactions to media
　by 12-month-olds, 101
　coverage of September 11 attacks,
　　91, 107
　identifying key features, 104,
　　106–109
　parental approaches suggested,
　　110–111
Federal Trade Commission (FTC), 48,
　220, 224, 242
Fedoruk, Dennis, 48
Fernald, Anne, 100
Finding Nemo movie, 104, 109
Fisch, Shalom M., 124, 126
Fite, Katherine V., 50
Fitzgerald, Julia, 47
Fivush, Robyn, 96
flashbacks and scene cuts, 124, 125,
　126, 131
Flavell, John, 55
Flintstones, 180
food marketing
　and childhood obesity, 219–226
　commercialized characters studied,
　　226–227
"Food Marketing to Children and Youth"
　(Institutes of Medicine), 224
food pyramids, 218–219, 220(illus),
　221(illus)
foreign-language DVDs. *See*
　second-language acquisition
Foulkes, David, 97–98
Friedman, Amy, 113
Friedrich, Lynette, 183
frightening movies, videos. *See also* fear
　reactions to media

fantasy events perceived as real, 93,
　95–96
　and movie rating system, 103–104
From Neurons to Neighborhoods (Shonkoff,
　Phillips, eds.), 4–5
Fun with Languages DVD, 145
functional magnetic resonance imaging
　(fMRI scan). *See* brain imaging

Gardner, Howard, 91
Gass, Stephen, 141, 142
Gee, James Paul, 211
Gifford, Chris, 107–108, 157
Gilligan's Island television program, 163
Goles, Wendee, 87–88, 89
Golin, Josh, 48
Golinkoff, Roberta Michnick, 71, 78
grammar development, 148. *See also*
　language skills
G-rated movies, 103
Greenough, William T., 5, 6, 64
Grela, Bernard, 168, 169, 170
Gupta, Sanjay, 8

habituation, 31, 32, 82
Hamel, Elizabeth, 228
Hampton, Russell, 48
Harris, Sara Kay, 189
Harrison, Kristen, 95
Harry Potter movies, 102, 103
Hart, Betty, 154–156, 173
Head Start, 153, 189
head-turn preference procedure, 78–79,
　146, 165–166
Healy, Jane M., 27, 28, 30
heart rate of babies and attentional
　inertia, 37
Henry J. Kaiser Family Foundation, 2, 47,
　88, 184, 228, 230
Hersey, James C., 230
Hirsh-Pasek, Kathy, 71, 78, 140,
　204, 205
Hollich, George, 81–82
Hostel movie, 87

Howard, Susan, 38–39
Huesmann, L. Rowell, 184
The Hurried Child (Elkind), 71
Huston, Aletha, 162, 163, 183

I Like Animals!/Me Gustan Animales
    DVD, 145
illusions of children, 93, 94
imitation of on-screen activities, 59, 63
    by babies, young children, 253
    vs. real life actions, 60–62
    violence of, 184
impulse-control problems, 189
inconsiderate hotspots on online
    games, 213
The Incredibles, 104
Indiana Jones movies, 88, 102, 103
interactive media, 193–213, 245–246
    for babies, 194–195
    for children with special needs,
        259(app)
    computers with touch screens, 197
    reviewed on Web sites, 257(app)
    software for children, 198, 199,
        202–205
interactivity, child-controlled, 205, 207
    vs. participation, 200–202
InteracTV system, 246
Internet, 147, 223, 245

James, William, 27
Jeopardy television program, 72, 73
Jetsons, 180
Jim (boy with speech anomalies),
    135–138, 148, 149
Johnson, Marie, 136
joint attention approach, 143–144,
    168, 169
JoJo's Circus television program, 56,
    64, 250
Jordan, Amy B., 120, 132, 229–230
JumpStart Preschool Advance, 197,
    202–204
Jusczyk, Peter W., 78

Kai Lan television program, 148
Kaiser Family Foundation. *See* Henry J.
    Kaiser Family Foundation
Kanter, Nancy, 162
KidPix graphics program, 212
Kirkorian, Heather, 74, 75, 76
Koenig, Phyllis, 167
Kohlberg, Lawrence, 175
Krcmar, Marina, 168, 169, 170
Kuhl, Patricia K., 144, 145, 147
Kunkel, Dale, 217, 220

language skills, 63, 146, 148. *See also*
    second-language acquisition
    and blocks vs. TV viewing, 22
    and elicited responses from children,
        119, 142
    impacted by noise of background
        television, 77–80, 81–82
    require person-to-person contact,
        118–119, 135–138, 143–144
    through videos, TV, 138–140,
        158–159, 161–167
    tied to level of chaos in home, 81
LeapFrog, 194
LeapPad, 206, 246
learning, 52
    cause and effect, 196
    contingency, 196
    factors for videogames, 211, 212–213
    impaired in presence of noise, 82
    not effective with passive viewing,
        listening, 146–147
    and preschool TV programming,
        113, 115
    pro-social behavior, 176
    from real-life imitation, 60–62
    through interactive media, 195
    tracked from on-screen teaching
        moments, 127–128
    from videos/DVDs, 57–58, 59–60, 63,
        165–170, 195
Left Brain video, 46
Lerner, Claire, 42

Levin, Stephen, 33
licensing of media characters for
    merchandise, 104, 157, 241, 242
  by Disney Corporation, 226, 227–228
  on high-fat, -sugar foods, 224
  by Sesame Workshop, 227
Linebarger, Deborah, 29, 131, 158, 160,
    162
Linn, Susan, 226
The Lion King movie, 104, 110
Little Einsteins television program, 45,
    148, 162
Little Leaps Grow-with-Me Learning
    System, 194
location of television, 230
Lorch, Elizabeth, 11
low-income children
  engage in pretend play with violent
    themes, 190
  language skills, vocabularies, 22,
    153, 155
  positive influence of educational
    programming, 122–123, 163
  with TVs in shared bedrooms,
    242–243
Lyle the Kindly Viking King videotape, 125

Madagascar movie, 104
magazine format, 121, 122
Mandarin Chinese, 146, 148
manners, civil. *See* on-screen etiquette;
    social skills
Mares, Marie-Louise, 181, 182
marketing of children's merchandise, 104,
    157, 242. *See also* commercials
    aimed at children; food marketing
Marsh, Jackie, 226
McIlrath, Mary, 224
Meaningful Differences in the Everyday
    Experience . . . (Hart, Risley), 155
meaningfulness. *See* comprehensibility of
    television/videos
media, guidelines for selecting, 109–111,
    236–252

  amount of viewing time, 250–251
  communicating with babysitters,
    248–249
  in families of multiple children,
    246–247
  integration of non-TV media, 245–246
  limiting background television, 67–84,
    243–245
  location of television as factor,
    242–243
  parents control content, 104,
    239–241, 250
  reality and make-believe perceptions,
    91–93
  in single-parent families, 70, 247–248
  using TiVo, on-demand systems,
    249–250
media, violent, 87–89
  creates self-regulation difficulties, 190
  distinguishing between reality and
    fantasy, 91–93, 94
  leading to children's violence, 103
  viewed by infants and children, 87–89
Mega Bloks, 21–22
Meltzoff, Andrew, 59–60
memory, 51, 96–97
Mi Casa/My House DVD, 145
Mister Rogers television program, 55, 115,
    136, 162
  with child-directed language, 163, 164
  compared to superhero shows, 183
  promotes pretend play, social skills,
    177, 190
Mommy, I'm Scared (Cantor), 95
Moose character, Noggin TV, 114
moral reasoning of children, 175–176, 182
Morison, Patricia, 91
movies
  fear reactions to, 104, 106–111
  moral lessons of, 182
  ratings, 88, 103
  Web site reviews, 255(app)
The Mozart Effect (Campbell), 45–46
MRI scans. *See* brain imaging

Mulsow, Miriam, 15
Mumme, Donna, 100, 101
The Muppet Movie, 37

Naigles, Letitia, 167
Namdi, Kojo, 82
narratives
    consistent with action on screen, 125
    deficiency of very young children, 117
    format of *Sesame Street*, 123
    linear quality as crucial, 124, 126
    and pro-social messages, 182
    studied, 34, 39, 40, 63
    videos vs. on-air shows, 160
National Association for the Education of
    Young Children, 28
National Autistic Society, U.K., 18
nature vs. nurture debate, 6
New York Times newspaper, 4, 21
Newman, Rochelle, 41, 78, 147, 165, 166
news programs, 72–73, 83, 244–245
Nick Jr., 30, 46, 62
Nickelodeon, 35, 69, 108, 113, 156, 157,
    158, 239
NickJr.com, 241
Nigg, Joel T., 14–15
nightmares, 97, 99
9/11. *See* September 11 terrorist attacks
Noggin TV, 113–114, 116, 123, 250
noise of always-on television, 77
    and auditory challenges of babies,
        78–79
    and babies' use of visual cues, 80
    impact on older children, 81
novelty preference, 31

obesity of children, 215–231
    and eating while watching TV, 231
    linked to televisions in children's
        bedrooms, 229–230
Ochs, Elinor, 239
online games controlled by children, 210,
    212–213, 223–224
on-screen etiquette, 129, 173–174

orienting response, 32
over-parenting, 191
OyBaby DVD, 216

parental attitude toward TV, 235
    impacts children's learning, 131–132
    as predictor of heavy television use,
        69–70
parent-child interactions
    and baby videos, 253
    with background television, 74–75
    displaced by TV, 21, 22
    and DVDs on car trips, 243
    and pro-social behavior, 175, 186–187
    required for language development,
        141–142, 155
    and *Sesame Beginnings*, 24
    TV as divisive element, 238–239
    when parent is in control, 207
Parish, Julia, 206
The Passion of Christ movie, 89
PBS. *See* Public Broadcasting
    Service (PBS)
PBSKids.org, 210, 245
Peabody Picture Vocabulary Test, 161, 162
pediatricians and child-development
    specialists, 9–10
Pediatrics journal, 8–9, 14, 20, 28, 29, 217
Peep and the Big Wide World online game,
    210, 212
Pempek, Tiffany, 37, 40, 73, 74
"Pestering Parents" (Center for Science in
    the Public Interest), 225
PG–13 movie rating, 103, 104
Piaget, Jean, 90, 104, 106
pictorial competence, 54–55, 62
    of symbolic representations for
        children, 57–58, 63
    and upside-down orientation of young
        children, 53
Pierroutsakos, Sophia, 54
Pinker, Steven, 153
Pinky Dinky Doo, 250
Playhouse Disney, 56

playtime, creative
 affected by background TV, 70–72
 develops pro-social behavior, 176,
 187–190
 falls when displaced by TV, 21, 73–74
 leads to self-regulation, 188–189
 maturity of, 74
 with media themes, 190
 with parental interactions, 75–76
 used to intervene for fear
 reactions, 110
The Plug–In Drug (Winn), 27–28
Poland, Cory, 140
politeness. *See* on-screen etiquette;
 social skills
Power Rangers, 177
PowerTouch Learning System ebook,
 206, 207
preoperational stage (Piaget), 90
preschool software programs, 198–199,
 202–205
 designed to be controlled by child, 210,
 212–213, 243
pretend play. *See* playtime, creative
pretend vs. real, distinguishing between,
 91–94, 106. *See also* reality and
 make-believe, perceptions of
programming for children. *See also*
 educational programming
 age-specific, 102, 119–120, 240, 251
 with conflict-resolution, 181–182
 effective characteristics, 131
 frightening features, 104, 106–109
 innocuous, 240
 preschool television, 114–120
 pro-social, 180–181
 and vocabulary development, 159
 who are low-income, 122, 123
pro-social behavior
 and conflict-resolution programming,
 181–182
 imitated from *The Wonder Pets*,
 185–186
 linked to *Barney*, 186–187

 negative impact of superhero
 shows, 183
 programming for, 180–181, 190
 scripts, 184
 stages, 175
 studied using *Dragon Tales*, 178–179
Public Broadcasting Service (PBS), 37,
 124, 210, 241–242

question-asking as language acquisition
 technique, 119, 142

radio as background noise, 69, 82, 83
Raymond television program, 75, 76
reading
 of images upside down, 53–54
 and vocabulary development, 153
Ready to Learn program, 130, 253
reality and make believe, perceptions of,
 91–93. *See also* pretend vs. real,
 distinguishing between
real-life activities
 compared to video actions, 60–62, 64
 complete memories of, 96
recontact study of educational program
 viewers, 129–130
Redbook magazine, 29
Rehm, Diane, 82
repetition
 dissipates video deficit, 119
 enabled by TiVo, video-on-demand
 systems, 249
 of fearful images, 101
 of new words, 170
 required for learning from videos, 49,
 62, 159
Revelle, Glenda, 197
Rice, Mabel, 163
Richard Scarry videos, 115, 126
Richards, John E., 36, 37–38, 96
Rideout, Victoria, 228
Risley, Todd R., 154, 155, 173
Road Runner television program, 163
Roberts, Susan, 38–39

role models, television characters as, 175, 176
Rovee-Collier, Carolyn, 196, 197
R-rated movies, 88
Rust, Langbourne W., 177, 178, 179, 180, 181

Sachs, Jacqueline, 135, 136, 137, 148
Salomon, Gavriel, 131
Samuels, Adrienne, 93
Santomero, Angela, 130
Saylor, Megan, 117, 118, 142
scale models, concept of, 56–58
scene cuts. *See* flashbacks and scene cuts
Scheibe, Cynthia, 218
Scholastic videos, 240
screen time. *See also* television viewing; violence on-screen
  amounts, time limits on, 152, 236–237, 251
  and brain connections for motor, spatial skills, 19
  and children vulnerable to ADHD, 14
  combined with pretend play, 187–190
  impact on social skills, 177
  limited by using pre-recorded videos, 250
  of online games, children's software, 213
  and *Sesame Beginnings*, 24
  timing of, 237–239
second-language acquisition, 144
  head-turn preference tests, 145
  in-person teaching vs. passive DVD viewing, 146–147
selecting media for children. *See* media, guidelines for selecting
self-regulation, 188
Selig, Josh, 185–186
September 11 terrorist attacks, 107
  television coverage viewed by children, 91, 243–244
Sesame Beginnings videos, 22, 23–24
Sesame Street, 120–122, 160, 250
  and attentional inertia, 35
  cognitive on-screen teaching moments, 128
  and habituation, 32
  impact on social skills, 177
  linked to later academic success, 129–130
  as means for learning English, 147
  studies showing benefits to children, 22
  used for research on fixation, 33
  uses Spanish words, 148
  videos compared to on-air shows, 160
  and vocabulary/language development, 155–156, 159, 160–161, 163
Sesame Workshop, 23, 47, 178
  and children's fears of the dark, 106
  content on the plot line, 126
  promotes children's nutrition, 226, 227
sharing, 125, 126, 174
Shifrin, Donald, 3, 4
Shonkoff, Jack, 3
Shrek movies, 104
Shribman, Bill, 210, 211
sign language, 135, 140, 174, 244
Simensky, Linda, 124, 180
Singer, Dorothy, 122, 127, 128, 162, 186, 191
Singer, Jerome, 122, 128, 162, 186, 191
Slate online magazine, 16
Snow White and the Seven Dwarfs movie, 104
social interactions, 143, 148, 170
social responsibility, 188–189
social skills, 173–174. *See also* on-screen etiquette; pro-social behavior
  environment as critical factor, 175
  importance of make-believe play, 176, 187–191
  increased by viewing *Dragon Tales*, 178–179
  influenced by television, videos, 177, 180–188

Society for Research in Child
Development, 3
socioeconomic factors
and Early Window Project, 163
and locations of TVs, 242–243
and *Sesame Street*, 122, 123, 128
and vocabulary development, 153
socio-emotional awareness, 128
software. *See* interactive media,
software for children; preschool
software programs
The Sopranos television program, 99
sound effects/music, 253
Spanish as second-language, 148, 162
spatial IQ increased by listening to
Mozart, 45–46
speech development
of babies, 79, 80, 81, 164
and bird song studies, 143
impacted by background noise,
81–82
through certain educational TV
programs, 159, 160–161
through DVDs, 138–140, 148
Spider Man movies, 104
split screen paradigm, 166
Spongebob Square Pants, 241
Square One TV television program, 126
Sroka, Iris, 120
Star Trek television program, 95
Star Wars movies, 88, 102, 103
Stevens, Tara, 15
Stewart, Cherie, 194
stories
childrens' understanding of, 116–117
importance of linear qualities, 124,
126, 131, 170
interrupted by computer
navigation, 201
superheroes, 94, 183–184
Superman, 183
Swiper the fox. *See Dora the Explorer*
The Sword and the Stone movie, 182
symbolic information, 56–58

symbol-mindedness, 59, 63
synapse-pruning of brain development,
6–7

Tarantino, Quentin, 87
Taylor, Marjorie, 93
"A Teacher in the Living Room" report, 47
Teletubbies, 17, 63
negative correlation with language
growth, 159
research on babies' attention,
understanding, 34, 37–39
and toddlers' word-learning, 167–170
Teletubbies Go video, 128
television as background. *See* background
television
television trance. *See* zombie effect
of TV
television viewing. *See also* background
television; screen time; violence on-
screen
AAP edict for children under 2 years
old, 1–4
and ADHD, 9–10, 11, 15–16
and attentional inertia, 35–36, 37
and childhood obesity, 215–231
children identify with characters, 176
in child's bedroom, 229–230
cognitive engagement with, 34
in daycare centers, 129, 132
and emotional contagion of babies, 101
guidelines for selecting media,
236–252
illusory world of, 93
and language/second-language
development, 135–138, 147,
148–149, 158
learning from, 52, 57–58, 59–60, 132
as meaningful, with parents'
interactions, 24, 155
related to playtime, 20, 21
as toxic, 11
used as babysitter, 70
while eating, 230–231

Thomas & Friends, 17–19
and autism spectrum disorder, 18
Thompson, Richard, 105
time limits imposed on screen time,
236–237
suggestions, 251
by using pre-recorded videos,
249, 250
Titzer, Robert C., 47
TiVo and video-on-demand systems, 245,
249–250
Toy Story movie, 102, 103, 104
trance from television viewing. *See* zombie
effect of TV
The Transporters DVDs, 19
Troseth, Georgene, 54, 58, 117, 118,
119, 142
Truglio, Rosemarie, 23, 107, 121,
122, 160
Turner, Erin D., 37

under-parenting, 191
United Kingdom bans children's junk food
commercials, 221

Vandewater, Elizabeth A., 20–21, 29,
69, 217
Veggie Tales, 115, 125
video deficit, 61, 62, 64
lessened by parent-child interaction,
117–119
videogames, 241
as interactive programs for
preschoolers, 202–205, 210–211
self-leveling, 211
using buttons instead of joysticks, 198
violent, 94
videos
attributes of, 152
babies' vs. children's interaction with,
54–55
as babysitters, 25, 70, 248
compared to imitating real-life actions,
59, 60–62

compared to on-air shows, 160–161
and emotional information of
babies, 100
as lasting a set amount of time,
249, 250
and long-term learning, 166
as pictorial, symbolic representations,
57–58
as social partner for language
acquisition, 119, 170
as thematic story lines, 160
two-dimensional nature of, 62
used to test toddlers' word-learning,
167–170
violence on-screen
of Cartoon Network, 103
linked to children's aggression, 103,
177, 183–184, 239
negative impact on children, 15, 94
violent media. *See* media, violent; violence
on-screen
visual capabilities, 53, 106
vocabulary growth. *See also* word-learning
critical factors of, 170
linked to level of talking in
families, 155
linked to linear narrative structure,
160–161
of low-income children, 153,
156, 163
meaning attached by babies, 166
as predictor of academic
performance, 153
testing of preschoolers, 161–164
V.Smile, 194, 198, 246
VTech, 47
Vygotsky, Lev, 187–188, 209

Wachs, Theodore, 81
Walker, Dale, 158
Walt Disney Company, 45, 120
and age-inappropriate media, 104
and food marketing of licensed
characters, 225–226, 227

The Washington Post Magazine, 105
Wellman, Henry M., 93
What Causes ADHD: What Goes Wrong and Why? (Nigg), 14
What's Going On in There? (Eliot), 31
white noise, effects on language learning, 82
The Wiggles television program, 62
Winn, Marie, 27
Winnie the Pooh video, 109, 126, 250
Wizard of Oz movie, 94
The Wonder Pets television program, 173, 184–186, 250, 252
Wood, Anne, 38
Woodard, Emory, 181, 182, 186
Woolley, Jacqueline, 93
Wootan, Margo G., 225, 226

word-learning, 253
by babies, toddlers, 164–170
with child-directed language, 163
and polite behavior, 174
research, 153
in Spanish, 162
summarized, 170
via video, 96, 118
Wright, John, 162, 163

Yogi Bear, 180
Your Baby Can Read video, 46–47

Zero to Three journal, 127
Zero to Three organization, 23, 42
Zimmerman, Frederick J., 10
zombie effect of TV, 27–28, 29, 30, 34, 36